Power to the Partners

Power to the Partners

Organizational Coalitions in Social Justice Advocacy

MARAAM A. DWIDAR

The University of Chicago Press
Chicago and London

The University of Chicago Press, Chicago 60637
The University of Chicago Press, Ltd., London
© 2025 by The University of Chicago
Published 2025

34 33 32 31 30 29 28 27 26 25   1 2 3 4 5

ISBN-13: 978-0-226-84036-9 (cloth)
ISBN-13: 978-0-226-84038-3 (paper)
ISBN-13: 978-0-226-84037-6 (e-book)
DOI: https://doi.org/10.7208/chicago/9780226840376.001.0001

Library of Congress Cataloging-in-Publication Data

Names: Dwidar, Maraam A., author.
Title: Power to the partners : organizational coalitions in social justice advocacy /
    Maraam A. Dwidar.
Description: Chicago : The University of Chicago Press, 2025. |
    Includes bibliographical references and index.
Identifiers: LCCN 2024044676 | ISBN 9780226840369 (cloth) |
    ISBN 9780226840383 (paperback) | ISBN 9780226840376 (ebook)
Subjects: LCSH: Social justice—United States. | Coalitions—United States.
Classification: LCC HM671 .D95 2025 | DDC 303.3/720973—dc23/eng/20241014
LC record available at https://lccn.loc.gov/2024044676

*To Bryan Jones, who believed in me long
before I believed in myself*

Contents

1

The Power of Partnership

On the evening of August 2, 2022, Ashley All, an organizer with Kansans for Constitutional Freedom (KCF), was nervous.[1] Kansas had become the first state in the nation to vote on abortion rights through referendum on the heels of the US Supreme Court's landmark decision in *Dobbs v. Jackson Women's Health Organization*. On the ballot was a constitutional amendment allowing Kansas lawmakers to ban abortion—the first of many efforts to restrict reproductive rights in the post-*Dobbs* era. If passed, the amendment would open the door to a near or total ban on abortion in the state.

Republican lawmakers had led a campaign based on misdirection: they drafted confusing ballot language, refused to say what policies they would enact if the amendment were passed, and strategically scheduled the vote on a day with historically low turnout. Organizers for KCF, a bipartisan coalition of roughly forty reproductive rights organizations and allied groups including Planned Parenthood, the American Civil Liberties Union, the Trust Women Foundation, and URGE: Unite for Reproductive & Gender Equity, had worked for months to combat their efforts. By election day, the coalition had spent over six million dollars—in a state won by Donald Trump by nearly fifteen points in 2020—and later that evening, triumphed in a landslide victory. All, a veteran political organizer, could scarcely believe it.

While the outcome of their work may have come as a shock, KCF's tactics were tried-and-true. Across local, state, and national organizing, coalition work is ubiquitous. In 2018, a coalition of environmental justice groups and oil industry associations formed to oppose changes to an Environmental Protection Agency regulation affecting the sale of gasoline with 15 percent Ethanol (E15)—and successfully rescinded the rule.[2] In 2020, a broad-based coalition of business groups, religious organizations, and Black Lives Matter activists successfully lobbied Mississippi state lawmakers for the removal of the Confederate battle emblem from their state flag.[3] And in 2023, a decades-long ban on awarding Pell Grants to incarcerated individuals was lifted by the US Congress—the result of years of advocacy by a coalition of social and economic justice organizations led by the Vera Institute of Justice.[4] This book is about what makes coalition work by these kinds of advocates succeed.[5] To understand why some coalitions triumph and others fall short, I spent seven years observing and recording the behavior of more than 1,700 coalitions advocating for social and economic justice in American national politics. I measured their differences—in membership, money, messaging, and goals—and compared those with successful outcomes to those that failed. In doing so, I tried to tease out the micro- and macro-level conditions surrounding organizations' successful efforts collectively to shape public policy. Do coalitions succeed when they have deep pockets? When they have an opportunity, like the chance to capitalize on a moment or movement? Or maybe the ability to recruit just the right kinds of partners, with specialized skills and friends in high places?

All of these things matter. But most of all, what truly distinguishes successful coalitions is their ability to build partnerships with strong architectures and mobilize many different, crosscutting interests in pursuit of a shared ideal. These organizations, keenly aware of their competitors and constraints, use coalition work to compensate for individual shortcomings and progressively build movements. They partner with longtime allies and former opponents, strategically invest their resources, and make careful compromises. Some of these partnerships are long standing and formal, like Voces Verdes (founded in 2009), a coalition of Latinx community organizations and businesses fighting for clean air, energy, and water policy. Others are more ad hoc and fleeting, like the Coalition Against Religious Discrimination, which united a fluctuating set of organizations to promote religious rights and liberties in a dozen advocacy initiatives beginning in the late 1990s. Regardless of their form, these coalitions are always united by a single goal: to produce meaningful change. This book focuses on their efforts to shape political institutions and public policy in pursuit of social and economic justice.

In the coming pages, I tell a story of how social and economic justice organizations strategically respond to their communities' needs and their operational constraints with coalition work. Most of these advocates face day-to-day challenges: they have fewer members, smaller budgets, and more limited issue agendas than the private and professional interest groups of K Street (Han, McKenna, and Oyakawa 2021; Schlozman, Verba, and Brady 2012). They are beholden to their patrons and paying members to keep the lights on and thus must respond to patron preferences, even if these run counter to that of the organization (English 2019, 2020; Marchetti 2014). So they turn to partnerships, old and new, to do the hard work of advocacy. In doing so, they face a natural tension. They worry about balancing their organizations' autonomy and interests with investments in coalition work. To survive in a competitive political environment, they must protect their records and reputations as individual groups. But in a crowded arena, making friends is also vital. I argue that social and economic justice groups consciously thread this needle. They work strategically in coalitions when the benefits of partnership outweigh the costs. By investing in these partnerships, they advance more effective and more equitable advocacy. This book explains how.

Understanding Advocacy

Many historically marginalized communities in the United States struggle to gain political access, find the time to politically engage, or to garner the attention of their advocates in government (Brady, Verba, and Schlozman 1995). These long-standing dynamics have substantial consequences for representation. Lawmakers, for example, have few incentives to take up the concerns of communities with low rates of political participation (Mayhew 1974). More often than not, their work responds to the interests of wealthy Americans and big business—those who participate politically at high rates—disenfranchising millions in the process (Gilens 2004; Gilens and Page 2014). To put it simply: American government privileges the interests of those with the most advantage.

Social and economic justice organizations—interest groups seeking to influence government policymaking on behalf of historically marginalized communities—try to mediate this disparity (Martinez 2009; Phinney 2017; Pinderhughes 1995; Strolovitch 2007). Many of these groups have roots in protest movements that decry government shortcomings to social and political grievances, such as those for women's rights and civil rights in the early and mid-twentieth century (Strolovitch 2007). The National American Woman Suffrage Organization (NAWSO, founded in 1890), the National Association for the Advancement of Colored People (NAACP, founded in 1909), and the League of United Latin American Citizens (LULAC, founded in 1929), for example, all formed during critical moments in American history to mobilize their communities and lobby policymakers in support of suffrage and civil rights. Their efforts led to monumental policy changes, including the ratification of the Nineteenth Amendment, the passage of the Civil Rights Act of 1964 and the Voting Rights Act of 1965, and the overturning of the

"separate but equal" doctrine in US constitutional law (Gelbman 2021; Pinderhughes 1995).

In the second half of the twentieth century, over a thousand organizations
were founded to advocate for vulnerable communities, such as UnidosUS
(formerly the National Council of La Raza, founded in 1968), GLAAD (formerly the Gay and Lesbian Alliance Against Defamation, founded in 1978),
and the Black Women's Health Imperative (formerly the National Black
Women's Health Project, founded in 1983) (Strolovitch 2007). Alongside their
predecessors, their efforts led to historic policy achievements protecting and
promoting the interests of marginalized communities, including the Equal
Pay Act's prohibition on sex-based wage discrimination in 1963, the estab-
lishment of social welfare programs supporting poor Americans in 1964 and
1965, and the passage of labor protections through the Age Discrimination
and Employment Act of 1967 (McConnaughy 2013; Skocpol 1992).

Organizations like the NAACP, LULAC, GLAAD, and their compatriots
share a common factor: they developed in response to moments of social
reckoning and deepening needs for better representation of their communities. These organizations remain one of the very few sources of political representation for vulnerable groups in American society (Schlozman, Verba, and
Brady 2012). They take many forms, including citizen groups, labor unions,
legal advocates, nonprofit service providers, and think tanks (Baumgartner
et al. 2009a; Schlozman and Tierney 1986). They engage in policy advocacy—
lobbying—and serve their constituents at a grassroots level. They offer community services such as legal aid, share educational resources such as voting
guides, and politically empower their constituents by encouraging them to
make their voices heard—and helping ensure they do so. They are key advocates for their constituents in public policymaking and service.

But they face an uphill battle. Despite their role as "compensatory representatives," many organizational advocates for vulnerable communities have
limitations. While their constituents' needs are boundless, these organizations' time and resources are not. They must often balance different motivations, such as a much-needed win, with the countervailing interests of different constituent groups. Some constituents have "easier" needs, or interests
that align more closely with dominant groups and shifting political winds.
Other constituents require advocacy that noisily disrupts the status quo and
fights against stigmatized policy images and frames. The outcome is a tale
as old as time: their advocacy successes are fleeting and mainly promote the
interests of their more advantaged constituents while neglecting those with
intersecting disadvantage (Brower 2024; English 2019, 2020; Marchetti 2014;
Strolovitch 2007).

Compensating by Collaborating

Organizations consciously respond to these disparities and biases. They are aware of their many constraints and turn to specific tools to compensate for them. Collaborating—which I also refer to as coalition building—is one of these tools, and the most common lobbying strategy in organizational politics (Baumgartner and Leech 1998; Baumgartner et al. 2009a; Hula 1999). While effective, it is also complex, and groups do not deploy it lightly. Information about potential partners—such as common interests, past successes, and reputation/stature—is paramount in the decision to work with others (Hojnacki 1997, 1998).

This intricate relationship has led to a small but growing body of research about coalitional advocacy. Scholars of organizational coalitions largely fall into two camps. The first argues that coalitions are unlikely, since organized interests require autonomy to survive and coalition building presents inherent risks to autonomy (Wilson 1973; Berry 1977; Browne 1990). The second contends that coalitions are advantageous because they allow groups to enhance their effectiveness in a crowded political environment (Salisbury 1990; Hojnacki 1997). Regardless, organizational coalitions *do* form—and often. Hula (1999), for example, reports that groups with policy-oriented goals regularly join coalitions in order to reduce expenditures, shape policy proposals, and define issue debates. Others do so to obtain insider information or to publicly demonstrate allyship (Hula 1999). The broader policy environment, of course, also plays a role. When opponents in a policy debate are strong, organizations derive greater benefits from lobbying in a coalition and are thus more likely to join one (Hojnacki 1997). Coalitions are most likely to break when differences in ideology, priorities, or lobbying style among partners collide (Staggenborg 1986; Levi and Murphy 2006).

Research findings on the outcomes of coalition building are more mixed. Heinz et al. (1993), Gray and Lowery (1998), Mahoney and Baumgartner (2004), and Haider-Markel (2006), for instance, find either no connection or an inverse relationship between coalition building and policy outcomes. McKay and Yackee (2007), Baumgartner et al. (2009a), Nelson and Yackee (2012), Phinney (2017), and Lorenz (2019), on the other hand, observe positive relationships between collaborative lobbying and policy influence and note that certain characteristics—such as coalition size and group consensus—can magnify the impact of coalition work.

I argue that coalition work provides unique and significant benefits to social and economic justice organizations. These groups are widely known to have limited resources relative to their mainstream counterparts. Only a small proportion—fewer than 30 percent—retain a legal staff. Only 25 percent employ lobbyists, and a mere 20 percent have political action committees (PACs). In contrast, among mainstream interest groups, 50 percent retain a legal staff, 54 percent employ lobbyists, and 60 percent have PACs (Strolovitch 2007). These characteristics and differences tell a story of limited tactical, social, and financial capacity among organizational advocates for vulnerable communities.

Despite its risks, working in coalitions allows social and economic justice organizations to expand their capacities while reducing costs. Policy advocacy is an expensive task, requiring copious time and expertise that can be hard to come by (Baumgartner and Leech 1998; Baumgartner et al. 2009a). Coalition work enhances the abilities of organizations with limited resources and political connections to surpass this hurdle (Hojnacki 1997, 1998; Hula 1999; Lorenz 2019; Mahoney and Baumgartner 2004; Phinney 2017). By partnering with others, these groups develop new social ties, gain access to policy experts and a wider array of information, and profit from greater political credibility by association. With these benefits in hand, developing effective policy recommendations becomes more feasible. Collaboration should thus be a highly attractive and effective advocacy tactic for social and economic justice groups, particularly in comparison to their mainstream counterparts (who have far less ground to make up in the advocacy landscape).

But coalitions vary widely in their characteristics. They might contain two groups or twenty groups, they might unite loosely or in formalized partnerships, or they might bring together diverse interests—such as a group representing unhoused people allying with an organizational advocate for LGBTQ+ youth. Take, for example, Students Lead Students Vote (SLSV, founded in 2016), a formal coalition of nonprofit organizations and philanthropic leaders dedicated to increasing voter turnout among college students. SLSV maintains a fixed membership of approximately 150 organizational partners, a staff of seven, an executive committee, and an advisory board composed of leaders from its membership alongside prominent policy experts.[6] Formal coalitions like SLSV tend to be long standing and retain staff, leaders, and a mission separate from those of their individual organizational members. But these characteristics barely scratch the surface of the breadth and consequence of formal coalition work. By way of their formality, they have something that ad hoc coalitions systematically lack: *architecture*, a set of agreed-on rules and procedures that govern all aspects of decision making in a coalition—from who is (and is not) in the coalition to what issues to advocate on to proceedings dedicated specifically to unpacking the lessons of successful and unsuccessful advocacy (Gelbman 2021; Zack et al. 2023; Zack and Smithson-Stanley 2024). These processes facilitate collective learning and adaptability and should magnify the potential for advocacy success. In coalition work, architecture surely matters.

And so, too, does diversity. Diverse coalitions take myriad forms, from coalitions of organizations representing a range of constituent communities—such as RISE St. James (a faith-based group founded in 2018), Downwinders at Risk (an advocate for communities of color founded in 1994), and the Ironbound Community Corporation (ICC, a nonprofit service provider for low-income families founded in 1969)—to coalitions of "strange bedfellows" that unite advocates for social justice and big business—such as the National Fair Housing Alliance (NFHA, founded in 1988) uniting with the Mortgage Bankers Association (MBA, founded in 1913).[7] These sorts of coalitions tend to get a lot of attention, and for good reason: they catch the eye and make for a snappy news story. For instance, in December 1999, following the World Trade Organization (WTO) protests organized by labor and environmental groups, the *Los Angeles Times* ran a story titled "Teamsters and Turtles: They're Together at Last."[8] In August 2017, following the United States' exit from the Paris Climate Agreement under President Trump—a move opposed by the oil industry and climate activists alike—one headline read, "Greens and Big Industry Are the Baptists and Bootleggers of Climate Policy: What Could General Electric and the Environmental Defense Fund Possibly Have in Common?"[9] In both cases, these alliances brought together groups with distinct and sometimes competing interests and received an enormous amount of public attention: more than five thousand national news stories were published describing the above-mentioned union of "turtles and Teamsters," and as of the publication of this book, over 1,500 stories have reported on the 2017 alliance of climate activists and industry representatives.[10] More importantly, these coalitions sent important signals of concern and consensus to public policymakers—not despite, but *because* of their differences.

Diverse coalitions also have a strategic advantage: when many different groups decide to form an alliance, they bring together all their skills, expertise, and connections. Together, they have far greater tactical and informational capacity than any single member organization (Lorenz 2019; Nownes 2007; Schlozman and Tierney 1986). But of course, there's a catch: coalitions that unite diverse interests are far more complex than others. When groups without a clear and common interest work together, they must justify the union to their boards of directors and funders. These leaders are likely to express some concern for the partnership or, in the case of strange bedfellows such as the Environmental Defense Fund (EDF, founded in 1967) and General Electric, disapprove entirely. So when social and economic justice groups build diverse coalitions, they do so for a reason: after careful calculus and deliberation, they decide that the benefits outweigh the costs (Hojnacki 1997, 1998). I argue that these kinds of coalitions enjoy greater influence over public policymaking. By their very nature, they have the unique ability to signal consensus and credibility to policymakers and offer substantially better, more well-rounded policy recommendations.

In building this argument, I acknowledge that coalition work is a valuable tool for all kinds of organizations, not just those advocating for social and economic justice. Many other groups, including those with limitless resources and unfettered access to political institutions, also benefit from collaborative advocacy and building diverse coalitions. And they consistently engage in coalition work: approximately 40 percent of advocacy efforts by the broader lobbying population—including industry groups, business corporations, and governmental associations—occur in coalitions, 25 percent of which retain formal architectures. And approximately 75 percent of these coalitions contain some degree of membership diversity (Dwidar 2022a). Unlike their social and economic justice–oriented counterparts, their focus on building coalitions is not based on conserving resources but on achieving greater credibility and signaling consensus. In 2020, for example, a coalition of sixteen businesses—including AT&T, Coca Cola, Microsoft, and the Metro Atlanta Chamber—came together to lobby the Georgia General Assembly in favor of a bill imposing additional sentencing on individuals who commit hate crimes.[11] Their partnership was an attempt to signal unified corporate support for the bill. Thus, a central part of my theory is that while coalition building benefits all kinds of groups, it has greater benefits for organizational advocates for social and economic justice.

Coalition work also offers a chance for social and economic justice groups to advocate more equitably. These groups seldom promote the interests of their most vulnerable, intersectionally disadvantaged constituents (Brower 2024; English 2019, 2020; Marchetti 2014; Strolovitch 2006). An organization representing a racial minority group, for example, is far more likely to represent its higher-income rather than its lower-income constituents. The reason is simple: these groups rely heavily on funds from patrons and paying members to do their work and are thus beholden to their preferences (Imig 1996; Walker 1983). These funders, who typically represent organizations' most advantaged constituent groups, often disapprove of intersectional advocacy, labeling it as "narrow" and "controversial" (Staggenborg 1986; Strolovitch 2006). They far prefer for their patronages to pursue more expedient and "winnable" policy campaigns (Marchetti 2014).

Some of the oldest women's organizations in the United States have recently come under fire for this dynamic. In 2020, the National Organization for Women (NOW, founded in 1966), the Feminist Majority Foundation (FMF, founded in 1987), and the American Association of University Women (AAUW, founded in 1881) were the subjects of exposés in the *Washington Post* and the *Daily Beast* for their systemic promotion of white women's political interests at the expense of those of women of color.[12] Staffers of these organizations attributed this trend to their disapproving members and patrons, stating explicitly that "the folks [providing] funding [. . .] were less interested in women of color and more interested in more quote-unquote 'neutral' topics" (Kitchener 2020).

But these groups *do* want to pursue intersectional work. Many highlight intersectional advocacy as central to their goals but note that it is difficult to go it alone (Strolovitch 2007). The nature of partnership, involving many groups and smaller individual investments, offers a strategic and lower-profile solution—ideal for pursuing advocacy that is considered important to an organization's mission without expending significant individual resources and drawing the ire of funders. Thus, I argue that social and economic justice organizations strategically build coalitions in order to pursue this particular form of advocacy. This deliberate choice makes clear to disapproving actors that intersectional advocacy is not occurring at the expense of broader organizational priorities—their utmost concern (Strolovitch 2007).

Collaborating helps organizations compensate, whether for limited resources, a lack of political credibility, or constrained advocacy agendas. When social and economic justice organizations build coalitions, they carefully balance their organizational priorities and strategically promote more effective advocacy and more equitable policy ideas. Their successes mean that policy choices made by political institutions account for the interests of marginalized communities—offering a semblance of hope for democratic legitimacy.

Advocacy and the Fourth Branch

Most talk about lobbying is negative. It is no secret that special interest groups spend copious time and money courting lawmakers. Their PACs, meanwhile, ensure that allies in Congress keep their seats and thus, their office doors open to their causes. Who do these special interest groups represent? Are they persuasive? Do they "buy" votes? Hundreds of research articles and dozens of books discuss these questions (Baumgartner and Leech 1998). This concern is so potent that everyday Americans recoil at the mention of special interest groups in Washington—52 percent, in fact, view the work of lobbyists and interest groups to be a "very serious problem" in government.[13]

The positive contributions of these groups get little attention. While some lobbyists and groups do skirt legal boundaries, most interest groups

deal in honest advocacy. The information they provide—about voter preferences, district needs, and the outcomes of potential policies—is much needed
(Baumgartner and Leech 1998; Hansen 1991; Hall and Deardorff 2006). As
congressional capacity has declined, basic legislative functions such as select-
ing policy priorities, debating the merits and pitfalls of policy provisions, and
crafting the language of the law are now the work of interest groups (Drutman
and Teles 2015; LaPira, Drutman, and Kosar 2020). But their work does not
stop there—after policy ideas are enacted into law, the process of *implementing* these ideas begins. This work falls to an unassuming but sophisticated
political institution: the American federal bureaucracy or "fourth branch" of
government, responsible for 90 percent of US law, and a secondary character
of this book (Haeder and Yackee 2015; Warren 2018; Yackee 2006).

The reach of the American federal bureaucracy is wide—and growing (Potter 2019; Warren 2018; Yackee 2006). As the major political parties have polarized, substantive lawmaking by the US Congress has declined, and legislative
language has grown increasingly vague (Lewallen 2020). The bulk of modern
policymaking has thus steadily fallen to bureaucrats serving in federal agencies as they craft and promulgate rules implementing provisions of the law
(Potter 2019). But bureaucrats do not do this work alone. They work with and
are overseen by a variety of political principals and other actors, including the
president, members of Congress, and organized interest groups. These latter
actors are a particularly vital source of power and information in agency policymaking (Truman 1951; Schattschneider 1960; Olson 1965; Berry 1989; Salisbury 1992; Baumgartner and Jones 1993; Gray and Lowery 1996; Baumgartner
et al. 2009b). They are active players in this venue; the majority of all organizational advocacy targets a federal agency (Baumgartner et al. 2009a), and their
work helps bureaucrats sway public opinion (Hrebenar 1997), raise awareness
of policy issues facing agencies (Rourke 1984; Hrebenar 1997), resist political
control (Carpenter 2002), secure budgets (Berry 1989), and even craft regulatory language (Carpenter et al. 2022; Haeder and Yackee 2015).

Most agency policymaking—and most organizational advocacy—takes
place through a process called "notice-and-comment" rulemaking. This process derives from the policymaking authority of the Congress and the president and is governed by the Administrative Procedure Act of 1946 (APA).
The APA stipulates that after bills are signed into law by the president, their
component parts must be sent to the appropriate federal agencies to implement their content by writing rules regulating their enforcement. This process begins with agencies drafting "proposed rules." Once drafted, these proposed rules must be made public for specified notice-and-comment periods.
During these periods, members of the public—including organized interest

groups, private citizens, or political actors—may submit written public comments regarding the proposed rule. Interest groups dominate submissions made during this process, and their comments are considered an important source of expertise and information for federal agencies (Croley 1998; Golden 1998; West 2004; Kerwin, Furlong, and West 2011). When these periods come to a close, agencies must review all comments and issue final rules. Upon issuance, these rules become legally binding.

The work of advocacy organizations is paramount in this process. Agency rulemaking is lengthy and tedious. The average agency rule goes through at least eight different stages and is written over a period of two to three years (Potter 2019). This long process leaves room for errors and oversights. These mistakes, as simple as an outdated statistic or an incomplete definition, can have significant downstream consequences when agency rules are implemented by street-level bureaucrats. Consider, for example, the Federal Emergency Management Agency's (FEMA) National Flood Insurance Program (NFIP). In October 2021, FEMA issued a request for public comments with input on revising the NFIP's floodplain management standards. In response, a national coalition called the Anthropocene Alliance (A2, founded in 2017) mobilized.[14] A2 consists of roughly twenty nonprofit organizations advocating on behalf of 140 climate-changed communities nationwide—many of which are home to low-income people and communities of color. In their public comments to FEMA, A2 leaders reiterated a pervasive feeling among many affected communities and climate activists: that out-of-date NFIP standards put climate-changed communities in harm's way and make it difficult for them to obtain insurance from flooding. They argued that these unsuitable standards, ranging from the data sources used to evaluate the effects of NFIP regulations to a list of exceptions for home building on low-lying land, have serious consequences, from the loss of a home to the loss of a life. As of the publication of this book, FEMA is still in the process of revising these standards, but the implication is simple: that agency efforts to implement policies and revise existing rules are *extremely* consequential. A2, along with many other social and economic justice organizations, recognize this reality and work hard to inform agency decisions on behalf of their constituent communities.

Study Design

Working out what differentiates coalitions that succeed from those that fall short is a difficult task. Researchers have struggled to study organizational coalitions. Unlike individual interest groups and lobbyists, which are required to submit tax documents and disclosure reports, most coalitions develop on an ad hoc basis without fixed or named memberships. This limited documentation means that most existing research on collaboration in lobbying focuses on a small set of groups or policy issues and works in unison with organizations through qualitative or survey methodology. But my goal in this book is to provide explanations that span all kinds of organizations and issues, so that practitioners and scholars can develop a *general* understanding of how to build coalitions successfully.

To do so, I took on a simple solution. When people work in teams, they take credit where credit is due—organizations are no different. They might issue a joint press release, send a series of tweets mentioning their partners, or cosign a collaboratively written public comment. Since this book centers on advocacy in regulatory policymaking, I developed the *Collaborative Advocacy Dataset*, an original dataset tracking coalitions through cosignature patterns on public comments submitted to federal agencies. This dataset—the culmination of seven years of work—contains information on roughly twenty thousand organizations advocating on approximately 2,800 rules issued by 116 federal agencies between 2000 and 2016. Among other things, it details each organization and coalition's structure, mission, constituency, financial backing, and membership (in the case of coalitions) along with the subject and characteristics of the agency rules targeted by their advocacy. These data allowed me to track the activities of approximately 1,700 coalitions over a seventeen-year period.

As a complement to these quantitative data, I also conducted more than two dozen elite interviews with organizational leaders and agency bureaucrats in the years of 2022 and 2023. These leaders are currently employed, or were recently employed, by national-level advocacy organizations varying in staff size, financial resources, maintenance of paying membership, constituency, and policy orientation. These bureaucrats are currently employed, or were recently employed, by federal agencies and engaged in rulemaking-oriented activities. They represent a range of agencies, spanning both independent and executive branch agencies, levels of professionalization and size, perceived ideological leans, and policy orientations. In the coming chapters, I offer insights from these conversations as I describe my theoretical expectations and contextualize my empirical findings.

To measure the two central concepts of this book—the *effectiveness* and *equitability* of advocacy, I turned to modern text analysis tools. Organizations often use the notice-and-comment process to pursue their advocacy, in large part by suggesting regulatory language. This choice is intentional. If agency bureaucrats are persuaded by interest groups' advocacy, they often lift and place their suggested language, verbatim, into the final agency rules.

So to measure the effectiveness of their work, I used plagiarism detection software to determine the extent to which each public comment's language overlapped with that of its corresponding final rule. Then, to operationalize equitability, I developed a novel and hand-coded measure of the occurrence of intersectional advocacy. Together with the *Collaborative Advocacy Dataset*, these measures allow me to directly test my arguments: that coalition work promotes more effective, and more widely representative, policy advocacy.

Chapter Overview

Policy advocacy is expensive and arduous, particularly in the regulatory context. Because the arguments I make rest on collaboration as a means of compensation for social and economic justice organizations, it is important to begin with an overview of what we know about interest group politics and the regulatory process. Thus, in chapter 2, I historicize the role of organized interests to explain their prominence in our current governmental system. I describe the origins of social and economic justice interest groups in social movements for women's rights and civil rights in the early to mid-1900s, their unique role as "compensatory representatives" in American politics, and the barriers they face in political advocacy. I conclude with a discussion of how organizations strategically build coalitions to compensate for these barriers and how their targets—in this case, agency rules—guide their use of coalition tactics. In describing the unique relationship between coalition tactics and targets, I trace the manner by which federal agencies develop, publicize, and finalize their rules and the entry points for organizational advocacy in this process.

Chapter 3 tackles the challenge of collecting data on organizational coalitions—an informal activity with little to no documentation. I describe the impact of this data problem on prior scholarship and introduce my innovative solution: the *Collaborative Advocacy Dataset*, an original dataset tracking coalitions through cosignature patterns on public comments and comprising information on over twenty-thousand organizations advocating on approximately 2,800 rules issued by 116 federal agencies over a seventeen-year period (2000–2016). Using these data, I explore patterns of collaboration across organizational and policy characteristics.

Chapter 4 develops and tests the first portion of the book's theoretical argument—that coalition work boosts the influence of social and economic justice groups lobbying federal agencies. I describe the expectations of regulatory advocacy and the incentives of agency bureaucrats to emphasize the unique capabilities of organizational partnership. I show that while organizational advocates for social and economic justice often build coalitions, collaboration alone is not a sufficient condition for achieving greater advocacy influence. Instead, I demonstrate that building coalitions with *formalized structures* significantly increases the regulatory influence of these advocates. This simple analysis highlights the importance of an understudied phenomenon—coalition architecture—in elevating policy ideas and mediating representational disparities in rulemaking and lobbying.

Coalitions come in many forms. The most striking collaborations unite diverse memberships—from religious organizations partnering with racial justice groups to unions of far stranger bedfellows, such as consumer advocates uniting with big business. These diverse collaborations are common and, when formed, attract attention. Chapter 5 examines common types of diverse coalitions and their influence over lobbying outcomes. I argue that coalitions with membership diversity exert greater influence over the rulemaking process than their homogeneous counterparts. I show that the most influential coalitions are those that contain representational diversity (i.e., a plurality of interests), rather than those that unite strange bedfellows. I also find evidence of a threshold effect—wherein the entry of representational diversity, rather than a greater degree of diversity, is most consequential for advocacy influence. In contrast to the popular narrative of bureaucratic imperialism, this chapter offers evidence of a more legitimate and participatory policy process in which the proposals of representationally diverse—pluralistic—coalitions are favored.

The American lobbying environment is crowded, competitive, and costly. The wealthiest and most privileged interests often reign supreme. Can strategic collaboration level the playing field? Chapter 6 tackles the next portion of this book's theoretical argument—that collaboration lends greater benefits and outcomes to social and economic justice–oriented interest groups than their mainstream counterparts. By replicating the analyses of chapters 4 and 5 using data on collaborative regulatory advocacy by a sample of private, professional, and general interest groups, I show that coalition building does indeed uniquely benefit organizations representing historically marginalized communities.

Chapter 7 develops and tests the final portion of the book's theoretical argument. I explain how, from an organizational perspective, collaboration is a complex but useful tactic for *intersectional* advocacy. Because of stringent resource limitations, social and economic justice organizations are often beholden to the preferences of their patrons and active members, many of whom represent the identities and promote the priorities of the groups' most advantaged constituents. As such, their advocacy on behalf of their most vulnerable constituents—those with intersectional disadvantage—falls short. I argue that collaborative strategy allows these groups to advocate on behalf of issues concerning these constituents by conserving resources and avoiding the ire of members and patrons through the "cover" provided by coalitions. Using the *Collaborative Advocacy Dataset* in conjunction with a novel, hand-coded measure of the occurrence of intersectional advocacy, I demonstrate that coalition work moderates organizations' pursuit of intersectional advocacy.

In the concluding chapter, I discuss the implications of my findings for the study and practice of advocacy-based representation in American policy-making. While efforts to promote the interests of marginalized communities are often unsuccessful, this book sketches a portrait of resolute and conscious organizational actors that strategically collaborate to compensate for barriers to representational equality. The evidence demonstrates that this tactic is, in fact, an effective tool for mediating representational bias in organizational agenda setting and public policymaking. I conclude by prescribing a series of practices that organizational leaders and activists may apply to enhance their collaborative advocacy. Now let's get started.

Collaboration as Compensation

In the summer of 2020, the Black Lives Matter movement (BLM) shook the world. Within a span of twelve days in late May and early June, between fifteen and twenty-six million people took to the streets during a deadly pandemic to participate in demonstrations across the United States—later declared the largest movement in American history (Civis Analytics 2020).[1] As the reader may well know, these demonstrations were triggered by the murder of George Floyd at the hands of Minneapolis police on May 25, 2020. But the work of organizing this activity and associating it with concrete policy demands was years in the making. At the forefront of this work was a coalition of about fifty racial justice organizations representing the movement for Black civil rights and dignity, the Movement for Black Lives (M4BL, founded in 2014).

M4BL and its partners prefer not to take too much credit—as a movement, their vision is local, grassroots oriented, and decentralized. They seek to build activists by providing frameworks, materials, and guidance. As a coalition of organizations, however, they have a policy agenda. On July 7, 2020, they released a proposal for the BREATHE Act, a bill divesting taxpayer dollars from policing and suggesting alternative approaches to public safety.[2] Policy change is a long path, and as of the publication of this book, their work is ongoing. But their efforts to build a long-lasting movement have been historic. Since June 2020, for example, over eleven million philanthropic dollars have been pledged to support the work of racial justice organizations, old and new.[3]

Many social and economic justice organizations have roots in movements like BLM. The Civil Rights Movement and women's rights movement in the 1950s, 1960s, and 1970s, for example, led to a monumental increase in the number of groups representing vulnerable communities in national politics (Berry 1989). Between 1960 and 1999, 65 percent of existing women's organizations, 56 percent of existing racial justice organizations, and 79 percent of existing economic justice organizations were formed, including advocates such as the Center for Law and Social Policy (CLASP, founded in 1969); MANA, a National Latina Organization (formerly the Mexican American Women's National Association, founded in 1974); and Asian Americans Advancing Justice (AAAJ, formerly the Asian American Legal Advocacy Center, founded in 1983) (Strolovitch 2007). Throughout the mid- to late twentieth century, these groups worked tirelessly, simultaneously pursuing legal action and legislative change and closely following policy implementation by the executive branch. Many of their efforts were fruitful. In 1964, the Economic Opportunity Act established social welfare programs supporting poor Americans. In 1964 and 1965, the Civil Rights Act and Voting Rights Act (respectively) became law, barring discrimination in public life, employment, and government and racial discrimination in voting. In 1974, the Equal Credit Opportunity Act was established, prohibiting discrimination on the basis of race, gender, class, religion, national origin, age, or marital status in credit practices. And in 1984, AAAJ's legal efforts led to the reversal of Fred Korematsu's 1944 Supreme Court conviction in *Korematsu v. US*.

These achievements changed the course of American social and civil rights policy. They also funneled greater resources, political power, and access to advocacy organizations representing historically marginalized communities. Consequently, these groups became known as "emergent contenders" in the American political landscape—groups that have been historically compromised in American politics because of their constituents' stigmatized identities and histories of political and social marginalization, but who have steadily gained degrees of power and influence resembling those of mainstream lobbying organizations (Schneider and Ingram 1997). Decades after their early feats, their numbers continued to grow. By the turn of the twenty-first century, there were over one thousand such organizations, including more than 150 economic justice groups, one hundred women's organizations, fifty Black organizations, and thirty organizations representing women of color (Strolovitch 2007). Scores more—including labor unions, nonprofit service providers, legal advocates, think tanks, and citizen and public interest groups—have since been established. Figure 2.1 depicts this monumental increase in the number of these advocates registered to lobby at a national level. These groups dually represent and activate those mobilized by the movements that birthed them, and their work continues today.

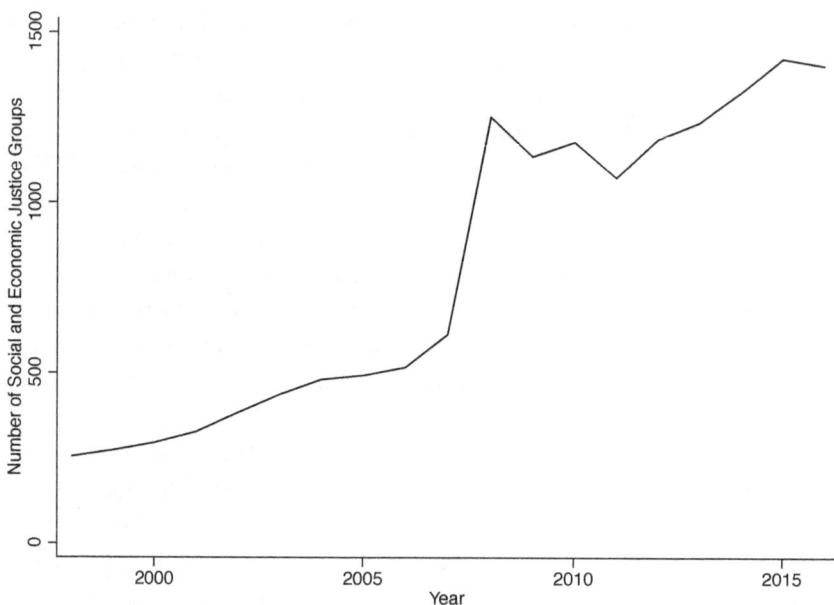

F I G U R E 2.1. Social and economic justice lobbying registrants, 1998–2016. Data compiled by the author from CRP records (available at https://www.opensecrets.org).

Compensatory Representatives

Social and economic justice organizations occupy a unique space in American politics. They respond to the representational disparities discussed in chapter 1; namely, that their constituent communities often do not receive representation through formal, electoral avenues. The reason is simple. Members of historically marginalized groups in the United States face steep barriers to political participation. Activities such as voting, contributing to campaigns, engaging in political protests, and joining political membership organizations require individual and institutional resources (Brady, Verba, and Schlozman 1995). These resources are unevenly distributed across demographic populations, with fewer resources concentrated among historically marginalized groups and intersections thereof (Gilens 2004). Legislators have few incentives to take up the concerns of populations with low political participation rates (Mayhew 1974; Gilens 2004; Gilens and Page 2014). Thus, elected officials rarely advocate on their behalf; instead, these officials more often respond to the interests of their wealthiest and most politically active constituents. And even as the body of elected officials serving in national government has diversified—the 117th Congress, for example, was the most racially and ethnically diverse group in its history—these trends have held true.[4] In fact, scholars have repeatedly demonstrated that descriptive representation rarely leads to *substantive* representation (Bratton and Haynie 1999; Brown 2014; Guinier 1994; Minta 2011; Reingold, Haynie, and Widner 2020; Swain 1993).

As a result, many marginalized individuals' primary opportunities for political representation occur through advocacy by social and economic justice interest groups (Martinez 2009; Pinderhughes 1995; Strolovitch 2007; Phinney 2017). Because of their origins, they straddle political boundaries between "insider" politics and "outsider" movements (Costain 1992). They serve as conduits for the representation of communities that have been underrepresented and underserved by American electoral politics and the two-party system, such as women of all races, people of color, and low-income people (Costain 2005; Frymer 1999; Strolovitch and Forrest 2010). Their work offers a promise of formal political access to these otherwise neglected groups, a dynamic coined "compensatory representation" by Dara Strolovitch (2007). Over time, many have succeeded in looking the part of a political insider. A majority of social and economic justice organizations are headquartered in the Washington, DC, metropolitan area, and many have offices on or near K Street, a corridor home to some of the most powerful lobbying outfits in Washington (Strolovitch 2007).

But they differ from their neighbors in fundamental ways. Despite massive gains in their numbers following the "long 1960s," social and economic justice organizations occupy a small proportion—a little over 3 percent—of the broader national lobbying population.[5] In addition to being outnumbered, they are vastly out-resourced by industry associations, business groups, and corporate interests (Baumgarter and Leech 1998; Berry 1989; Schlozman 1984; Walker 1991)—a trend that has been compounded by the US Supreme Court's 2010 decision in *Citizens United v. FEC* (Hertel-Fernandez and Skocpol 2015), and is illustrated, strikingly, in figure 2.2.[6] For instance, in 2016, national social and economic justice lobbying registrants spent a total of approximately $15 million on lobbying activities. In comparison, their mainstream counterparts spent over $3.5 *billion*. Unsurprisingly, these disparities have downstream consequences; as many scholars have demonstrated, social and economic justice organizations are generally unable to match their moneyed counterparts in lobbying breadth and volume (Costain 2005; Frymer 1999; Heaney 2004; Martinez 2009; Pinderhughes 1995; Strolovitch and Forrest 2010; Strolovitch 2006, 2007; Walker 1991).

However, there are exceptions to this relationship. While business and professional interests hold a lobbying advantage, they are often limited by

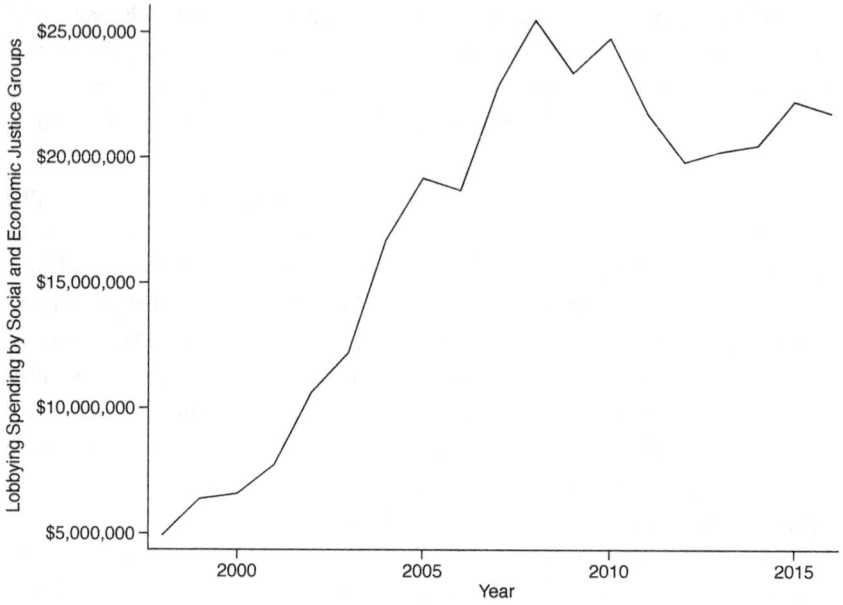

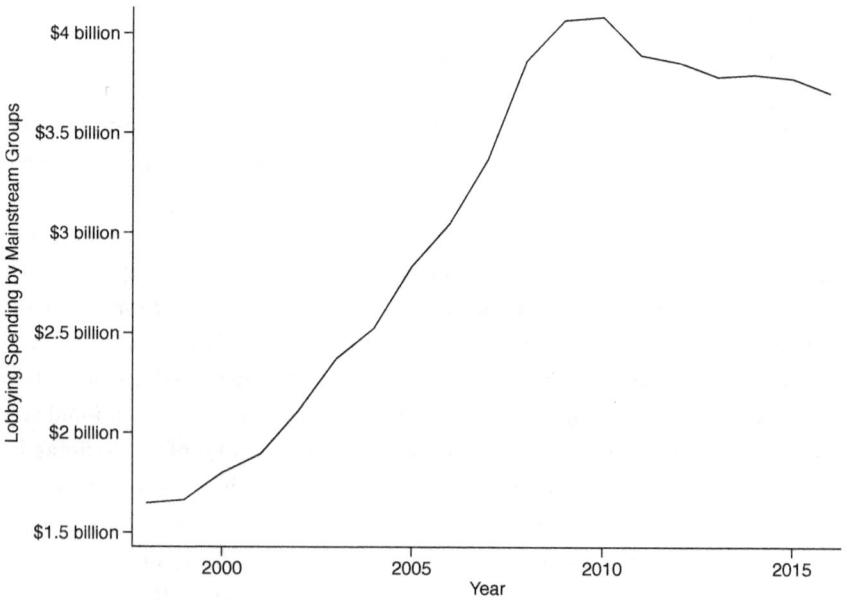

FIGURE 2.2. National lobbying spending, 1998–2016. Social and economic justice groups (*top*) and mainstream groups (*bottom*). Data compiled by the author from CRP records (available at https://www.open secrets.org).

processes and institutions that require popular majorities. Laws that pass by initiative or referenda, for instance, are more likely to reflect the priorities of citizen groups than business groups (Gerber 1999). When business interests succeed, it is mainly on issues that have broad public backing or garner limited attention and opposition because of their narrow scope (Baumgartner et al. 2009a; Smith 2000). And social and economic justice organizations *do* have successful track records. Like other groups, they are served by certain institutional and political conditions. They are more likely, for instance, to achieve their goals when advocating for the status quo; when their policy positions align with those of economic, political, and organizational elites; and when they are able to mobilize popular majorities (Amenta 2006; Baumgartner et al. 2009a; Gilens and Page 2014; Piven and Cloward 1977; Smith 2000). They are also more likely to exert influence when they share advocacy goals with others working in their sector (Hero and Preuhs 2013; Pinderhughes 1995; Weldon 2011). In the words of Anne Costain, their advocacy is "unique and worthy of study" because of its "demonstrated capability to deliver access to the excluded" (Costain 2005, 111).

But admittedly, these conditions are rare. For example, while defending the status quo *is* a favorable advocacy strategy, most long-standing policies—which reflect and reinforce sociopolitical arrangements rooted in white privilege—are not in line with the missions and interests of progressive organizations. And because social and economic justice groups often represent stigmatized and politically unpopular communities, it can be difficult for them to earn the support of elites and popular majorities as well as find aligned partners within their sectors (Schneider and Ingram 1993). Thus, despite large gains in number and stature, disparities in the lobbying and policy environments make it difficult for social and economic justice groups to uphold their promise of delivering access.

These inequalities are both extra-organizational—such as those discussed in earlier paragraphs—and intra-organizational—having to do with decision-making structures, staff politics, or funding models. For instance, the federal tax-exempt status that many social and economic justice groups hold—a 501(c)(3) nonprofit status—compels many of these groups to lobby at lower rates than they are legally permitted to out of fear of losing the status (Berry and Arons 2005). Additionally, complex relationships with funders often incentivize these organizations to cater to middle-of-the-road issues (Zack et al. 2023; Zack and Smithson-Stanley 2024). Over time, for instance, liberal advocacy groups have largely abandoned their work on redistributive issues (e.g., paid family leave, universal health care) in favor of postmaterialist issues (e.g., menu labeling, protections for near-threatened species) (Berry

1989). This relationship has been compounded by a decline in the number of civic associations and an increase in staff-led groups (Hertel-Fernandez and Skocpol 2015), which often neglect the needs of their most vulnerable constituents: those who experience intersectional disadvantage (English 2019, 2020; Marchetti 2014).

An Intersectional Lens

These trends have led to a burgeoning approach in the study of social justice advocacy—one that applies theories of intersectionality to better understand agenda-setting choices and lobbying outcomes among social and economic justice groups. Theories of intersectionality were originally introduced by Black feminists (Truth 1851; Combahee River Collective 1977) and coined by Kimberlé Crenshaw (1991), and they came about because of the frustrations of women of color with feminist movements that prioritized the experiences, positions, and interests of white women—framed as those of "all women"—and a Black civil rights movement that did the same with the experiences and positions of Black men (Collins 1990; Crenshaw 1989; Davis 1981; hooks 1981). The intersectional framework recounts the manner in which different biological, cultural, and social categories—such as race, gender, class, and sexuality—intersect to create compounding systems of discrimination and oppression. It emphasizes that intersectionality is inescapable, structuring every facet of an individual's life experiences and manifesting in "interlocking" or "simultaneous" oppressions.

Unsurprisingly, the representational choices of advocacy organizations—even those that represent marginalized communities—can reinforce or mediate these oppressions. And indeed they do, as documented by a range of scholarship highlighting majoritarian bias in interest group advocacy (Brower 2024; English 2019, 2020; Marchetti 2014; Schattschneider 1960; Strolovitch 2006). Scholars have observed that advocacy organizations representing marginalized communities routinely prioritize the interests of their more advantaged constituents—such as white women rather than women of color—at the expense of their intersectionally disadvantaged constituents (Strolovitch 2007). Intersectional advocacy thus makes up a small proportion of policy advocacy, and its occurrence is largely governed by organizational contexts. For example, some social and economic justice organizations exist exclusively to promote intersectional advocacy, and, while this population of groups is small, it has grown steadily over time (Strolovitch 2018).

Scholars have also speculated that state- and local-level advocacy organizations may be more likely than national-level groups to promote intersectional advocacy (Skrentny 2002; Berry and Arons 2005) and that national-level groups with connections to state-level affiliates may more frequently attend to intersectional issues (Strolovitch 2007). However, recent work has found that state- and local-level advocacy groups largely perpetuate the same biases as their national-level counterparts. Marchetti's 2014 survey of state-level organizations, for example, reports that while these groups frequently pursue intersectional advocacy surrounding issues of class, they systematically neglect intersectional advocacy surrounding issues of gender, race, sexuality, and ability. Scholars have thus suggested that intersectional advocacy is largely governed by organizational priorities, centered on the need to appeal to the interests of active—and more advantaged—supporters (Marchetti 2014).

The Power of Partners

Social and economic justice groups are well aware of these various biases and constraints. To mediate them, they turn to tried-and-true lobbying strategies. As I described in chapter 1, one of the most common tactics they rely on is *coalition work*. Coalition work is extremely common—and effective—across areas of social and political life. Community organizers, activists, interest groups, candidates for political office, and elected officials often build coalitions in pursuit of solutions to public problems. The reason is simple: public problems often affect broad communities of people, and developing effective solutions to these problems typically requires collective action. Organizations advocate in coalitions because they believe they can achieve a greater impact by working together than by working alone.

Organizational coalitions vary widely in form and function. They may include both groups and individuals, such as interest groups, civic associations, think tanks, service providers, political organizations, companies, community leaders, government actors, charitable foundations, and more. Some coalitions become formal entities with distinct names, paid staff, and governance models, like the Alabama Coalition for Immigrant Justice (ACIJ, founded in 2006), a coalition of six statewide grassroots organizations advocating for immigrant rights in Alabama, and the Campaign for Better Health Care (CBHC, founded in 1989), a national coalition of three hundred nonprofit organizations, health care advocates, and labor unions organizing for accessible and affordable health care for all. Other coalitions remain informal working arrangements that may come together only once or recur over time. They can contain just two groups or—as they more often do—unite tens of separate entities.

But building coalitions is undoubtedly complicated. Coalitions often bring together actors with varied interests. Coalition partners may have vastly

different cultures, missions, theories of change, and possibly even conflicting political and policy ideologies. Bridging these differences is a challenging task, and many potential partnerships are unable to surpass this hurdle
(Levi and Murphy 2006; Staggenborg 1986). Structural characteristics can
also pose obstacles to sustaining coalitions, such as unequal levels of power
across member organizations, the "free rider" problem, concerns about reduced autonomy, and complications surrounding partnerships with "strange"
or "uncomfortable" bedfellows (Zack et al. 2023; Zack and Smithson-Stanley
2024). For instance, scholars have argued that groups with the greatest political power often hold outsized leadership roles within coalitions, excluding
groups with less power—typically those advocating on behalf of historically
marginalized communities—through a dynamic termed the "iron law of oli-
garchy" (Agranoff and Mcguire 2001; Ansell and Gash 2007; Cheyns and Riisgaard 2014; Levine 2022). In larger coalitions, members may be tempted to
shirk their individual responsibilities while still reaping the benefits of the
broader collective action—a tendency that limits the ability of coalitions to
achieve their goals (Olson 1965). Finally, when organizations join coalitions,
or join in coalitions with "uncomfortable" bedfellows, they sacrifice some
degree of autonomy in setting goals, strategy, and credit claiming, and they
may be subject to blowback from their constituencies, staff, and funders (Mc-
Cammon and Campbell 2002; Olson 1965; Walker 1983). While working with
groups that are very different from their own in terms of policy orientation
or priority may be beneficial to organizations, it may also come at a political
or social cost.

However, coalitions can still be a powerful tool with the capacity to both
strengthen individual partners and bring about significant social and political change. As I noted briefly in the previous chapter, for individual organizations, coalition work can expand material and nonmaterial resources and
increase legitimacy in the eyes of political and policy actors. They can expand
member organizations' social networks and deepen their relationships with
coalition partners, establishing patterns of trust, buy-in, and commitment—
feelings that are critical to coalition recurrence (Staggenborg 2015; Bryson,
Crosby, and Stone 2006; Alexander, Comfort, and Weiner 1998; Szulecki,
Pattberg, and Biermann 2011). Tactically, these partnerships also pay dividends. Working with others increases access to information and widens the
strategic tool kits and tactical expertise available to member organizations.
Together, these characteristics build credibility and influence. For instance,
scholars have demonstrated that coalition work not only increases the likelihood of short-term gains but also reinforces the durability of any changes
achieved (Zack et al. 2023; Zack and Smithson-Stanley 2024).

Lobbying the Federal Bureaucracy

As you may now be thinking, organizational tactics are also certainly influenced by the broader political environment. Most prominently, the "great broadening" of American government—the vast expansion of American policymaking into many new areas beginning in the 1950s and continuing through the 1970s—contributed to a rapid growth in the American interest group population (Baumgartner and Jones 1993, 2009; Baumgartner and Leech 1998; Baumgartner et al. 2009a; Leech et al. 2005; Hojnacki 1997, 1998; Jones, Theriault, and Whyman 2019). This growth was not without consequence; a larger number of competitors meant that organizations became increasingly compelled to specialize, strategize, and fundraise in greater volumes in order to enhance their effectiveness in a crowded decision-making environment (Hojnacki 1997, 1998).

Declining analytic capacity in Congress has also contributed to changes in the strategic nature of American lobbying. Strapped for time and information, lawmakers have historically relied on staff and nonpartisan legislative support offices such as the Congressional Research Service (CRS), the Congressional Budget Office (CBO), and the Government Accountability Office (GAO) to make complex policy decisions (Baumgartner and Jones 2015; Drutman and Teles 2015; Fagan and McGee 2022; LaPira, Drutman, and Kosar 2020). But staff levels and institutional expertise in Congress are declining. From 1995 to 2015, the number of staff employed by Congress decreased by 66 percent—while Members' constituencies continued to increase in number. The CRS, CBO, and GAO had their budgets progressively slashed and, in this same period, lost 37 percent of their own staff (Drutman and Teles 2015; LaPira, Drutman, and Kosar 2020). Moreover, turnover in expert positions across chambers of Congress continues to break records—staff departures reached a two-decade high in March 2022.[7] Together, these patterns signal that institutional knowledge in Congress is dangerously low. And the outcome is twofold: the number of issues that Congress can attend to has steadily decreased and now, more than ever, lawmakers rely on "subsidies" provided by interest groups to do the work of policymaking (Baumgartner et al. 2009a; Hall and Deardorff 2006; Hall and Miler 2008; LaPira, Drutman, and Kosar 2020).

But these subsidies do not make up for the steady decline in congressional capacity. As I noted briefly in the previous chapter, this trend has led to the displacement of most national policymaking authority to the American bureaucracy—the mass of agencies, departments, and commissions that make up the administrative body of the federal government, colloquially known as the "fourth branch" (Warren 2018; Yackee 2006). The work of these offices is extraordinarily consequential. Agency policymaking has enormous breadth, touching nearly every provision of every law and executive action. While lawmakers in Congress often do not focus on "nitty-gritty" policy details, agencies *do*. Bureaucrats' choices to define a population, revise a standard, or specify how a public good will be delivered may seem small, but their outcomes are far reaching, and advocacy organizations are well aware of their significance. In fact, the majority of American lobbying targets a federal agency—and agencies often seek out the expertise of interest groups in crafting and promulgating provisions of the law (Baumgartner et al. 2009a; Cropper et al. 1992; Golden 1998; Haeder and Yackee 2015; Hrebenar 1997; McKay and Yackee 2007; Nelson and Yackee 2012; Yackee 2006, 2012).

An unintended consequence to this particular trend has been a rise in the power of American interest groups. For decades now, interest groups have helped bureaucrats to sway public opinion (Hrebenar 1997), raise awareness of policy issues facing agencies (Rourke 1984; Hrebenar 1997), resist political control (Carpenter 2002), secure budgets (Berry 1989), and craft regulatory language (Haeder and Yackee 2015). This relationship is facilitated, in part, by federal law, which requires agencies to solicit opinions from outside groups and private citizens when writing rules. Similarly, courts have historically encouraged agencies to be more responsive to groups and citizens who express opinions during this process (Rabin 1986; Shapiro 1988; McGarity 1992, 1997). Federal agencies thus have strong incentives to consider the policy recommendations of interest groups, and often do.

Over time, scholars have sought to better understand the relationship between organized interests and agencies. Some conceived of interest groups as partners with Congress in influencing the bureaucracy (see McCubbins and Schwartz 1984; McCubbins, Noll, and Weingast 1987, 1989; Epstein and O'Halloran 1996, 1999). McCubbins, Noll, and Weingast (1987, 1989) suggest, for instance, that the imposition of administrative procedures by Congress drives bureaucrats to work toward the enacting Congress's—and its favored interest groups'—goals by constraining agency behavior. McCubbins and Schwartz (1984) argue that Congress and interest groups work together in pursuit of shared policy goals. They theorize that Congress uses interest groups to "police" the activity of the bureaucracy and alert Congress of problematic bureaucratic actions by sounding "fire alarms." They find that Congress often waits for these "fire alarms" from interest groups before conducting oversight over agencies' policy choices. Similarly, Epstein and O'Halloran (1996, 1999) report that when Congress delegates policymaking to the bureaucracy, it often elicits support from interest groups in overseeing ("policing") the administrative branch.

However, a growing body of work has pointed to the *direct* influence of interest groups over bureaucratic policymaking. For instance, interest groups independently assist the bureaucracy by providing expert information during notice-and-comment rulemaking and are often successful in shaping its policy outputs (Carpenter et al. 2022; Cropper et al. 1992; Hrebenar 1997; Golden 1998; Yackee 2006; McKay and Yackee 2007; Yackee 2012; Nelson and Yackee 2012; Haeder and Yackee 2015). This expert information alerts bureaucrats to problems with proposed regulations, and when taken in context (i.e., when there is a consensus across the information sent to bureaucrats), agencies are better able to use interest group comments to alter proposed rules (Croley 1998; Golden 1998; McKay and Yackee 2007; Nelson and Yackee 2012). Further, Nixon, Howard, and DeWitt (2002) report that "privileged" interest groups do not dominate influence in notice-and-comment rulemaking.[8] At any given point in time, a wide range of organizations are actively engaged in agency policymaking (Golden 1998; Yackee 2006).

In addition, the role of judicial review in bureaucratic proceedings underscores interest groups' direct influence over agency decisions. All agency rules are subject to judicial review to ensure that they follow their legislative mandates and procedural requirements. In support of this oversight mechanism, federal courts have required the bureaucracy to keep a meaningful written record (encompassing proposed and final rules, public comments, relevant studies or data, and more) to assist in this process and to enhance the responsiveness of the bureaucracy to public participants in rulemaking (Seidenfeld 1997; Magat, Krupnick, and Harrington 1986). The "threat" of potential court action, as well as courts' reliance on the written record, have thus increasingly provided opportunities for outside groups to influence agency rulemaking and strongly incentivized agencies to carefully consider their comments (Chubb 1983; West 1984).

Take, for example, the American Rescue Plan Act of 2021. This act provided approximately $1.9 trillion in COVID-19 relief to state, local, and tribal governments; schools; employers; small businesses; and individuals. One of its most salient provisions was the Child Tax Credit, which offered eligible families monthly payments of up to $300 for each child under age six and up to $250 for each child aged six to seventeen—the largest such tax credit in American history. But delivering this tax credit was easier said than done. How would recipients be identified? Where would the money be delivered? What if eligible families hadn't filed taxes recently? These questions of implementation were basic but consequential, and covered *a lot* of eligible recipients—many low-income families, for example, simply don't make enough money to be required to file federal taxes. To effectively deliver the tax credit, the implementing agencies—the Internal Revenue Service (IRS) and the Treasury Department—consulted with advocacy organizations to think through the options, cover their bases, and raise awareness of the relief.[9] They partnered with a nonprofit organization, Code for America, to develop a sign-up tool for families who hadn't recently filed taxes. Together with another group, the United State of Women, they publicized the availability of the tax credit and developed sign-up guides in multiple languages. In a matter of months, they had delivered $15 billion in payments to the families of about sixty million children.

A History of Rulemaking

When advocacy organizations try to directly influence the federal bureaucracy, they face several entry points. They may be invited to offer informal consultations before the issuance of a proposed rule (either behind closed doors or during "listening meetings"), volunteer policy guidance in response to an Advance Notice of Proposed Rulemaking (ANPRM), or submit a public comment upon publication of a Notice of Proposed Rulemaking (NPRM). Across these stages, organizations' access and influence vary widely and are structured by relationships, policy issues, and administrative history.

Early administrative governance was largely clerical—the first agency rules likely developed when agencies tasked with regulating the economy, such as the Interstate Commerce Commission (ICC) and the Federal Trade Commission (FTC), were established in the late nineteenth and early twentieth centuries. Rulemaking during this period was not particularly salient. For instance, in 1911, the US Supreme Court heard the case *United States v. Grimaud*, involving a shepherd who had been fined by the US Department of Agriculture (USDA) for allowing his sheep to graze in a national park without a permit. The court upheld the agency rule that triggered the fine without much attention or controversy.

Over time, rulemaking became a much more prominent policymaking tool. As the federal government grew substantially in the early 1930s as the result of New Deal programs and initiatives, agencies responded in kind. The American bureaucracy quickly professionalized, due in part to the uptake of the Pendleton Act, which awarded civil service positions on the basis of merit rather than patronage. This growth in government and bureaucratic skill led to new responsibilities for federal agencies—namely, the development of more general regulations rather than rules developed on an individual, case-by-case basis. This shift in approach led to the 1936 passage of the Federal Register Act, developing a *Federal Register* archive in which all agency policies with "general applicability and legal effect" were required to be published. However, this new requirement did not standardize regulatory policymaking procedures, which varied considerably across agencies, and over the following decade lawmakers debated whether, and how, to implement greater structure.

In 1946, the US Congress passed the APA, which described—in only nine pages—the steps that agencies must follow in implementing new law. This act continues to govern agency policymaking today, through only three requirements. First, it requires agencies to publish notices of proposed rulemaking in the *Federal Register* describing the statutory backing for each new rule as well as a summary of the subjects and issues at stake. Second, agencies must provide all members of the public—private citizens, businesses, advocacy organizations, elected officials, and so forth—with an opportunity to participate by offering public comments. Third, agencies are required to publicly state the date that any given rule would go into effect (normally, no less than thirty days following the publication of the final rule).

Rulemaking became more frequent under the APA but remained a fairly uncontroversial process. Agency work was considered "expert" and left largely undisturbed by Congress and the president. But beginning in the 1960s, rulemaking took on a more salient role in government policymaking. In response to public demands for greater consumer protection and government regulation of health-adjacent sectors, agency action became more aggressive. In 1965 and 1971, for example, the FTC required tobacco companies to add warning labels to cigarette packages and banned broadcast cigarette advertising. Later, in 1977, the Environmental Protection Agency (EPA) developed regulations limiting lead air emissions. During this period, judicial involvement in agency rulemaking increased and courts frequently struck down agency rules. These decisions shared a common theme: that agencies were beholden to procedures that required robust public participation. They reiterated that agency rules must be developed in close consultation with stakeholders and affected parties such that their policy outcomes would "promote participation [. . .] and reflect the preferences of all involved" (Bressman 2007, 1761).

In the 1980s, the rulemaking process changed yet again. President Ronald Reagan issued an executive order in 1981 creating a new executive office—the Office of Information and Regulatory Affairs (OIRA)—responsible for the review of agency rules. This office, housed within the White House Office of Management and Budget (OMB), was given the authority to review agencies' draft regulations before publication and solicitation of public feedback. While several key changes followed—for example, the 1984 Supreme Court case *Chevron v. Natural Resources Defense Council* established the doctrine of

Chevron deference, which compels courts to defer to agencies' expertise, and a 1993 Executive Order required agencies to conduct cost-benefit analyses for "economically significant" rules—the APA remains the backbone of agency rulemaking.

Agency Rulemaking Today

Today, most agency policymaking happens through a process called notice-and-comment rulemaking.[10] This process is challenging and lengthy—so much so that the average agency only produces about twenty-three proposed rules and twenty-six final rules each year (about three thousand rules are published annually in the *Federal Register*) (Potter 2019). Figure 2.3 illustrates the steps that a given agency must follow in developing a new rule. The first significant step, deciding whether to write a new rule, can be triggered by several sources. The US Congress can, for instance, pass a new law directing an agency to write a specific rule. Through executive action, the president can direct agencies to develop rules enforcing aspects of their administration's agenda. Agencies can also initiate discretionary rules—rules that they write of their own volition—in response to policy needs that they observe.

The next step involves developing a draft proposal, one of the most consequential stages in this process. Because agencies have an incentive to "get it right the first time" in order to avoid reputational damage or legal consequences, they tend to take their time with this phase (West 2004). In a 2004 study of agency rulemaking, for example, West reports that the average length of proposal development was approximately five years. During this stage, both agency actors and organizational actors can be involved. The process typically begins with a small rule-writing team including program staff, economists, general counsel, and even political leadership. To inform their policy choices, this team might decide to conduct reviews of academic research or develop their own original research, either internally or through a contractor.

Depending on the subject of the proposed rule, the agency may be required to produce impact analyses or cost-benefit analyses—another complex and time-consuming hurdle. This stage presents one of the first opportunities for organizational advocates to influence policy direction. At this pivotal point, agencies often consult stakeholders and experts. A formal avenue for doing so is through an Advance Notice of Proposed Rulemaking (ANPRM)—a notice published in the *Federal Register* formally requesting guidance. ANPRMs, however, are optional, and thus fairly uncommon. Agencies are far more likely to gather information in a less public manner through "informal and

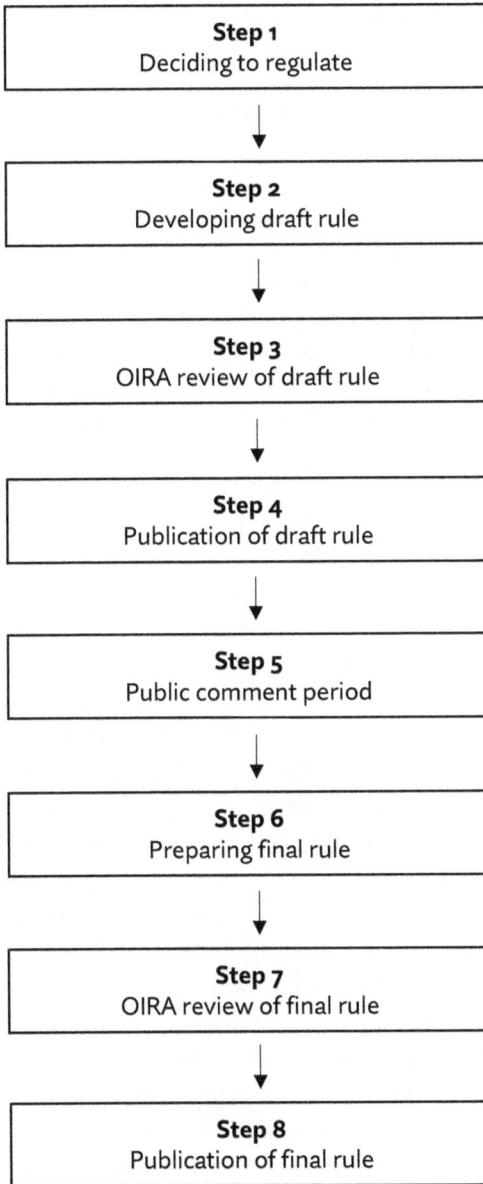

FIGURE 2.3. Stages of notice-and-comment rulemaking

idiosyncratic" conversations with invited groups (West 2009, 577). In fact, some evidence suggests that most organizational influence occurs during this stage (see Chubb 1983, Yackee 2019).

The next significant step involves OIRA review. This stage, mandated by executive order, allows OIRA to conduct a review of any "significant" draft rule. Under the order, agency rules are subject to review if OIRA determines whether they:

1. Have an annual effect on the economy of $100 million or more or adversely affect in a material way the economy, a sector of the economy, productivity, competition, jobs, the environment, public health or safety, or State, local, or tribal governments or communities;
2. Create a serious inconsistency or otherwise interfere with an action taken or planned by another agency;
3. Materially alter the budgetary impact of entitlements, grants, user fees, or loan programs or the rights and obligations of recipients thereof; or
4. Raise novel legal or policy issues arising out of legal mandates, the President's priorities, or the principles set forth in this Executive order.[11]

If OIRA chooses not to review a draft rule, or upon clearance of OIRA's review, the rule is published in the *Federal Register*, along with a set period (typically thirty days) during which written comments can be submitted by members of the public.

The volume of comments received on a draft rule varies widely—some rules receive no comments, and some receive hundreds of thousands. In extreme cases, such as a 2012 EPA rule addressing greenhouse gas emissions, millions of comments are sent in. Most often, comments are submitted by advocacy organizations with specialized expertise or private groups with vested interests in the outcome. But sometimes, mass public attention can turn to agency activity. In 2014, for example, comedian John Oliver encouraged his *Last Week Tonight* viewers to submit comments on a proposed Federal Communications Commission (FCC) rule regarding net neutrality. The volume of responses was so high—hundreds of thousands of people responded to his call to action—that the FCC website crashed.[12]

During these periods, agencies are discouraged from the type of ex parte communication (off-the-record conversations) with outside actors in which they might engage during proposal development. Instead, if agencies decide to gather information or seek guidance while a rule is out for public comment, they might hold public hearings or listening forums. Upon the closing of the comment period, agencies are required to review *every* comment received and issue a written response. These written responses are published along with the final rule, explaining the agency's rationale for incorporating or disregarding the comments' recommendations. Existing research holds mixed positions on the value of these periods—scholars of bureaucratic politics note that since agencies often publish draft rules in a near-final form, comments received during the subsequent periods will have little sway (Potter 2019; Yackee 2020). Thus, they suggest that commenters largely engage with these periods to pursue judicial review at a later point in a rule's lifespan. Scholars of interest group politics, however, have consistently found evidence of influence during notice-and-comment periods, and several agencies have begun to pilot programs designed to increase public involvement from a more diverse array of organizational advocates during these periods (Golden 1998; Haeder and Yackee 2015; McKay and Yackee 2007; Nelson and Yackee 2012; Yackee 2006, 2012).

In the last stage, agencies finalize the rule. First, they review all comments received, a task that is easier said than done. While this exercise can be trivial—many rules receive a small number of comments—it can occasionally be extremely taxing. For example, when the FTC proposed significant regulations on cigarette packaging and advertising in the late 1990s, the agency rented a warehouse to process the hundreds of thousands of comments that it received. Former FDA commissioner David Kessler described a frantic, yet orderly, scene: "The first group registered the responses and entered data into computer banks. The stacks of paper were then rushed into a second group, where each individual comment was read and categorized into one of hundreds of topics. . . . Finally, the responses were sped to a third team of professional FDA staff for careful analysis" (Kessler 2001, 337). Today, reviewing public comments does not look much different. While some agencies turn to federal contractors and modern text analysis tools (like plagiarism detection) to speed up parts of this process, it remains extensive. For instance, an agency official I spoke with in 2022 said to me, "Reviewing comments is a very manual process. Maybe [my agency] is just old school, but our process is to literally print out the comments, divide them by category, and assign each category a lead who is in charge of reading and drafting the response to that set of comments. It's hard work!"[13]

Upon sorting through all public comments, agencies begin the task of deciding which recommended changes—if any—they will make to the proposed rule. Importantly, this exercise centers around creating the *best possible* final policy. Agencies do not necessarily follow the majority opinions of commenters. Instead, they search comments for valuable information to inform their policy choices. They may look for certain signals across or within comments—such as consensus or credibility—but their final choices are driven by a desire to develop the best implementation protocol for the provision of law they have been tasked with implementing. After reviewing and incorporating feedback from public comments, agencies send the draft final rule through an internal clearance process and then on once again to OIRA. If OIRA clears the policy or chooses not to review it, the final rule is published in the *Federal Register* and, after a short waiting period, becomes legally binding.

Summary

Over the last several decades, social and economic justice organizations have become critical representatives for their constituents in national policymaking processes. As formalized advocates in American politics, they play an important role in sustaining the policy goals of the campaigns that birthed them. To this day, for example, women's organizations continue to fight for the Equal Rights Amendment (ERA), a policy initiative introduced by the women's suffrage movement in 1923. Over time, these organizations have become active contenders in the American political system; many now maintain offices in the Washington, DC, metropolitan area, have formidable reputations, and boast connections to elected officials and political institutions. Despite these gains, however, they struggle to match their private and professional counterparts in breadth, presence, and resources. Their advocacy agendas are limited and characterized by a pervasive majoritarian bias. To compensate, they strategically leverage advocacy tactics and carefully select targets.

As the American lobbying environment has grown increasingly saturated, reliance on one particular strategy—coalitional advocacy—has become more common. In this chapter, I introduced a core idea of this book—that building partnerships with other organizations allows social and economic justice groups to conserve their resources, expand their tactical and informational capacity, and increase their legitimacy in the eyes of policymakers. In doing so, I reiterated that coalition work presents a unique solution to problems of competitive lobbying contexts, limited organizational capacity, and advocacy biases. But of course, policy process matters. To this end, I also discussed my focus on regulatory lobbying—advocacy organizations' efforts to influence federal agency policymaking—along with the steps by which federal agencies execute their policy responsibilities and entry points for advocacy organizations seeking to shape outcomes. I emphasized that agency rulemaking matters a great deal, particularly in the modern policy environment—a reality of which social and economic justice organizations are well aware. In the next chapter, I pick up with a discussion of the novel measurement approach developed to answer the questions I pose in this book: the *Collaborative Advocacy Dataset*.

3

Studying Coalitions

Much like building coalitions, *studying* coalitions is complex. As of the publication of this book, only a handful of studies have explored the subject of coalitions in American lobbying, the majority of which focus their empirical efforts on a small number of cases. There is good reason for this limited attention: it is difficult to collect comprehensive data on coalitional advocacy. Coalitions, like other social ties, are dynamic and often informal. They occur and recur in response to unique political and policy contexts. And they leave no clear trace; unlike lobbyists and interest groups, organizational coalitions are not required to disclose their presence or activity to government offices. Lobbying disclosure reports, campaign contributions, and independent expenditures allow scholars to answer questions of individual-level interest group activity and influence; coalition-level questions, however, have historically been beyond the scope of existing data.

Scholars have thus relied on survey experiments, elite interviews, and other qualitative methodologies to study collective action and collaboration in American lobbying. Hojnacki's (1997) foundational work, for example, analyzed data on coalition activity reported by organizations active on five policy issues through questionnaires and in-person interviews conducted in September 1993. Hula's (1999) book surveyed and interviewed interest groups active on three policy issues—transportation, education, and civil rights—in the 101st Congress. Others have turned to qualitative and mixed methods approaches to study coalitions; Levi and Murphy's (2006) work, for instance, relied on archival records to trace the processes and mechanisms of coalition building in a single case: the 1999 World Trade Organization (WTO) protests in Seattle. In her 2017 book, Phinney deployed a mixed-methods approach to study coalition activity surrounding the passage of federal welfare reform in

1996. These varying strategies underscore that "there is no easy way to compile primary data about coalitions" (Hula 1999, 12). In this chapter, I describe my own approach.

The *Collaborative Advocacy Dataset*

The problem of collecting comprehensive data on organizational coalitions is challenging but not insurmountable. Since the publication of many of the works on coalitions mentioned in the previous section, significant advances in the technological landscape have altered the interaction between organizations and government. These advances, like the advent of the internet and social media applications, offered new opportunities for organizations to publicly build reputations, stake claims over issue areas, and associate with other organizations. Nowadays, an advocacy organization *without* a sophisticated website—one that articulates a mission, lists their staff and advisors, describes ongoing projects, and champions positive press—is an extreme outlier. The same is true for elected officials and branches of government, including the American federal bureaucracy. In fact, one of the most consequential outcomes of these advances was the federal government's launch of Regulations.gov in January 2003, part of an e-rulemaking transparency initiative by the Bush Administration.[1] This website provided a repository for all regulatory actions and rulemaking materials—past, present, and future—and served as a portal for public participation in the notice-and-comment process.

Regulations.gov fundamentally changed the nature of American regulation. Its purpose was simple: to make public participation in rulemaking more accessible. The new website housed information on every agency action and adjudication by every federal agency—from proposed rules to supporting materials. It further offered members of the public a one-stop shop for offering public comment. Under the new website, any individual or group—private citizen, elected official, interest group, corporation, and so forth—could read about proposed agency actions and submit comments online. These changes had monumental implications. Under the previous systems, information about agency rules was disseminated through paper announcements and comments were submitted by mail, a process that privileged political insiders. Regulations.gov, on the other hand, created universal access to the regulatory process. Anyone with access to the internet could read about and be a part of the rulemaking process. As an added bonus, agencies also uploaded archives of past dockets—including regulatory documents and public comments dating back to at least 1980.

The primary benefit of these changes is, of course, clear. Greater access to information, more equitable communication channels, and a commitment to transparency all bolster democratic legitimacy—particularly in a branch of government run by unelected officials. Another, less clear, advantage is a unique opportunity to capitalize on data made newly available by Regulations.gov to expand our knowledge of the relationship between public participants and agency rulemaking. My work takes advantage of this treasure trove of data by introducing a new dataset, called the *Collaborative Advocacy Dataset*, the product of seven years of meticulous effort.[2] This dataset tracks coalitions through cosignature patterns on public comments and measures the nature and outcomes of organizational advocacy using modern text analysis tools. To answer the different questions I pose in this book, this dataset contains two subsets: a subset of data on coalition behavior and outcomes by a sample of social and economic justice organizations and a subset of identical data concerning a sample of "mainstream" organizations—groups representing private, professional, and general interests. These data contain information on over twenty thousand organizations advocating on approximately 2,800 rules issued by 116 federal agencies over a seventeen-year period (2000–2016).

SAMPLING ORGANIZATIONS AND AGENCY RULES

The first step to compiling the *Collaborative Advocacy Dataset* involved gathering two samples of organizations: one containing social and economic justice organizations, and one containing mainstream organizations. To produce these samples, I turned to data from lobbying disclosure reports. Under the Lobbying Disclosure Act (LDA) of 1995, any person or entity engaged in national-level lobbying is required to register their presence quarterly with the clerk of the United States House of Representatives and the secretary of the United States Senate. These reports require groups and lobbyists to disclose, among other things, the general policy area in which they typically lobby and the specific policy issues on which they lobbied during these periods—both of which typically remain stable over time (Baumgartner et al. 2009a; LaPira and Thomas 2020). These reports are made publicly available by government offices, and in recent years, a few different nonpartisan research groups have compiled, coded, and publicized data from these reports. Today, the most prominent such group is called the Center for Responsive Politics (CRP), also known by the moniker OpenSecrets.

To produce the first sample, I used data from these reports compiled by the CRP. More specifically, I first assembled a list of all organizations that submitted at least one lobbying disclosure report (LDR) during my period of study and maintained an advocacy focus in any of five general policy areas: racial/ethnic minority groups, Native American tribes, women's issues, anti-poverty issues, and LGBTQ+ issues.[3] These policy areas derive from the CRP's category codes—classifications of organizations' main policy emphases.[4] These category codes are assigned by the CRP on the basis of information from registrants' websites, annual reports, and financial filings, alongside news articles discussing their advocacy. In ambiguous cases, coders may turn to registrants' self-reported general issue area codes and specific lobbying issues, as provided on their LDRs.[5] To assign these codes, the CRP relies on a hierarchical coding system consisting, at the highest level, of thirteen sectors, at the middle level of approximately one hundred industries, and at the most detailed level of approximately four hundred categories.[6] The five above-mentioned policy areas were sourced from the CRP's most granular level of coding (i.e., the four hundred plus categories) and represent all possible categories in the CRP's coding scheme that explicitly reference the policy interests of historically marginalized communities in the United States. A codebook with the complete list of category codes may be accessed through the CRP's Bulk Data repository.[7] An archived copy of this codebook is also available for download on my website.[8]

I then drew a stratified random sample of one hundred organizations from this list.[9] This sample was stratified according to organizations' advocacy foci; for instance, the proportion of groups with an advocacy focus on women's issues in this sample is roughly equivalent to the proportion of such advocates in the broader sampling frame. To produce the second sample, I assembled a list of all organizations that submitted at least one lobbying disclosure report during my period of study and maintained an advocacy focus on any general policy area *except* those five areas used to select the first sample.[10] I then drew a stratified random sample of fifty groups from this list.[11,12] As with the first sample, this sample was stratified according to organizations' advocacy foci; for instance, the proportion of advocates with an advocacy focus on issues of energy and natural resources in this sample is roughly equivalent to the proportion of such advocates in the broader sampling frame. Importantly, as such, neither sample is intended to be equally representative of all types of groups, agencies, and policy domains. Rather, they are intended to be representative of the policy landscape as it pertains to *advocacy*—by social and economic justice–oriented groups and mainstream organizations, respectively. Group types, agencies, and policy domains are present in the data at rates commensurate with the degree to which they are active and present in national lobbying and policymaking. My results should therefore generalize to modern lobbying activity by both sets of advocates. In the coming pages, I will discuss the characteristics of the sample of social and economic justice organizations—the main subject of this book. I discuss characteristics of the mainstream sample in chapter 6.

THE PARTICULARITIES OF LDA AND CRP DATA

The use of data from reports submitted under the LDA—and compiled by the CRP—to capture the nationally active interest group population comes with advantages and disadvantages. The primary advantage is simple: LDA data represent one of the only reliable and publicly available sources of national-level lobbying activity in American politics (Baumgartner and Leech 2001; Baumgartner et al. 2009a; LaPira, Thomas, and Baumgartner 2014; LaPira and Thomas 2020). Moreover, their nature necessitates the use of data compiled, cleaned, and coded by a third party such as the CRP (LaPira and Thomas 2020). Relying on raw LDA data (or similar primary data) to capture directly the bounds of the lobbying population would require coding hundreds of thousands of disclosures and directory entries by hand—a task that is unrealistic for many researchers, myself included. For reference, during the period under study in this book, more than six hundred thousand LDRs were filed.[13] Many scholars have documented these challenges and thus rely on CRP data to sample and study the national interest group population; LaPira and Thomas's (2020) retrospective on the twenty-fifth anniversary of the LDA, for instance, identified more than six dozen peer-reviewed articles, chapters, and books relying on LDA data—commonly compiled by the CRP—to draw samples or study the full population of lobbying organizations.

The primary disadvantage of these data relates to a fundamental characteristic of the LDA—which requires organizations to meet a minimum level of spending in order to file a lobbying registration. At the time of sampling, the Lobbying Disclosure Act of 1995, alongside the Lobbying Disclosure Technical Amendments Act of 1998, required organizations employing in-house lobbyists to file lobbying registrations if their total expenses for lobbying activities exceeded $5,000 during a quarterly period.[14] Some organizations, particularly less resourced advocates and groups with a tax status that disincentivizes them from reaching this threshold—that is, a 501(c)(3) status—*may* be nationally active policy advocates but may not reach this spending threshold—and therefore may not file LDAs and may have been excluded from my sampling frames. While my definition of *nationally active*— all advocates that filed at least one disclosure report during the seventeen-year period under study—sought to address this concern by establishing a low standard of national-level lobbying activity for inclusion in the sampling frames, this reality represents an important condition of the sampling procedure. Scholars have noted that despite this limitation, the LDA data remain the most valid source of capturing the national-level lobbying population, as other data sources (e.g., commercial directories such as the *Washington Information Directory* (Walker 1983) or the *Washington Representatives Directory* (Schlozman 1984; Schlozman and Tierney 1983, 1986) do not document actual advocacy activity (LaPira and Thomas 2020).

Additionally, the reliance on organizational classifications assigned by a third party (i.e., the CRP's category codes) to establish the bounds of the populations under study in this work presents a similar limitation. It is likely that there are some nationally active organizations that *could* be considered social and economic justice–oriented groups that presented classificatory difficulties for CRP coders and thus did not appear in my sampling frame. Scholars have documented the porousness of organizational constituencies and orientations and thus the challenges of reliably classifying interest groups in social science research (Berry 1989; Baumgartner and Leech 1998; Strolovitch 2007). The CRP's coding procedure is designed to minimize these classificatory difficulties by relying on a wide range of information to minimize ambiguity in coding (e.g., organizational websites, annual reports, financial filings, news articles, and LDRs—see the previous section). Moreover, their codes are applied consistently over time—unless organizations undergo a significant change in orientation or mission, they reliably receive the same code. However, the porousness of boundaries remains an important reality—and limitation—of any research that seeks to make binary classifications among advocacy organizations.

THE SEJ SAMPLE

The sample of social and economic justice groups (SEJ sample) includes a variety of organizations (table 3.1) advocating on a range of policy issues (table 3.2).[15] To start, 49 percent of the sample consists of Native American tribes and their organizational representatives, such as the National Congress of American Indians (NCAI, founded in 1944), the Alaska Federation of Natives (AFN, founded in 1966), and the Catawba Indian Nation. Thirty-eight percent of the sample is made up of citizen groups such as Asian Americans Advancing Justice (AAJC), the Feminist Majority Foundation (FMF), and the Human Rights Campaign (HRC, founded in 1980). Finally, charitable foundations, think tanks, and professional associations—such as Catholic Charities USA (CCUSA, founded in 1910) and the American Council on International

TABLE 3.1. SEJ sample by organizational type

Organizational type	Frequency	Percent
Charitable foundation/think tank	7	7.00
Citizen group	38	38.00
Native American tribe	49	49.00
Professional association	6	6.00
Total	100	100%

TABLE 3.2. SEJ sample by policy focus

Policy focus	Frequency	Percent
Anti-poverty	26	26.00
LGBTQ+	4	4.00
Native American tribes	49	49.00
Racial/ethnic minority	16	16.00
Women's issues	5	5.00
Total	100	100%

Personnel (ACIP, founded in 1972)—make up the smallest proportions of the sample, at 7 and 6 percent, respectively. No businesses, business groups, governmental associations, or unions are present in the sample.

Table 3.2 depicts the primary policy foci of the sample of social and economic justice groups, according to data compiled and coded by the CRP. This breakdown demonstrates, most prominently, that organizations advocating on issues of Indigenous policy make up nearly half of the sample, at 49 percent. This finding reflects the same feature portrayed in table 3.1, which I will discuss in more detail in a few paragraphs. This analysis also illustrates that organizations focusing on issues of economic justice (anti-poverty) compose approximately 26 percent of the sample. Groups advocating on issues of racial justice make up approximately 16 percent of the sample. Finally, those lobbying primarily on women's and LGBTQ+ issues compose 5 and 4 percent of the sample, respectively.

Finally, the sample contains organizations advocating on behalf of many different constituencies.[16] Twelve distinct constituencies are present, as illustrated in table 3.3. Fifty-five percent of the sample consists of organizations advocating on behalf of racially minoritized groups, including Black/African American, Asian American, Latino/Hispanic, and Native American/American Indian individuals. Thirteen percent of the sample is made up of groups representing children and youth. Five percent of groups in the sample

TABLE 3.3. SEJ sample by constituency

Constituency	Frequency	Percent
Children/youth	13	13.00
Elderly	1	1.00
General interest	3	3.00
Immigrant	5	5.00
LGBTQ+	2	2.00
Low-income	4	4.00
Racial minority	55	55.00
Religious community	4	4.00
Student	2	2.00
Veteran	1	1.00
Women	4	4.00
Other	6	6.00
Total	100	100%

represent immigrant communities, 5 percent represent low-income people, 4 percent represent religious communities, and 4 percent represent women. Groups championing the interests of LGBTQ+ individuals (2 percent), students (2 percent), veterans (1 percent), and elderly people (1 percent) compose the smallest constituent categories in the sample.

THE PARTICULARITIES OF NATIVE INTERESTS

There are a substantial number of Native American tribes in my sample. At first glance, this trend may seem surprising—and maybe even disconcerting. But it captures an important feature of American lobbying: that Indian nations and their organizational advocates compose a significant proportion of the interest group population. In fact, these groups make up approximately 40 percent of all lobbying advocates for women, people of color, Indian nations, low-income people, and LGBTQ+ people in national-level politics (Dwidar 2022b).[17] Thus, this characteristic of my sample should lend confidence to the representative nature of my sampling strategy.

Nevertheless, it is worth taking a moment to discuss the particularities of Native interests as lobbying entities. Indian nations differ from traditional interest groups in key ways, including, prominently, their statuses as sovereign nations and correspondingly, their unique relationships with the federal government. However, despite these characteristics, Native American tribes are not entirely autonomous decision-makers. Federal policymaking can significantly affect the functions and needs of Indian tribes. As such, they are active contenders in American lobbying.[18] In particular, since the passage of the Indian Gaming Regulatory Act (IGRA) in 1988—which provided many tribes with the financial resources to become players in the American political system—Indian nations have consistently engaged in lobbying efforts to protect and improve their treaty, land, resource, and civil and political rights (Mason 1998, 2000; Steinman 2004; Witmer and Boehmke 2007; Corntassel and Witmer 2008; Witmer, Johnson, and Beohmke 2014).

This choice to invest in lobbying was decidedly strategic. Research on tribal political activity has repeatedly highlighted a fundamental tension: that traditional political participation, such as seeking and holding nontribal office, remains contested within tribal communities (Carlson 2022; Evans 2011). While turnout by American Indian voters has increased substantially in recent election cycles (see Sanchez 2021), some tribal leaders, advocates, and scholars argue that such participation undermines tribes' designations as sovereign governments (LaVelle 2011; Oeser 2010). Instead, scholars have observed that tribes and their members often seek political representation through diplomacy, using interest group tactics such as lobbying government officials and testifying before Congress to advocate for their rights (Carpenter 2017; Hoxie 2012; Wilkinson 2006). Indeed, Indian nations, American Indian nonprofit organizations, tribal consortia, and tribal businesses routinely leverage traditional interest group techniques to influence policymaking across levels and branches of American government (Boehmke and Witmer 2012, 2020; Carlson 2021; Cowger 2001; Dwidar and Marchetti 2023; Hoxie 2012; Viola 1995; Wilkinson 2006).

Thus, there is strong scholarly support for the inclusion of Native American tribes in works examining interest group representation of marginalized populations. Scholars of tribal political activity report that tribal lobbying is motivated by the same factors that motivate traditional interest groups (issues, access, ideology, and constituent interests) and is both common and substantively similar to lobbying by traditional groups (Witmer and Boehmke 2007; Boehmke and Witmer 2012; Witmer, Johnson, and Boehmke 2014). Relatedly, it is worth emphasizing that existing scholarship on interest group politics—including the small number of works examining organizational representation of historically marginalized populations—has largely neglected the study of tribal lobbying. For example, in their examinations of social and economic justice organizations in American politics, Strolovitch (2006, 2007) and Marchetti (2014) assess advocacy organizations that serve Native interests (rather than Indian nations themselves) and merge tribal interests with broader racial/ethnic minority interest groups, respectively. Thus, I consider the prevalence of Native American tribes and their organizational advocates in my data to be both empirically appropriate—as it approximates a broader trend in the population—and theoretically valuable, as it allows me to make inferences on behalf of an understudied but important subset of groups.

The second step to compiling the *Collaborative Advocacy Dataset* involved collecting a corpus of regulatory documents: all applicable public comments, proposed agency rules, and final agency rules. To collect these documents, I relied on Regulations.gov's interactive Application Programming Interface (API).[19] For every organization in my samples, I built a search query containing parameters for docket type (rulemaking), comment period (closed), received date range (January 1, 2000, to December 31, 2016), and keyword (name of the organization). I then read each comment returned by the query and removed false positive results.[20] For all comments determined to have been submitted by the organizations in my samples, I collected the corresponding proposed and final rule documents. I then used optical character recognition (OCR) software to transcribe each document, which I augmented with manual transcription and error correction where necessary. Finally, I preprocessed all public comment, proposed rule, and final rule documents. This involved the conversion of all words to their stems[21] and removal of capitalization, stop words,[22] graphics, figures, and appendixes—in line with standard conventions for text analysis (Grimmer and Stewart 2013).

Across both subsets of the *Collaborative Advocacy Dataset*, this process ultimately produced a corpus of 3,580 public comments submitted on 2,917 proposed rules issued by 116 federal agencies. Of these proposed agency actions, 55 percent corresponded to a published final rule.[23] Within the data on the sample of social and economic justice organizations, the agencies appearing in the data span a range of sizes and policy specializations—from agencies such as the Bureau of Indian Affairs to the Department of Health and Human Services to the Equal Employment Opportunity Commission—as well as a mix of independent (25 percent) and executive branch (75 percent) agencies.[24] The proposed rules within this subset of the data also span a wide range of policy topics. As illustrated in figure 3.1, twenty out of the twenty-one major topics proposed by the Policy Agendas Project's common policy coding scheme are present.[25] Many of the proposed rules in the data fall in the areas of health and education policy—approximately 23 percent and 13 percent of all proposed rules, respectively. This trend reflects the policy environment, as health care and education reform were ubiquitous on the national government's agenda during the period under study. The rules are also characterized by ranges of complexity and salience. They include straightforward,

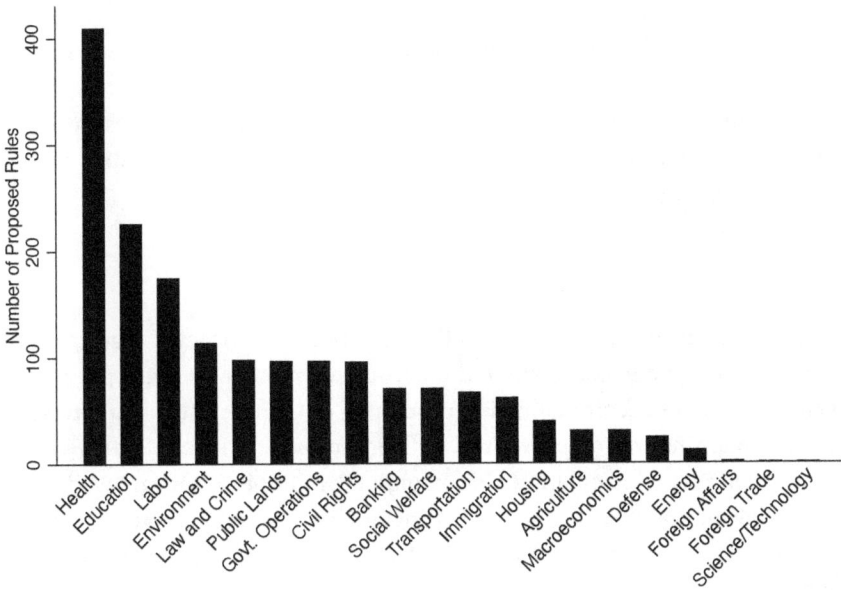

FIGURE 3.1. Proposed rules by policy topic (SEJ sample)

low-salience proposals, such as a revision to a rule governing Women, Infants, and Children (WIC) food packages' dietary guidelines, and more technical and salient efforts, such the proposition of a rule governing the coverage of certain contraceptive services under the Public Health Service Act.

Measuring Advocacy Influence

To operationalize social and economic justice organizations' *advocacy influence*, I compared the text of each comment submitted by each organization to its corresponding final rule and produced a measure of global textual similarity between the documents.[26] I did so by using a plagiarism detection software called WCopyfind, a tool that compares textual documents and reports similarities in their words and phrases. WCopyfind allows users to select and edit comparison rules before execution. I adopted the following comparison rules to detect all perfectly matching phrases between comment–final rule pairs.[27]

- Shortest phrase to match[28]: six words
- Most imperfections to allow[29]: two
- Minimum percent of matching words[30]: 100 percent

- Skip nonwords[31]
- Skip words longer than twenty characters[32]

I then counted all words contained in perfectly matching phrases for each comment–final rule pair, which represents my final operationalization of advocacy influence.[33]

MEASURING INTERSECTIONAL ADVOCACY

To operationalize the occurrence of intersectional advocacy, I read the entirety of each public comment and determined whether or not it promoted a concrete policy recommendation pertaining to the interests of an intersectionally marginalized population. I defined an *intersectionally marginalized population* as any population that contained multiply disadvantaged subgroups of marginalized groups. This included any combination of populations marginalized on the basis of gender, race, income, age, sexual orientation or identity, ability, and immigration/citizenship status. Examples of such populations include women of color, children living in poverty, or LGBTQ+ youth.

More specifically, I searched for two signals: an explicit reference to an intersectionally marginalized population (e.g., "economically disadvantaged women") *and* an explicit policy position or recommendation pertaining to the interests of this group (e.g., "we recommend that [the Small Business Association] use in its disparity calculations [. . .] other data sources that will allow for a more complete picture of the availability of women-owned businesses").[34] This position or recommendation could have taken any form so long as it specifically identified the desired policy output (such as generally supporting or opposing policy direction/content; recommending the striking, amending, or adding of policy language; or requesting greater context or detail regarding the proposed policy). This recommendation could have constituted the entirety of a comment or could have been one of several policy recommendations.[35] This variable is binary in nature.

MEASURING GROUP AND COALITION CHARACTERISTICS

In many of the analyses to come, my key predictor variable is the *formation of a coalition* in the submission of a public comment. I operationalized this variable by manually examining the signature line of each comment in my corpus.[36] If the comment was signed by more than one organization, I assigned the *coalition* variable a value of 1; otherwise, I assigned it a value of 0. I also coded each coalition observed in the data for whether it maintained a formal structure—defined by the presence of coalition architecture (maintenance of a name and staff separate from those of member organizations, along with a fixed membership). If the coalition maintained a formal structure, I assigned the *formal coalition* variable a value of 1; otherwise, I assigned it a value of 0.

I also gathered information on the *formation of a diverse coalition*. As some scholars have speculated—and as I theorize in this book—coalitions that unite diverse interests are often more influential (Lorenz 2019; Junk 2019). This relationship should hold exceptionally true in the two settings I examine: administrative policymaking and advocacy by social and economic justice organizations. For a range of reasons, diverse coalitions are more equipped to produce expert and balanced proposals backed by broad consensus; agency bureaucrats are uniquely incentivized to search for and prioritize proposals of this nature (Nelson and Yackee 2012). I thus developed two measures of the presence of diversity in each coalition's membership. I conceived of this diversity first by way of the presence of *representational diversity* within coalitions—defined as the presence of a plurality of constituent interests represented among coalition partners. To operationalize the occurrence of representational diversity in coalitions, I classified each coalition member into one of twenty-six categories demarcating their primary constituency.[37] I classified coalition members by examining their mission statements in the year of comment submission using archives of their organizational websites accessible through the Wayback Machine. The scheme consisted of the categories displayed in table 3.4.

Using these data, I then calculated normalized Shannon's H—a standard diversity index for instances where there are a set number of categories across which diversity can occur[38]—as a measure of the level of representational diversity in each coalition, defined as:

$$H(X) = -\frac{1}{\ln(n)} \sum_{i=1}^{n} (p(x_i)) * \ln p(x_i)$$

Where x_i represents the ith constituency type, $p(x_i)$ is the proportion of total attention the ith constituency type receives, and n is the total number of constituency types.[39] This value—which ranges from zero to one—ultimately reflects the spread of members in each coalition across different constituency types. A normalized Shannon's H of zero indicates that a coalition is composed entirely of members of a single constituency type, while a normalized Shannon's H of one indicates that a coalition is composed of an equal

TABLE 3.4. Constituency coding scheme

Constituency
Asian American
Black/African American
Business/industry
Children/youth
Religious (Christian denomination)
Chronically ill
Differently abled
Elderly
Environment
General public interest
Immigrant
Profession/industry
Jewish
Latino/Hispanic
LGBTQ+
Low-income
Muslim
Native American/American Indian
Other racial minority
Other religious minority
Political party
Student
Unhoused
Veteran
Women
Other

proportion of members of all constituency types (Boydstun, Bevan, and Thomas 2014). To measure the *presence* of representational diversity in coalitions, I then created a binary variable reflecting whether each coalition contained a non-zero level of representational diversity.[40]

Then, I captured the occurrence of a *coalition of strange bedfellows*—defined as a coalition uniting advocates for social and economic justice with business- or industry-oriented partners. I did so by classifying all coalition members in the *Collaborative Advocacy Dataset* into one of seven categories demarcating their organizational type.[41] I classified coalition members by examining their organizational websites in the year of comment submission using archives accessible through the Wayback Machine, alongside conducting searches for their organizational tax statuses in the year of comment submission using data provided by ProPublica.[42] The scheme consisted of the categories displayed in table 3.5.[43] I ultimately operationalized the occurrence of a "strange bedfellow" coalition by creating a binary variable reflecting the formation of a coalition that contained at least one "business or business group" partner, as captured by the above-mentioned organizational type coding scheme.[44]

Next, I collected information on the *capacity* of the organizational author(s) of each comment. As I described in earlier chapters, interest groups may be more influential and more likely to pursue intersectional advocacy when they have greater financial resources. To account for these possibilities, I recorded a measure of the *financial capacity* of each comment author. If a comment was submitted in a coalition, I aggregated this measure across the coalition. If not, I recorded the data for the single author. I operationalized this measure through each group's total revenue in the year of comment submission.[45] I collected this information from 990 forms available through ProPublica. As an additional measure of capacity, I recorded the *size* of each coalition, operationalized through the total number of members.[46]

Finally, among the sample of advocates for social and economic justice, I identified organizations with explicitly *intersectional missions*. Groups with intersectional missions—those that exist solely to represent an intersectionally marginalized population—are, by virtue of their identity, more likely to pursue intersectional advocacy. To account for this relationship, I identified the presence of an intersectional mission for each organization in this sample. I did so by navigating to the website of each group in the sample and reading their mission statement in the year of comment submission using archives of their organizational websites accessible through the Wayback Machine. If a group's mission statement purported solely to represent an intersectionally marginalized population—such as the Black Women's Health Imperative (BWHI), which advocates on behalf of the health and reproductive rights of

TABLE 3.5. Organizational type coding scheme

Organizational type
Business or business group
Charitable foundation or think tank
Citizen group
Governmental association
Native American tribe
Professional association
Union
Other

Black women—I identified the group as intersectional and assigned the variable a value of 1; otherwise, I assigned it a value of 0.[47]

MEASURING COMMENT AND RULE CHARACTERISTICS

To account for the nature of the underlying policy and attentiveness of the surrounding subsystem, I collected a number of policy-level variables. First, I recorded information on the *salience* of each proposed rule. Not all proposed rules are equally important or visible to subsystem actors. When a proposed rule is more consequential or salient, more actors may enter the debate, often by submitting public comments. In this more crowded and visible policy environment, advocacy organizations may experience lesser influence and intersectional advocacy efforts may be less likely to occur. To account for these likely relationships, I operationalized the *salience* of each proposed rule by collecting the total number of comments submitted in response.

Second, I developed a measure of the *complexity* of each proposed rule. Organizational coalitions may be more influential, and intersectional advocacy may be more likely, on proposed rules that are more complex in nature. More complex agency rules necessarily require more laborious lobbying efforts, and collaborative efforts are likely to have the capacity and skills to respond to such rules more effectively. Moreover, more complex proposed rules often span multiple policy domains and constituencies. By nature, intersectional advocacy is more likely to be concerned with such rules. To account for these possibilities, I operationalized the complexity of each proposed rule through the number of distinct policy subtopics encompassed by each proposed rule.[48]

Third, I developed a measure of *textual similarity between each public comment and its corresponding proposed rule*. Some proportion of language from proposed rules almost certainly remains in their corresponding final rules. Public comments occasionally quote language from the proposed rules they address. They may do so to direct bureaucrats to the sections of the rules they are referencing or as a comparison to the changes they recommend. Importantly, this quoted language may remain in the final rule and thus may contribute to an overestimation of the primary dependent variable. To address this potential measurement issue, I computed this measure using the same methodology and comparison rules used to measure the primary dependent variable.

Finally, public comments that contain more text are surely more likely to share language with the final rule. I thus recorded the *length* of each public comment, operationalized through the total number of words in each comment after preprocessing.

Before transitioning to my empirical analyses, it is important to note one aspect of the data. As previously mentioned, the number of all public comments submitted by the 150 groups in my samples during my period of study is 3,580. However, portions of chapters 4, 5, and 6 seek to understand how characteristics of *coalitions* of organizations may moderate successful advocacy. Thus, the data considered in these chapters are, in part, a subset of this greater sample—all public comments submitted by *coalitions*.

In addition, I did not collect and code membership-level data for every coalition observed. Instead, I collected and coded membership data only for coalitions containing less than fifty-one members. This choice was both theoretically and practically motivated. Theoretically, I adopted this rule to control for the appearance of superficial/symbolic coalitions, which typically contain hundreds of members and seldom pursue substantive policy advocacy. Second to this theoretical consideration, I sought to adopt this rule because of the time-intensive nature of the coding process. For reference, to collect the membership-level data presented in the book (all coalitions of fewer than fifty-one members), over twenty thousand coalition members were hand coded across seven attributes, yielding a dataset of approximately one hundred forty thousand observations. This effort required seven years of continuous work by eighteen research assistants. Thus, the data appearing in my models are all observations of coalitions of less than fifty-one members—an additional subset.

Finally, not every comment in the data was a response to a proposed rule on which a final rule was ultimately issued (required for the measure of my primary dependent variable). The notice-and-comment process can take years to resolve, and in rare cases, proposed rules may be dropped at the agency's discretion. Thus, the data appearing in the forthcoming models are also limited by this final characteristic, that they are based on *comments submitted on a proposed rule on which a final rule was issued.* This funneling process is illustrated by the diagram in figure 3.2.

This final set of comments—those submitted by coalitions of less than fifty-one members on a proposed rule on which a final rule was issued—are the data underlying portions of the analyses in chapters 4, 5, and 6.

```
┌─────────────────────────────────────────┐
│           All public comments            │
└─────────────────────────────────────────┘
                     ↓
┌─────────────────────────────────────────┐
│     All public comments submitted by     │
│                coalitions                │
└─────────────────────────────────────────┘
                     ↓
┌─────────────────────────────────────────┐
│     All public comments submitted by     │
│        coalitions of less than 51        │
└─────────────────────────────────────────┘
                     ↓
┌─────────────────────────────────────────┐
│                                          │
│             Final rule issued            │
│                                          │
└─────────────────────────────────────────┘
```

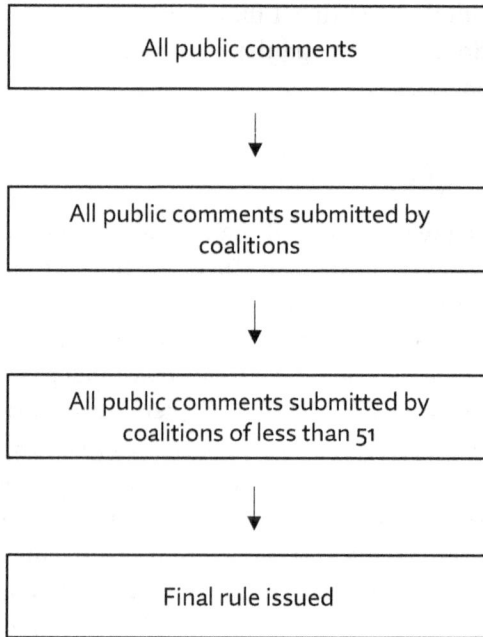

FIGURE 3.2. Data funneling process

Summary

In 1999, Kevin Hula published a groundbreaking book on coalitional lobbying in Washington. In it, he described that "the lack of readily available data pertaining to [...] political coalitions among interest groups is not surprising [...] [because] groups rarely publish objective accounts of their coalition behaviors" (Hula 1999, 12). In response to this challenge, Hula, along with other scholars writing about coalitional lobbying in the late twentieth century, deployed empirical strategies relying on mixed methods—combining survey questionnaires with elite interviews and focusing on advocacy within limited cases and temporal domains. Since the publication of Hula's book, only a handful of academic works have further explored the subject of coalition building in American lobbying—largely because of the lack of publicly available data on this behavior.

In this chapter, I have described my own methodological contribution to the study of coalitions in political advocacy. I have detailed my simple, albeit laborious, solution: using signature patterns on publicly available lobbying documents—public comments submitted by interest groups on proposed federal agency rules—to identify and track coalition behavior over time and

to conceptualize and measure organizational, coalition, and advocacy characteristics. Moreover, because of the nature of these documents, this approach
allows me to capture the intricacies of lobbying in an understudied but deeply
consequential policy process: federal agency rulemaking. These data thus allow me to offer the first comprehensive, book-length treatment of lobbying
coalitions in American national and regulatory politics.

Coalition Building, Architecture, and Influence

In May 2022, on the heels of the COVID-19 pandemic, an ongoing outbreak of Mpox (previously named "monkeypox")—a viral disease transmitted to humans from animals—was confirmed. After months of confusion, the Centers for Disease Control and Prevention (CDC) reported that the outbreak appeared to affect primarily gay and bisexual men and transgender individuals who have sex with men: as of early September 2022, this group accounted for approximately 93 percent of confirmed cases.[1] While the outbreak worsened, and as a vaccine became available, researchers began to report growing disparities in vaccine distribution among Black and Latinx communities and individuals living with HIV.[2] A press release issued by the North Carolina Department of Health and Human Services reported, for instance, that while 70 percent of Mpox cases affected Black men, only 24 percent of vaccines were administered to Black recipients; in contrast, while 19 percent of cases affected white men, 67 percent of vaccines were administered to white recipients.[3]

In response, a coalition of advocacy organizations mobilized. The coalition contained 115 groups, including the Human Rights Campaign (HRC), Advocates for Youth (founded in 1980), the Hispanic Federation (HF, founded in 1990), MomsRising (founded in 2006), and the National Women's Law Center (NWLC, founded in 1972). Together, they wrote a letter lobbying the CDC and the Department of Health and Human Services (HHS) to redirect existing funds to combat the virus, prioritize funding for sexual health clinics and community-based initiatives, increase rates of vaccine distribution among Black and Latinx communities, collect more comprehensive data regarding the spread of the virus, and cease referring to the virus as "monkeypox"—a term with racist connotations.[4] In a joint press release describing the call to action, Joni Madison, then interim president of the HRC, wrote,

The racial disparities we've seen in [Mpox] treatment and vaccine distribution highlight the need to change a deeply flawed health care system that historically best serves those with resources and connections. Government entities must do better to prioritize reaching BIPOC [Black, Indigenous, and People of Color], gay, bi+, and transgender and non-binary individuals, especially those individuals living with HIV.

A few weeks later, the Biden Administration formally requested $4.5 billion in emergency funding to support Mpox response efforts, including $1.6 billion to support vaccine manufacturing and hundreds of millions of dollars to support testing and public education.[5] Shortly thereafter, in tandem with the World Health Organization (WHO), government agencies and health organizations began a transition to a new name for the disease: Mpox.[6]

As I have described in earlier chapters, this kind of collective action—and collective success—in organizational advocacy is a familiar story (Phinney 2017; Gelbman 2021). Many political strategists and organizational leaders believe that building coalitions, complex as they may be, is fundamental to achieving influence over public policy. For instance, when the HRC hired a new president, Kelley Robinson, in late September 2022, they issued a press release lauding Robinson's commitment to "creating diverse winning coalitions [. . .] building political power with a focus on underserved and the most marginalized communities."[7] In this chapter, I test the notion that coalition work increases the policy influence of social and economic justice organizations.

Connecting to Theory

When do historically marginalized communities receive political representation? This question has been the center of a long tradition of research within and beyond political science. Scholars have most often evaluated this question by looking to the formal and informal activities of citizens, protest movements, and elected officials (Brady, Verba, and Schlozman 1995; Gause 2022; Gillion 2013; Grose 2011; McAdam 1982; Minta 2011; Piven and Cloward 1977). Few, however, have sought to answer this question by looking to the work of advocacy organizations. As I described in chapter 1, a growing body of research now suggests that organizational advocates for social and economic justice serve critical roles as "compensatory representatives" for their constituent communities (Brower 2024; English 2019, 2020; Marchetti 2014; Strolovitch 2006, 2007). Like the HRC and its allies' Mpox advocacy, their work elevates the interests of otherwise underserved groups and contributes to the development of more widely representative policy ideas and outputs in American politics.

But how? In this chapter, I make the case that coalition building allows these groups to advance more effective advocacy and achieve greater influence over public policy. I reiterate that social and economic justice groups, facing significant intra-and extra-organizational constraints, turn to coalition work to offset the costly nature of lobbying. By working with others, they gain legitimacy and receive greater attention. These partnerships serve as signals of consensus—an important heuristic for policymakers—and offer a reassuring sense of credibility. Moreover, by advocating collaboratively, they gain expanded informational, tactical, and financial capacities. Together, these collective resources allow them to surpass a fundamental hurdle of advocacy: developing effective policy recommendations.

Advocacy organizations can make many kinds of recommendations, ranging from advocacy that serves simply to "position-take" (establishing a written record) to symbolic submissions (showing their members and patrons that they did *something*) to lobbying that puts forth substantive policy ideas (Phinney 2017). This latter kind of advocacy is the most challenging and expensive lobbying content to produce—and the most fruitful. Decades of research on interest group activity demonstrates that policymakers privilege lobbying that provides an informational "subsidy" (Baumgartner and Leech 1998; Hall and Deardorff 2006; Golden 1998; Lorenz 2019; Junk 2019). In other words, advocacy that provides something useful, like public opinion or community context (e.g., how a policy design is likely to be received), a policy analysis (e.g., pointing out potential oversights and offering alternative or supplemental approaches), and empirical evidence (e.g., quantitative or qualitative data) is most likely to catch the eye of policymakers.

Alone, many social and economic justice organizations lack the tools to execute this kind of advocacy. These groups often struggle just to keep the lights on. Their budgets are tight, their teams are small, and their competitors have virtually no constraints (Strolovitch 2006, 2007). For many of these advocates, hiring political consultants and retaining a legal staff—two important tools to developing effective policy recommendations—is far beyond their capacity. A program manager for an economic justice organization said to me in an interview, "some of the challenges for smaller organizations like ours come out of funding. Funding's always a major issue."[8] Coalition work offers a resolution to this dilemma. By working with allies, these groups pool their financial and tactical resources. They gain access to the policy experts and legal teams they could not afford alone, along with the ability to purchase data, commission studies, and spread the burden of evaluating a policy debate and writing a response. They benefit, too, from the perspectives of others. By collaborating with organizations that may have different histories, orientations, and experiences, they increase their strategic capacity. These resources grant them the capability to put forward more widely informed, carefully analyzed, and technically written policy recommendations. In other words, coalition work allows social and economic justice organizations to produce more valuable policy advocacy.

The target of this advocacy, of course, plays an important role in moderating its outcomes. In this book, I evaluate social and economic justice organizations' attempts to influence policymaking by the American federal bureaucracy. Most agency policymaking occurs through notice-and-comment rulemaking, a largely transparent and open process that privileges public participation (Kerwin, Furlong, and West 2011). However, agency rulemaking is also one of the most technical and complex stages of American policymaking. The process of drafting and finalizing agency rules is intricate and driven by specific, enduring, incentives (Chubb 1983; West 2004). For instance, agents of the federal bureaucracy often have far greater expertise than their counterparts in other political institutions (Huber and Shipan 2002). They are typically among the foremost experts in the nation in their respective policy areas (Workman 2015). They have strong motivations to ensure that their policy choices are free from error, are unlikely to trigger scandal, are insulated from critique by political principals, and are protected from judicial review (West 2004; Workman 2015). They seek, unfailingly, the best and most informed implementation protocol for the provisions of the law they have been tasked with regulating (Potter 2019; West 2004).

And for good reason: regulatory language is extraordinarily consequential. The inclusion or exclusion of even a single sentence fragment can substantially change the way an agency rule is implemented. Take, for instance, the Coalition Against Religious Discrimination's (CARD) 2016 advocacy targeting a rule proposed by the Department of Veterans Affairs (VA). In August 2015, the VA published a proposed rule implementing Executive Order 13559—an executive order requiring agencies to prohibit religious discrimination in the delivery of social services by religious organizations in partnership with the federal government. The CARD submitted a public comment evaluating the VA's proposed rule. Their comment observed that while the VA's rule addressed many of the Executive Order's mandates, it contained one important oversight: it neglected to include language explicitly prohibiting religious discrimination. The CARD wrote,

The fix is simple. In order to be true to the Executive Order's principles, the Agency should adopt the following provision, which bars discrimination in both direct and indirect aid programs and mirrors the Executive Order's list of protections: "An organization that participates in [social service] programs funded by financial assistance from an awarding agency shall not, in providing services, discriminate against a program beneficiary or prospective program beneficiary on the basis of religion, a religious belief, a refusal to hold a religious belief, or a refusal to attend or participate in a religious practice."

Every choice a bureaucrat makes—from incidentally excluding an important provision (like the VA's proposed rule) to developing a definition (like that of "low-lying land") to establishing a standard (like an educational outcome)—has immediate and significant effects. As a result, agencies place a high premium on the information they receive throughout the notice-and-comment process. They carefully evaluate input from public participants and stakeholders—in part because they are required by law to do so, and in part because they believe that the rules they issue are better for it (Golden 1998; West 2004). They have strong incentives to privilege advocacy with high informational content (Carpenter et al. 2022; Nelson and Yackee 2012).

Finally, as trivial as it may seem, bureaucrats are people. And people are boundedly rational—we experience emotions, we face constraints on our time, and our attention spans are limited (Simon 1972; Workman and Shafran 2015). There are only so many hours in a bureaucrat's day, and like many other political actors, they must "satisfice" to maximize their working hours and reach their goals (Kingdon 1973; Workman 2015). For example, when agencies receive hundreds of thousands of public comments—as the FCC did following John Oliver's 2014 *Last Week Tonight* special—it becomes impossible for them to read and weigh each of these recommendations. Instead, they rely on certain tools to efficiently evaluate their content. In these unique cases, agencies deploy natural language processing tools to sift through and categorize comments en masse (Potter 2019). Most of the time, however, individual bureaucrats read through and evaluate each comment by hand. But still, they rely on heuristics—like writing style, citation patterns, and the names of the author(s)—to decide whether a comment is credible. In their eyes, one of the strongest signals of credibility is *consensus*. Coalition work sends this signal. It reflects uniformity among affected communities and groups. Because of the complexity of coalition building—requiring negotiation, compromise, and cost sharing—it indicates a heightened level of attention and concern from those with community knowledge and policy expertise. If many groups care so much as to advocate collectively, regulators take note.

Patterns of Collaboration

This story suggests that collaboration should be a highly attractive tactic for social and economic justice organizations. And it is. According to the *Collaborative Advocacy Dataset*, 54 percent of advocacy efforts by social and economic justice organizations occur in coalitions. These coalitions range widely in formality, size, and resource levels. Fifty-one percent are formal in nature—meaning that the coalitions themselves maintain names, fixed memberships, and staff separate from those of their member organizations—such as the National Coalition of LGBTQ Health, the Coalition for Homeless Youth, and the National Coalition for Women and Girls in Education. Across both formal and informal collaborations, the average coalition of social and economic justice organizations contains seventy-eight groups (median = 27 groups). Informal coalitions contain about thirty-six groups on average (median = 19 groups). Formal coalitions tend to be larger, averaging 119 member groups (median = 64 groups). Finally, collaborative advocacy pays dividends: the average financial backing of coalitions observed in the data—calculated by summing the total revenue of all coalition members in the year of comment submission, for each collaborative advocacy effort—is approximately $181,000,000 (median = $28,700,000). In contrast, the average financial backing of social and economic justice organizations advocating alone—calculated using the total revenue of all sample members in years of comment submission, for each solo advocacy effort—is approximately $26,500,000 (median = $10,600,000). In other words, on average, organizations' coalitional advocacy, despite its role as a cost-saving mechanism for many individual members, is resourced at a rate *more than 600 percent higher* than advocacy conducted alone.

Rates of coalition building are high and constant across different kinds of organizations. Table 4.1 presents rates of coalition work by members of the sample of social and economic justice groups, grouped by organizational type. It shows, strikingly, that nearly every organizational type observed in the data builds coalitions more than 50 percent of the time. Citizen groups and professional associations are standouts—building coalitions in 60 percent of all cases (public comment submissions). Native American tribes and charitable foundations and think tanks follow closely—building coalitions to facilitate 45 and 49 percent of their advocacy efforts, respectively. These trends demonstrate that the statistic presented in the previous paragraph—that social and economic justice organizations collaborate in their advocacy at high rates—is true for many different kinds of advocates representing historically marginalized communities. Moreover, these patterns reinforce a simple but foundational finding from existing research: that coalition building is a popular

TABLE 4.1. Coalition building by organizational type

Organizational type	Coalitional advocacy (%)
Charitable foundation/think tank	49
Citizen group	60
Native American tribe	45
Professional association	60

Note: These proportions represent rates of coalitional advocacy within organizational type categories. They were calculated as follows: number of public comments submitted in coalitions by members of the sample in each organizational type divided by the total number of all public comments submitted by members of the sample in each organizational type.

TABLE 4.2. Coalition building by group policy focus

Policy focus	Coalitional advocacy (%)
Anti-poverty	45
LGBTQ+ issues	69
Native American	65
Racial/ethnic minority	45
Women's issues	59

Note: These proportions represent rates of coalitional advocacy within policy foci. They were calculated as follows: number of public comments submitted in coalitions by members of the sample in each policy focus divided by the total number of all public comments submitted by members of the sample in each policy focus.

and ubiquitous lobbying tactic (Baumgartner and Leech 1998; Hojnacki 1997, 1998; Hula 1999; Levi and Murphy 2006; Phinney 2017; Strolovitch 2007).

These trends also hold true across organizations' policy orientations. Table 4.2 illustrates rates of collaboration in the data within groups' policy foci.[9] It demonstrates, once again, that nearly every policy advocacy category observed in the data is characterized by a high rate of coalition building, ranging from 45 to 69 percent. Groups lobbying on issues of economic justice (anti-poverty) and racial justice (racial/ethnic minority) built coalitions in 45 percent of all cases observed. Advocates for Indigenous policy issues (Native American) and women's issues collaborated in 65 and 59 percent of their advocacy efforts, respectively. Finally, organizations advocating on issues of LGBTQ+ policy pursued coalition work in nearly 70 percent of their public comment submissions.

Social and economic justice organizations with varying levels of financial resources, too, regularly deploy coalition tactics. Table 4.3 depicts rates of coalition building in the data by sample groups' total revenue in the year of comment submission. For purposes of simplicity, the total revenue data are presented in quartiles, where Quartile 1 corresponds to the lowest level of financial capacity among members of the sample and Quartile 4 corresponds to the highest level. As the table shows, the rate of coalitional advocacy across organizations falling into these financial capacity quartiles ranges from 51 to 57 percent. While popular opinion might suggest that wealthier organizations have little need for collaboration, the data demonstrate otherwise. Among social and economic justice organizations, coalitions are consistently utilized by advocates with the lowest and highest financial capacities. These patterns suggest that coalition building is not simply a story of conserving or gaining financial resources. Coalitions offer social and economic justice organizations, including those with greater financial backings, a range of strategic benefits—from access to new information to greater political credibility.

Finally, collaborative advocacy occurs regularly across topics of national policymaking. Figure 4.1 depicts rates of coalitional advocacy in the *Collaborative Advocacy Dataset*, broken down by the major policy topic of the corresponding proposed agency rules.[10] Most policy topics—fifteen out of twenty appearing in the data—are characterized by a high rate of coalition building, between approximately 40 and 60 percent. In other words, of all advocacy efforts targeting any one of these policy areas in the SEJ data, between 40 and 60 percent occurred in coalitions. Two policy topics, public lands and energy policy, are on the receiving end of comparatively lower levels of coalition work, at approximately 30 and 15 percent, respectively. One policy topic, foreign trade, appears to be characterized by an exceptionally high rate of collaborative advocacy, at 100 percent. However, of all observations in the

TABLE 4.3. Coalition building by group total revenue

Total revenue	Coalitional advocacy (%)
Quartile 1	57
Quartile 2	58
Quartile 3	53
Quartile 4	51

Note: These proportions represent rates of coalitional advocacy within revenue quartiles. They were calculated as follows: number of public comments submitted in coalitions by members of the sample in each total revenue quartile divided by the total number of all public comments submitted by members of the sample in each total revenue quartile.

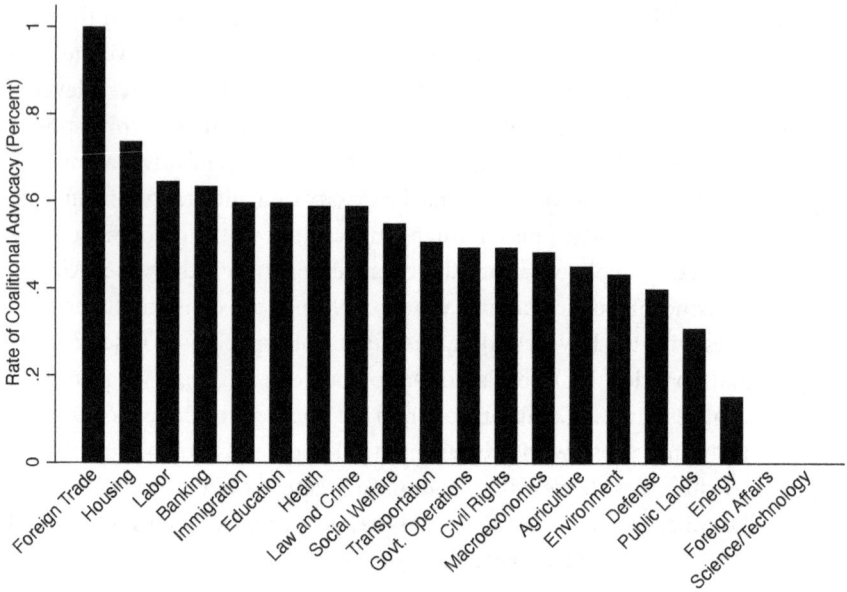

FIGURE 4.1. Coalitional advocacy by proposed rule policy topic

Collaborative Advocacy Dataset, only one concerned a proposed rule pertaining to foreign trade; this single observation happened to be submitted by a coalition. Finally, two policy topics received no collaborative advocacy: foreign affairs and science/technology policy.

Together, these trends demonstrate that collaborative advocacy is not the exception and does not discriminate. Across organizational types, policy advocacy foci, levels of financial resources, and areas of national policymaking, social and economic justice organizations build coalitions at high rates—in most cases, nearly half of their advocacy occurs in collaboration with others. These patterns lend support to a central tenet of my theoretical argument: that coalition work, as costly and complex as it may be, is a valued tactic for social and economic justice organizations. But is it effective for policy influence?

Assessing Advocacy Outcomes

I evaluate the fundamental argument of this chapter—that social and economic justice organizations have greater influence over public policy when they advocate in coalitions—using the *Collaborative Advocacy Dataset.* In this section, I estimate a series of generalized linear models (GLM)[11] but focus on the results of a single model: Model 1. Where appropriate, I refer to the appendix section of this book for models that evaluate alternative explanations. Model 1's dependent variable is the influence of organizational advocacy (textual similarity between comment–final rule pairs); its primary predictor variables are binary indicators of the formation of a coalition and the formation of a formalized coalition. The model controls for coalition size, financial capacity, characteristics of the targeted public policy (complexity, salience), and characteristics of the underlying public comment (textual similarity between the public comment and the original proposed rule, public comment length).[12] Additionally, I account for potential correlations within subpopulations of the data (organizations in the original sample) by clustering the standard errors by group. These relationships can be formally expressed by the following equation (eq. 1),[13] where $Y = \gamma(\mu|\phi)$:

$$
\begin{aligned}
\ln E(Y|X) = \beta_0 &+ \beta_1 \text{Coalition} \\
&+ \beta_2 \text{FormalCoalition} \\
&+ \beta_4 \text{CoalitionSize} \\
&+ \beta_5 \text{FinancialCapacity} \\
&+ \beta_6 \text{ProposedRuleComplexity} \\
&+ \beta_7 \text{ProposedRuleSalience} \\
&+ \beta_8 \text{ProposedRuleCommentSimilarity} \\
&+ \beta_9 \text{CommentLength}
\end{aligned}
$$

Figure 4.2 visualizes the results of Model 1.[14] This model evaluates whether advocacy by social and economic justice organizations is more influential when pursued through coalition work. It offers a few key findings. First, there is a statistically insignificant relationship between the formation of a coalition and advocacy influence. In other words, coalition building alone has no bearing on social and economic justice organizations' lobbying outcomes. However, there is a positive and statistically significant relationship between the formation of a formal coalition and advocacy influence. Put differently, social and economic justice organizations are significantly more influential when they pursue their advocacy in coalitions with *formalized structures* (collaborations with names, fixed memberships, and staff separate from those of their member organizations). Specifically, holding all other independent variables at their means, these results suggest that a shift from advocating alone or in an ad hoc coalition to advocating in a formal coalition more than doubles the shared word count in perfectly matching phrases between comment–final rule documents (fifteen to thirty-three words). This shift translates to approximately two additional shared sentences between document pairs, assuming an average sentence length of ten to fifteen words.

This effect size is extraordinarily meaningful. Consider the context: as I described in chapter 3, agency rules are highly technical. Thus, even minor changes in their language, like altering a standard or slightly expanding a definition, can profoundly affect their implementation. Take, for example, a 2016 advocacy effort by a formal coalition of thirty-two organizations including the NAACP Legal Defense and Education Fund (NAACP LDF, founded in 1940), the Southern Poverty Law Center (SPLC, founded in 1971) and the National Urban League (NUL, founded in 1910). Together, this coalition targeted a rule proposed by the Department of Education that sought to regulate the Every Student Succeeds Act (ESSA), a replacement to the No Child Left Behind Act (NCLB). Their public comment described a series of concerns and recommendations, one of which requested that the agency include a *single phrase*, "timely and meaningful consultation," to a subsection of the rule governing state plan peer reviews. Another part of their comment requested amending a definition embedded within the proposed rule. They wrote,

> We recommend striking section §200.19(c)(3) and replacing it with "§200.19(c)(3) Define a consistently underperforming subgroup of students in a uniform manner across all LEAs in the state such that this definition (i) Is based on the state's long-term goals and measures of interim progress, as established under §200.13 and (ii) Includes more schools than the definition of 'low performing subgroup' under §200.19(b)(2)."

In other words, the inclusion of a handful of phrases or sentences to an agency's policy can have monumental implications for its outcomes. In the case of the above-mentioned proposed rule, it may have meant the difference between requiring meaningful consultations with parents or offering services to a group of previously excluded students. Thus, taken in context, this result indicates that the effect of formalized coalition work is enormously substantively consequential. As I suggested in chapter 1, the architecture of coalition work does, in fact, matter a great deal.

Many of the remaining variables in Model 1 share directionally intuitive relationships with the dependent variable: social and economic justice organizations' financial capacity shares a positive, albeit insignificant, association with advocacy influence. This finding underscores existing research demonstrating that organizational resources alone are not predictive of lobbying outcomes (Baumgartner and Leech 1998; Baumgartner et al. 2009a; Lorenz 2019). Policy complexity, alternatively, shares a negative but insignificant association with the dependent variable. Finally, policy salience shares a negative and statistically significant relationship with advocacy influence, suggesting

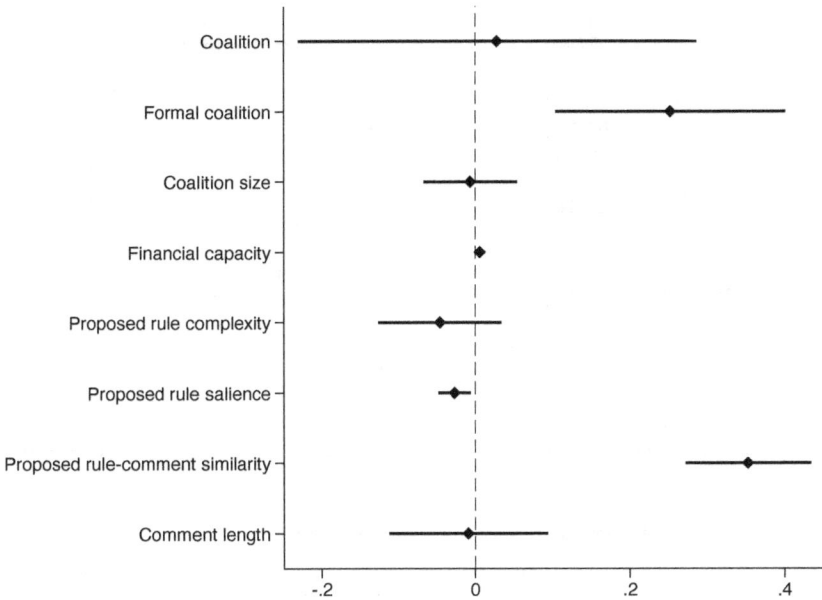

FIGURE 4.2. Coalition building and advocacy influence (Model 1). Generalized linear regression model (Gamma family, log link function) with group-clustered standard errors. $N = 869$. Diamonds indicate coefficient values. Lines indicate 95 percent confidence intervals.

that social and economic justice organizations are more influential when advocating on less salient public policies. This particular result reiterates a common theme in research on American lobbying—that organizations are often more successful when targeting policy areas with "narrower" scopes of conflict (Baumgartner et al. 2009a; Schattschneider 1960). These supplemental findings should lend confidence to the robustness of this model.

Now, back to the primary finding of this analysis: coalition work, alone, does not predict social and economic justice organizations' advocacy influence. In the first half of this chapter, I demonstrated that coalition work is liberally used by social and economic justice groups attempting to influence public policy. Model 1, however, suggests that the process of effectively deploying this tactic is more complicated. It implies that while coalition work is a common advocacy strategy, collaboration in and of itself is not sufficient for achieving influence. Simply building an alliance without sensitivity to its nature does not assist social and economic justice organizations trying to surpass the many hurdles to effective policy advocacy. Instead, this analysis indicates that successful coalitions have formal structures—separate from those of their member organizations—that govern their partnerships. This finding holds true both across all advocacy efforts by social and economic justice groups (solo and coalitional, as illustrated

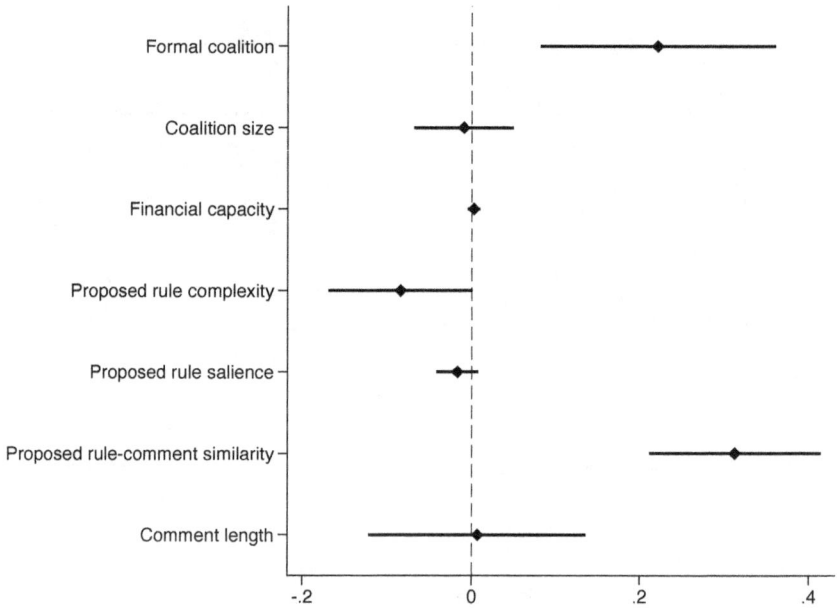

FIGURE 4.3. Formal coalition building and advocacy influence (Model 2). Generalized linear regression model (Gamma family, log link function) with group-clustered standard errors. $N = 428$. Diamonds indicate coefficient values. Lines indicate 95 percent confidence intervals.

in Model 1) and *within* coalitional efforts by these advocates. Model 2 demonstrates this latter finding by dropping all non-coalitional observations from the data and then replicating Model 1 in all other respects (see figure 4.3).[15] Together, these outcomes underscore the main takeaway of this chapter: building formal coalitions significantly increases the influence of advocates for social and economic justice, both generally speaking (across all advocacy efforts) and within coalitional advocacy efforts.

This discovery connects with a growing body of research on collaborative lobbying that recognizes that coalition work can take many forms. To study these variations, scholars of organizational behavior have often looked to coalition membership. However, as I suggested in chapters 1 and 2, one of the most distinct characteristics of coalition work has to do with their architectural choices. Most coalitions, for instance, are ad hoc—informal collaborations that unite friendly or disparate groups without a clear governing structure, demarcation of roles, or distribution of financial responsibility. In ad hoc coalitions, coalition leaders—the "first movers"—typically assume the most responsibility. While these alliances may come about because of a sense of shared fate, their deliberations occur without a clear configuration. Instead, organizational liaisons gather and discuss, often in a haphazard fashion. They disagree, suggest alternatives, and eventually reach a decision. Feelings can be hurt, egos bruised, and the free rider problem persists. In formal coalitions, however, processes are far more regimented (Gelbman 2021; Schroering and Staggenborg 2022; Staggenborg 2015; Zack et al. 2023; Zack and Smithson-Stanley 2024). Formal coalitions have names (and oftentimes staff) separate from those of their member organizations. Their membership rolls are typically fixed; while new members may be added and old members may leave, there is little uncertainty, at any given time, about who is (or is not) in the coalition. Within these coalitions, leadership roles are assigned and may rotate across member organizations to ensure fairness and accountability. They have clear missions, goals, and processes for decision making. For most decisions that need to be made, there are rules and structures that govern how the coalition will evaluate options and reach a conclusion. There is no confusion about whether, or how, to make decisions for the coalition.

Of course, not all formal coalitions model these exact characteristics. But many do—coalitions that go so far as to name themselves, establish a fixed membership, and maintain designated staff roles have given thought to their structure. By building or committing to a coalition with some semblance of architecture, organizations join a far more sophisticated enterprise of collaborative advocacy. Many of the challenges to coalition work and policy influence are alleviated by the rules and processes of these coalitions. Their governance provides the answers to questions that can trigger the downfall of other partnerships, such as, Who decides what? Who contributes what? and Who gets what? Moreover, because formal coalitions are designed to be long standing, they have the unique capacity to *learn*. As they build and invest in the collaboration over time, they can answer more complex questions that allow them to become better at their advocacy work, such as, Is the context changing? What's working (or not)? and What are we noticing? This ability (and desire) to learn as a coalition is extraordinarily important. It generates a more orderly and deliberative coalition environment that enables coalition partners to leverage their past experiences in developing future advocacy strategies and policy content. Informal collaborations, on the other hand, do not have these opportunities. Coming together a handful of times with partners that have varying levels of commitment, for instance, does not lend itself to systematic coalition-level learning and adaptability. A cofounder of a formal coalition of social justice organizations spoke to this point in an interview with me:

There are good actors [in coalitions], people who do good things even when it's hard . . . and there are . . . actors who free ride. And there are a bunch of people in the middle. If you don't have a good metronome, a good structure, you end up having all these people do unproductive stuff. You need to have that monthly meeting that starts and ends on time and has quality meeting notes sent out afterwards. That matters a lot. And [. . .] I think a core leadership team is really important too.[16]

In other words, architectures that allow partner organizations to learn, adapt, and act as a collective—along with the general benefits of coalition work (credibility signaling, greater informational content)—are built to resolve many of the difficulties of collaborative action. Their intentions and nature set formal coalitions apart from the crowd.

Alternative Explanations

But what if formal coalitions are just cover for something else? For example, maybe coalitions with formalized structures just happen to attract members with outsized influence in lobbying. Long-standing, reputable organizations might have the experiences, connections, and time that lead them to more frequently build or join formal coalitions over others. Based on their long histories as advocates, they might better understand the benefits of these partnerships, have greater opportunities to join formal coalitions, or enjoy the flexibility to pick and choose which coalitions they form. Or maybe formal coalitions tend to respond to policies where they are most likely to be influential, such as more complicated or publicly salient policies. These particular policies might require greater learning and adaptability by prospective advocates, which formalized coalitions are more equipped to facilitate than their ad hoc counterparts. Coalition partners might be aware of the benefit of a structured coalition under these advocacy conditions and turn to these partnerships accordingly. These concerns are valid and important to evaluate before proceeding to chapter 5.

To start, even among advocates for social and economic justice, interest groups with outsized influence in lobbying have one hallmark characteristic: a *lot* of money. For instance, while the NAACP and Black Girls Vote (BGV, founded in 2015) are both racial justice–oriented organizations focusing on the interests of Black Americans, one has far greater resources and connections than the other (in 2022, the NAACP reported a total revenue of $85 million; in the same year, BGV reported a total revenue of $230,000).[17] "Heavyweights" such as the NAACP might tend to build or join formalized coalitions more than other, less experienced, groups—an alternative explanation to the

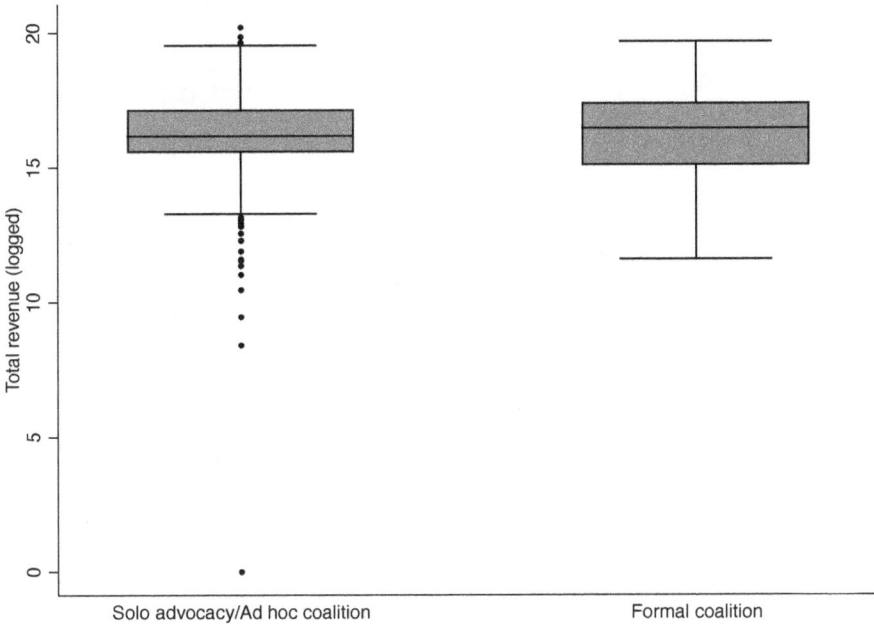

FIGURE 4.4. Distribution of total revenue over formal coalition building

conclusion I formed in the previous section. If this is the case, we should observe a series of patterns: first, that well-resourced organizations build formal coalitions at different rates than less resourced groups, and second, that upon accounting for coalitions containing heavyweight actors, Models 1 and 2 no longer demonstrate a statistically significant relationship between the occurrence of a formalized coalition and advocacy influence.

Figure 4.4 evaluates the first of these possibilities. It depicts a summary distribution of total revenue (logged) of organizations in the SEJ sample over the occurrence of formalized coalitions in the *Collaborative Advocacy Dataset*. This distribution demonstrates, plainly, that there is no difference between the total revenue of organizations advocating in formal coalitions versus those advocating alone or in ad hoc coalitions. Thus, this simple illustration should resolve the concern that formalized coalitions are simply a tool of resourced advocates who have greater experiences and strategic knowledge than others. To evaluate the second possibility, I look back to Models 1 and 2. As the reader may recall, these models depict the results of multivariate analyses with variables accounting for financial capacity at both the individual level (for observations of solo advocacy) and coalition level (for observations of collaborative advocacy). As I described in the previous section, these models' results demonstrate statistically insignificant relationships between financial

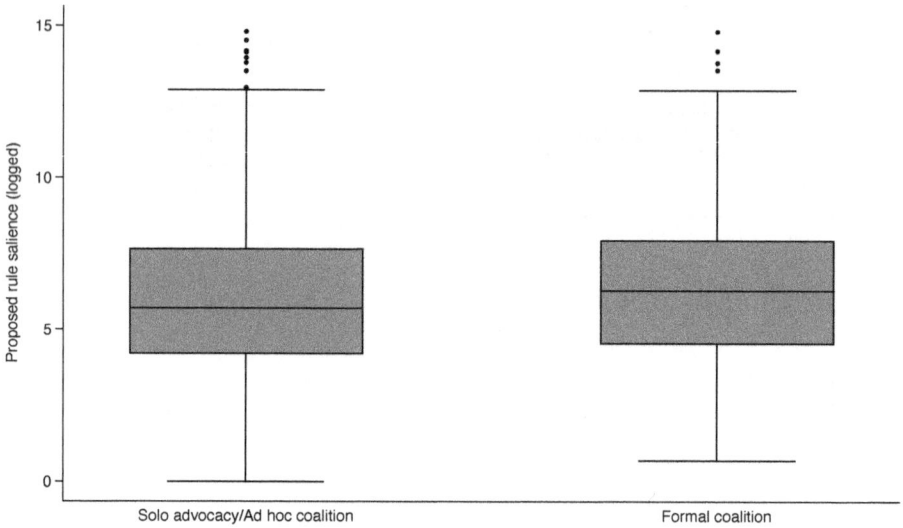

FIGURE 4.5. Distribution of policy salience over formal coalition building

resources—an appropriate proxy for the presence of a "heavyweight" actor within a coalition—and advocacy influence. In other words, even after accounting for a hallmark characteristic of experienced, reputable advocates (financial resources), formalized coalitional advocacy is strongly associated with social and economic justice organizations' advocacy influence.

But what about policy-level conditions? It could be the case, for example, that formalized coalitions largely respond to policies where member organizations believe they are most likely be influential. Formal partnerships—with their enduring lifespans, set structures, and fixed memberships—may be more equipped to address more complicated and salient policy proposals—such as those that span multiple policy areas and those that garner a great deal of organizational and stakeholder attention—than other, more straightforward implementations. If true, because of the very structures that set them apart, coalition leaders are likely to be aware of this dynamic. And if true, the data should reflect this behavior. But the data tell a different story. According to the *Collaborative Advocacy Dataset*, 41 percent of formal coalitions in the data occur in response to policies with the lowest possible level of complexity (out of six).[18] Moreover, 45 percent occur in response to policies with the second-lowest possible level of complexity. Figure 4.5 evaluates differences between the levels of salience of policies to which formal coalitions occur in response. This figure depicts a summary distribution of policy salience (logged) over the occurrence of formalized coalitions in the *Collaborative*

Advocacy Dataset.[19] It demonstrates, with clarity, that there is no difference between the levels of salience of proposed rules targeted by organizations advocating in formal coalitions versus those targeted by groups advocating alone or in ad hoc coalitions. Together, these statistics rule out the possibility that formalized coalitions are self-selecting into advocacy on public policies with characteristics that offer them a strategic advantage.

Summary

Social and economic justice groups constantly build coalitions. A former communications director for a social justice organization said to me in an interview, "frankly, the assumption is that you're going to work in coalition. I don't think I've ever been in a room with anybody who's said, 'we've got this' on their own. We understand that we *have* to work in coalitions."[20] The analyses of this chapter reflect this interviewee's mindset. In most cases, organizational advocates for social and economic justice work in coalition with others to facilitate their advocacy efforts. But the analyses of this chapter also show that their coalition strategies come with an important qualifier: collaboration in and of itself is not enough. Instead, building formalized, long-standing coalitions is pivotal for social and economic justice organizations' advocacy influence. This finding is an important contribution to organizers' tactical arsenals and researchers' theoretical understandings of cooperative advocacy. It suggests that influential collaborative advocacy requires building partnerships that enable their member organizations to pay attention to detail—by establishing structures for learning, adapting, and deciding.

As I stated at the outset of this section, coalitions come in many forms. In chapter 5, I evaluate the nuance of a different facet of coalition work: coalition membership. I propose that beyond the presence of architecture, for organizational coalitions to succeed in persuading policymakers of their ideas, they need to *look* a certain way. I argue that successful coalitions have memberships that uniquely enable them to respond to a core concern of policymakers—informational uncertainty. This claim is one that I have already begun to develop. As the reader may recall, part of the story of this book is that is that specific types of alliances greatly enhance social and economic justice groups' abilities to achieve influence over public policy. In the coming pages, I contend that coalitions with particular memberships—those that bring together groups representing a plurality of constituent interests and those that unite strange bedfellows (i.e., joining organizational advocates for social and economic justice with business or industry partners)—are more influential policy advocates than those without these characteristics.

I argue that simply evaluating coalition formation and architecture does not capture the full nuance of organizational teamwork. I suggest that in addition to coalitions that encourage members to be thoughtful by establishing structures, procedures, and hierarchies of decision making, collaborations with memberships that bring together many different types of expertise and experiences (even when it hurts) are more able to effectively meet policymakers' needs, thereby achieving greater advocacy influence.

5

Coalition Membership

At the time of its signing in March 2019, New Mexico's Energy Transition Act (ETA) was the most aggressive climate policy in the United States.[1] It charted a transition to 100 percent carbon-free energy generation by the year 2045 and allocated $40 million in assistance and workforce training for fossil fuel–dependent communities in the state. Governor Michelle Lujan Grisham described the significance of its enactment at the signing ceremony:

> This is a really big deal. In every corner of this state, advocates, utilities, young adults, unions, elected officials and families came together to push for and, today, enact this transformational law.[. . .] This legislation is a promise to future generations of New Mexicans, who will benefit from both a cleaner environment and a more robust energy economy with exciting career and job opportunities. Crucially, the Energy Transition Act does not leave affected workers and neighbors behind. We look out for each other. With this law, we seal that promise.

Her statement signaled to a crucial piece of the charge behind this policy achievement: that many different groups of people, including "utilities, young adults, unions [. . .] and families" had come together to "push for [. . .] this transformational law." The Governor's synthesis, however, barely scratched the surface. The campaign for this law had begun a year earlier, in 2018, and was led by a coalition of advocacy organizations and stakeholders in the state. As the governor alluded, it brought together some unusual allies: utility companies, Native American tribes, environmental groups, racial justice groups, and civic associations. Bringing together this collection of actors was a deliberate choice. The climate activists and grassroots groups involved in developing and championing the policy believed that only a broad-ranging coalition—with members representing different constituent groups and offering coverage across types of tactical skills—would lead them to success. A leader of this coalition, acting on behalf of the National Audubon Society, said to me in an interview,

> The New Mexico Energy Transition Act . . . happened because of a coalition of mainstream green [groups] like the League of Conservation Voters and the Sierra Club that very diligently and intentionally engaged social and racial justice organizations in these green issues when they hadn't originally conceived of themselves as [potential partners]. That story . . . was great because [the green groups] had a lobbyist presence and so we were able to extract all this intel from Santa Fe . . . but then we couldn't deliver on any kind of visibility on the ground and it was really the racial justice groups that did that. We couldn't have done it without a coalition like that.[2]

She continued, describing the challenges they faced in assembling the coalition: "This was a case where . . . there had absolutely been past harms [between coalition partners] . . . but there was also a sense of shared fate." The Navajo Nation, for example, had substantial reservations about the proposed law—one in five of their citizens live in poverty and at the time, 60 percent of coal workers in the state were Navajo citizens.[3] Both the potential for higher electricity prices and the threat of job loss among the local Indigenous community was a real, and valid, point of contention. For different reasons, utility companies shared a similar hesitation: the state's two largest power plants were coal fired, and before the ETA's enactment, nearly half of New Mexico's electricity was generated by coal.[4] Climate advocates, of course, wanted a big, news-grabbing win for clean energy. The leader I spoke to attributed the choices of these actors to join together in support of the ETA—despite distinct interests and histories of mistrust—to a shared understanding that unity was the only way to achieve a favorable policy outcome for any of their individual communities. The product of their collaborative effort was a groundbreaking law that simultaneously addressed climate, race, class, labor, and corporate concerns (Smithson-Stanley 2020).

Among organizers, the strategy behind this coalition's success is well understood. The program manager of an economic justice organization said to me in an interview, "it's absolutely fair to say that the dynamic of who [is] in these coalitions matters."[5] For example, a few years before the alliance behind the ETA, a coalition with similar features formed to target a rulemaking effort by the Small Business Administration (SBA). The proposed rule in question, issued in 2007, sought to implement the Women's Procurement Program, a federal contract assistance program created by the US Congress in 2000. The

program was, and still is, required by law to award at least 5 percent of all federal contracting dollars to women-owned small businesses each year.[6] In the
first of a series of public comments to the agency, the coalition acknowledged
at the outset the factors that united its fifteen members, which included business, religious, and racial justice groups. They wrote,

> While we represent organizations advocating diverse perspectives and con-
> stituencies, we all have a strong, common interest in ensuring that women-
> owned contractors have a full and fair chance to participate in federal pro-
> curement activities and that federal rules and programs are based on a sound
> understanding of statutory and constitutional law.[. . .] The SBA has now is-
> sued a proposed rule that appears to be designed specifically to deny most
> women-owned contractors a fair opportunity to participate in federal con-
> tracting. Most seriously, the proposed rule exceeds the SBA's rule-making
> authority by grafting new requirements onto the program that were neither
> intended nor desired by Congress—nor are they constitutionally required.

As their comment made clear, these organizations' choice to build a diverse coalition was decidedly intentional—just like the coalition surrounding the ETA. It was motivated by a "strong, common interest" among their
members in the ongoing policy debate. In this case, the SBA heeded a part
of their recommendation; they reissued the Notice of Proposed Rulemaking
(NPRM) in 2008 to address a series of technical corrections and reopened
the comment period to allow for an additional round of public input. This
coalition, together with the coalition of climate, industry, and community
groups surrounding New Mexico's ETA, reflects a series of distinct realities:
that building diverse coalitions is a more daunting task than forming an alliance with friendly groups; that member organizations nonetheless join these
coalitions because of their ability to offer coverage across different sets of organizational connections and skills; and that coalition partners believe that
these capacities will allow them to more effectively shape public policy. In this
chapter, I evaluate whether building diverse coalitions is, in fact, an approach
that rewards.

Connecting to Theory

Earlier in this book, I argued that social and economic justice organizations
have strong incentives to collaborate. Alone, many of these advocates have
limited financial, political, and tactical resources. They operate in crowded
and costly political environments that have become only more congested
and financially demanding over time. They are vastly outpaced by wealthier,

more well-connected interest groups. In chapters 3 and 4, using the *Collaborative Advocacy Dataset*, I found support for these foundational claims. Like other scholars (Strolovitch 2006, 2007), I demonstrated that organizational advocates for social and economic justice have substantially lower numbers and levels of resources than their private and professional counterparts. They build coalitions at disproportionately high rates—nearly half of their advocacy occurs in collaboration with other groups—suggesting that these organizations are aware of their limitations and believe that building coalitions enables their advocacy goals. Thus, I theorized that coalition work is an essential condition for the achievement of social and economic justice organizations' policy influence. However, I uncovered a caveat: simply building coalitions does not significantly increase organizations' advocacy influence. The key, instead, is building coalitions with formalized structures supporting collective learning and decision making. In the coming pages, I continue to unpack this finding. I suggest that beyond the presence of formal coalition architecture, the *composition* of coalitions—the diversity of constituencies represented among partners and the unification of strange bedfellows—matters for advocacy outcomes.

Second to formal structure, one of the most common coalition characteristics is the presence of "representational diversity" among member organizations—in other words, the unification of a plurality of interests (Junk 2019; Phinney 2017; Lorenz 2019). Public policies have wide-ranging effects. For myriad reasons, their target populations—broad or restrained—are often, if not always, multifaceted. The ETA, for example, touched on the interests of members of the Navajo Nation, utility companies, local fossil fuel–dependent communities, and climate activists. The coalition that championed the bill, correspondingly, contained representatives of each of these communities.

But not all coalitions choose to unite a diverse group of interests. In the case of the ETA, the coalition leader I spoke to described the intentional effort of legacy environmental groups such as the Sierra Club, the League of Conservation Voters, and the National Audubon Society to partner with social and racial justice organizations whose constituencies were also implicated in the bill.[7] The leader pointed out that the climate groups pursued these diverse partners for tactical reasons—while they had the political and policy acumen to negotiate with lawmakers in Santa Fe, they lacked the connections and tools to widen the proposed policy's visibility and support among other constituent communities. In their view, other organizations with interests in the policy, including local social and racial justice groups, had this leverage. And their efforts paid off, so much so that Governor Lujan Grisham referenced the composition of their coalition at the law's signing ceremony.

This characteristic of lobbying coalitions is also indicative of distinct theories of change—beliefs about the tools, mechanisms, and approaches that will enable them, as individual organizations and champions in a broader movement, to succeed in enacting social and political change. An immigrant rights group, for instance, might approach their work with a theory of change grounded in providing services to their local community or politically engaging their constituents. A professional association, on the other hand, might focus their efforts on national-level policy work by writing white papers and lobbying lawmakers. These theories of change lead different advocates to become experienced in certain spaces and well versed with certain strategies. While representational diversity most immediately provides partnerships with constituent-level context, differences among member organizations also provide alliances with more pronounced strategic resources—allowing for conversations about how to benefit from, and bridge, divergent structural specialties and experiences. This logic was echoed in my interviews with organizational leaders and activists. For example, a policy director for a racial justice group said to me, "groups like the one I work with right now [. . .] sometimes need to come together with groups that have expertise with policy work that we don't necessarily possess." He continued, "On the other hand, other groups want to work with us because they know that we can deliver constituents and information about people who are directly affected by the issues."[8]

Of course, uniting and sustaining representationally diverse coalitions is hard work. After all, if it were so simple, then all coalitions would contain diverse partners. Instead, many organizations largely choose to build partnerships with "friendly faces." Representationally diverse coalitions challenge their member organizations. They put groups with disparate histories, communities, experiences, and theories of change in conversation with one another. In doing so, even if coalition partners feel a sense of shared fate, they force difficult conversations. Member organizations must weigh, for example, which of them are more skilled at certain tasks (such as making a political connection or coordinating a social media campaign) and which are not. They must discuss which positions to champion (and how and why) and which institutions or processes to target. These deliberations require compromise, and in some cases, member organizations may recuse themselves from the partnership if they feel that they are giving up more than they are getting. If the coalition successfully advocates (say, by issuing a press release, writing an amicus brief, or submitting a public comment), it means that its members have reached a consensus. This outcome, from a set of partners with ranging interests, backgrounds, and orientations, is a significant accomplishment.

For instance, it should come as no surprise when a set of labor organizations unites. They have plenty in common. However, when a labor organization successfully unites with a student group or a religious group, it means far more.

My point here, however, is not about the symbolism of a representationally diverse partnership (though this signal also matters) but the work that these partnerships are wont to produce. By pushing through the challenges of negotiating with partners that represent many different communities, these kinds of collaborations produce advocacy that more directly and effectively responds to policymakers' most acute need: *information*. Here, my reasoning is simple. Unlike coalitions that consist of the same type of partner (e.g., a coalition of LGBTQ+ groups), representationally diverse coalitions accumulate extensive, broad-ranging intelligence that reflects their collective positionality (e.g., community-level context, social and political history, awareness of policy alternatives, political connections, tactical skills, and so forth). This intelligence is a direct by-product of their membership; a coalition consisting of an LGBTQ+ group and a Latinx group, for instance, will bring to bear context from each of these constituent communities along with their unique professional specialties and experiences. These coalitions' policy recommendations and strategies will therefore be more widely informed—and thus, more rigorous—than those of a coalition containing a homogenous set of advocates. And this rigor, substantive and symbolic, is important to policymakers, especially in the regulatory setting. For instance, an agency official said to me in an interview, "We definitely look to see who is submitting comments.[. . .] When a lot of different groups write comments together, that sends us a signal about the public pulse, and we notice that."[9] Thus, I argue that coalitions with representational diversity—defined as those that represent a plurality of constituent interests—are more influential policy advocates than their homogeneous counterparts.

However, as the reader may now be thinking, representationally diverse coalitions vary widely in their composition. They might unite a women's organization with a racial justice group, or a corporation with an advocate for consumer interests. This distinction matters. Many diverse coalitions bring together partners representing different interests but which typically fall on the same "side" of policy debates. A hypothetical coalition uniting Community Change Action (formerly the Center for Community Change, founded in 1968) with the Arab American Anti-Discrimination Committee Alliance (ADC, founded in 1980) and the Roosevelt Institute (founded in 1977), for instance, *is* diverse, but not shockingly so. Its partners, all social justice-oriented advocates, share a mission: to defend and promote the rights and liberties of Americans. Other diverse coalitions are more radical, uniting advocates that typically fall on opposite ends of policy battles, with polarized missions and constituencies—such as the union of the National Fair Housing Alliance and the Mortgage Bankers Association I described in chapter 1. For example, in early 2023, a coalition of industry groups and consumer advocacy organizations formed to lobby on a proposal by the Food and Drug Administration (FDA) to restructure its Human Foods Program, a program that handles inspections, laboratory testing, and investigative operations for the agency.[10] This coalition contained organizations that ordinarily fall on opposite ends of the policy spectrum, such as the Consumer Brands Association (an industry group representing manufacturers of consumer packaged goods, founded in 1908) and Consumer Reports (formerly Consumers Union, a nonprofit organization dedicated to consumer advocacy, founded in 1936)—decidedly "strange" bedfellows. In a press release describing the partnership, the groups described themselves as a "robust and diverse coalition [. . .] representing industry, consumer groups, and state and local regulators" brought together by a common concern.[11] A few years earlier, in July 2020, a coalition with similar characteristics formed in Mississippi to lobby lawmakers for the removal of the confederate battle emblem from their state flag. The *New York Times* ran a front-page story reporting on the partnership, which included the NAACP, the National Collegiate Athletic Association (NCAA, founded in 1906), and the Mississippi Prison Industries Corporation, a set of "seemingly unlikely allies."[12] Industry groups reported joining the coalition out of concern for the "economic repercussions posed by keeping the flag." The Black Lives Matter (BLM) activists that headed the coalition's charge, on the other hand, viewed the success as "part of the broader [racial justice] movement." Reflecting on the partnership, a local leader said, "they may be motivated by different reasons [. . .] but they're all working toward the same goal." After voting in favor of a bill to remove the emblem, lawmakers in the state—Republicans and Democrats alike—pointed to the coalition's "unity" as a key source of its persuasiveness.

As these cases illustrate, coalitions of strange bedfellows form for the same reasons that motivate other organizational collaborations: a sense of shared fate among partners, an understanding of the value that their members' distinct backgrounds and skills provide, and an awareness of the signal that their unions send to policymakers. But coalitions that contain strange bedfellows also go a few steps further. As challenging as building and maintaining a diverse coalition may be, sustaining a diverse coalition with *extremely dissimilar* partners—like a coalition uniting business or industry representatives with social and economic justice advocates—takes the cake. These partnerships, if successful, send a crystal-clear signal of need and consensus across a huge range of stakeholders and constituents—a range that is much wider than those of their conventional counterparts. By way of including business and industry partners (which drastically out-resource social and economic justice advocates), they also bring to bear a much deeper arsenal of financial resources. Meanwhile, like any diverse coalition, they benefit from the presence of informational and tactical diversity—an organic outcome of bringing many different groups together to deliberate. Thus, I argue that coalitions of strange bedfellows—defined as those that unite social and economic justice organizations with business and industry-oriented partners—experience significantly greater policy influence than their conventional counterparts.

Finally, there is strong evidence to suggest that not only do diverse coalitions lend themselves to more capable policy advocacy, but also that policymakers themselves view these coalitions favorably. As I wrote in chapter 4, rulemaking-oriented bureaucrats have strong incentives to consider public comments with high informational content. An agency official said to me in an interview, "The comments that are most useful to us [have] high expertise. They make detailed arguments with supporting evidence."[13] Another official said, "We don't just want to hear from industry. We already know what they think. We want to hear from other, more diverse voices . . . [and] we notice when industry and non-industry groups work together. That's a strong signal that . . . gives us helpful background as we make our decisions."[14] In other words, policymakers respond to the *composition* of coalitions—both directly and indirectly. By uniting different kinds of groups, diverse coalitions send a cue that speaks to the fundamental concerns of agency policymakers: information, public perception, and stakeholder consensus. This cue does not go unnoticed.

Coalition Characteristics

This context suggests that while they are not without challenges, building coalitions with diverse memberships is beneficial to organizational advocates for social and economic justice. The data support this notion. According to the *Collaborative Advocacy Dataset*, 58 percent of all collaborative advocacy efforts by social and economic justice groups contain some degree of representational diversity. These trends hold true across both formal and ad hoc coalitions; 42 percent of formal coalitions and 56 percent of ad hoc coalitions contain representational diversity. As these statistics suggest, ad hoc coalitions generally attract more representationally diverse partners than their formal counterparts. On average, ad hoc coalitions contain memberships that are 28 percent more representationally diverse than formalized partnerships.

TABLE 5.1. Coalition composition by organizational type

Organizational type	Representational diversity (%)	Strange bedfellows (%)
Charitable foundation/think tank	75	29
Citizen group	54	39
Native American tribe	61	19
Professional association	97	3

Note: These proportions represent rates of building representationally diverse and strange bedfellow coalitions, respectively, within organizational type categories. They were calculated as follows: number of representationally diverse/strange bedfellow coalitions formed by members of the sample in each organizational type divided by the total number of all coalitions formed by members of the sample in each organizational type.

In contrast, coalitions containing strange bedfellows (uniting social and economic justice advocates with business/industry partners) are few and far between. Only 18 percent of coalitional efforts by social and economic justice organizations contain a business- or industry-oriented partner. Twenty-seven percent of coalitions containing business or industry-oriented partners are ad hoc in nature; only 5 percent maintain formalized structures. Eleven percent of coalitions with representational diversity unite strange bedfellows.[15]

Table 5.1 depicts social and economic justice groups' rates of building representationally diverse coalitions and coalitions of strange bedfellows in the *Collaborative Advocacy Dataset*, grouped by organizational type. It demonstrates a series of trends in coalition composition: first, across coalitional efforts, all four organizational types build representationally diverse coalitions at high rates (in more than 50 percent of coalition cases). In contrast, social and economic justice organizations' patterns of building coalitions with business/industry partners vary widely. According to the *Collaborative Advocacy Dataset*, citizen groups join coalitions of strange bedfellows with regularity—approximately 40 percent of their coalitional efforts include business or industry partners. Charitable foundations/think tanks and Native American tribes join these coalitions at much lower rates, in roughly 30 percent and 20 percent of their collaborative advocacy efforts, respectively. Professional associations join in coalition with industry and business representatives at the lowest rate, across only 3 percent of their coalitions.

Table 5.2 depicts these same patterns of coalition work through the lens of social and economic justice organizations' policy foci.[16] It reflects many of the same trends illustrated in table 5.1. Organizational advocates active across all five policy categories—economic justice, racial justice, Indigenous issues, women's issues, and LGBTQ+ issues—build representationally diverse coalitions a majority of the time; more than 50 percent of coalitions formed by each of these policy-oriented advocates contained members representing two

TABLE 5.2. Coalition composition by group policy focus

Policy focus	Representational diversity (%)	Strange bedfellows (%)
Anti-poverty	69	27
LGBTQ+	50	9
Native American	59	14
Racial/ethnic minority	51	12
Women's issues	63	28

Note: These proportions represent rates of building representationally diverse and strange bedfellow coalitions, respectively, within policy foci. They were calculated as follows: number of representationally diverse/strange bedfellow coalitions formed by members of the sample in each policy focus divided by the total number of all coalitions formed by members of the sample in each policy focus.

or more distinct constituent categories. In contrast, rates of building coalitions of strange bedfellows are low across all policy categories. Organizations advocating for economic justice (anti-poverty) and women's policy issues join with business- and industry-oriented partners in 27 and 28 percent of their collaborative efforts, respectively. Racial justice (racial/ethnic minority, Native American) groups join with business and industry partners in 14 percent (Native American) and 12 percent (racial/ethnic minority) of their coalitions, respectively. Finally, LGBTQ+ groups join strange bedfellow partnerships in only 9 percent of their cases of coalition work.

Together with the findings of chapter 4, these statistics tell a simple yet important story: all kinds of social and economic justice organizations build coalitions at high rates and, in doing so, build coalitions with varying compositions. Across organizational types and policy orientations, these advocates often build coalitions with memberships that represent a range of constituent interests. Unsurprisingly, these groups seldom join coalitions with business or industry partners—in all cases, a minority of their coalition work unites them with strange bedfellows. Yet the question remains: Do these behaviors matter for their advocacy influence?

Coalition Membership and Influence

I test the fundamental claims of this chapter—that social and economic justice organizations exert greater influence over public policy when they advocate in coalitions with diverse memberships—using the *Collaborative Advocacy Dataset*. I estimate a series of generalized linear models (GLM) but largely focus on the results of Model 3. Where appropriate, I refer to the appendix section of this book for models and tests that evaluate alternative explanations. Like Models 1 and 2 (chapter 4), Model 3's dependent variable is the

influence of organizational advocacy by social and economic justice organizations (textual similarity between comment–final rule pairs). Its primary
predictor variables are binary indicator variables reflecting the formation of
a representationally diverse coalition and a coalition of strange bedfellows.
The model controls for the formation of a coalition, the formation of a formal
coalition, coalition size, financial capacity, characteristics of the targeted public policy (complexity, salience), and characteristics of the underlying public
comment (textual similarity between the public comment and the original
proposed rule, public comment length). The model also accounts for potential correlations within subpopulations of the data (groups in the sample) by
clustering the standard errors by group. These relationships can be formally
expressed by the following equation (eq. 2),[17] where $Y = \gamma(\mu|\phi)$:

$$
\begin{aligned}
\ln E(Y|X) = \beta_0 &+ \beta_1 \text{Coalition} \\
&+ \beta_2 \text{FormalCoalition} \\
&+ \beta_3 \text{RepresentationalDiversity} \\
&+ \beta_4 \text{StrangeBedfellows} \\
&+ \beta_5 \text{CoalitionSize} \\
&+ \beta_6 \text{FinancialCapacity} \\
&+ \beta_7 \text{ProposedRuleComplexity} \\
&+ \beta_8 \text{ProposedRuleSalience} \\
&+ \beta_9 \text{ProposedRuleCommentSimilarity} \\
&+ \beta_{10} \text{CommentLength}
\end{aligned}
$$

Figure 5.1 visualizes the results of Model 3.[18] This model evaluates whether
advocacy by social and economic justice organizations is more influential
when pursued by coalitions with diverse memberships. It illustrates several key
findings. First, as with Model 1, there is a statistically insignificant relationship
between the formation of a coalition alone and advocacy influence. Meanwhile, the effect of coalition architecture endures—as with Models 1 and 2,
there is a positive and statistically significant relationship between the formation of a formal coalition and social and economic justice organizations'
advocacy influence. This finding lends further support to the conclusions
made in chapter 4 by demonstrating that even upon accounting for coalition composition, the relationship between formal coalition architecture and
advocacy influence remains consistent. Second, there is a positive and statistically significant relationship between the formation of a coalition containing representational diversity and advocacy influence. Put differently, social
and economic justice organizations experience significantly greater policy
influence when advocating in coalitions with members representing a plurality of constituent interests. More specifically, holding all other independent

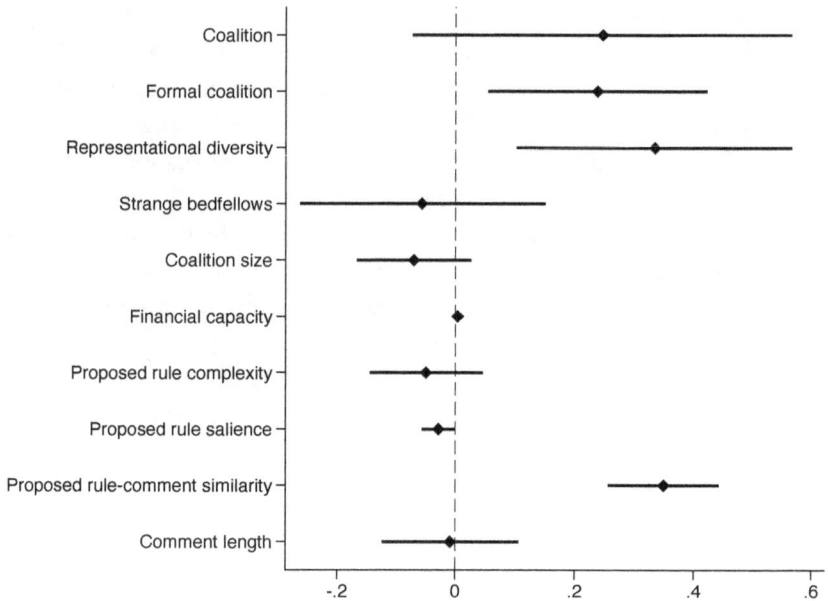

FIGURE 5.1. Coalition composition and advocacy influence (Model 3). Generalized linear regression model (Gamma family, log link function) with group-clustered standard errors. $N = 623$. Diamonds indicate coefficient values. Lines indicate 95 percent confidence intervals.

variables at their means, this finding suggests that a shift from advocating alone or in a homogeneous coalition to advocating in a coalition with a representationally diverse membership more than doubles the shared word count in perfectly matching phrases between comment and final rule documents (seven to eighteen words). As with the effects described in chapter 4, this effect size is both statistically and substantively meaningful. As the reader may recall, these results capture the outcomes of social and economic justice organizations' efforts to influence the content of final federal agency rules. These policies are highly technical and extraordinarily precise. In agency rules, every word counts. Thus, this finding lends strong support to a core tenant of my argument in this chapter.

However, the remaining predictor variable of interest—the formation of a coalition containing strange bedfellows—shares a statistically insignificant relationship with the dependent variable. In other words, coalitions that unite business/industry partners with advocates for social and economic justice are no more influential over policy outcomes than solo advocates or coalitions without this characteristic. While this result does not lend support to the latter component of my argument in this chapter, it is nonetheless telling. Along with the first pair of findings from this model, it suggests that while coalition architecture and composition are important factors for advocacy influence, certain coalition compositions are more consequential than others. Coalitions that unite partners with crosscutting *constituent interests* are most effective at achieving their goals. This finding remains true even after restricting the analysis to coalitions with formalized structures—which chapter 4's analysis demonstrated to be a pivotal architectural condition for advocacy influence. The results of this secondary analysis are available in figure 5.2, which depicts the results of an ordinary least squares linear regression model (Model 4) identical to Model 3 in all respects beyond sample size.[19]

These discoveries help clarify a picture of the mechanisms connecting coalition composition with advocacy outcomes. By demonstrating that advocates for social and economic justice are significantly more influential when they build coalitions with partner organizations representing a plurality of interests (rather than those that unite with business or industry partners), this analysis underscores the unique value of representational diversity in coalitional advocacy. According to the *Collaborative Advocacy Dataset*, coalitions with representational diversity do not appear to materially differ from their "strange bedfellow" counterparts. Both sets of coalitions are similar in size, similarly resourced (although coalitions with business or industry partners

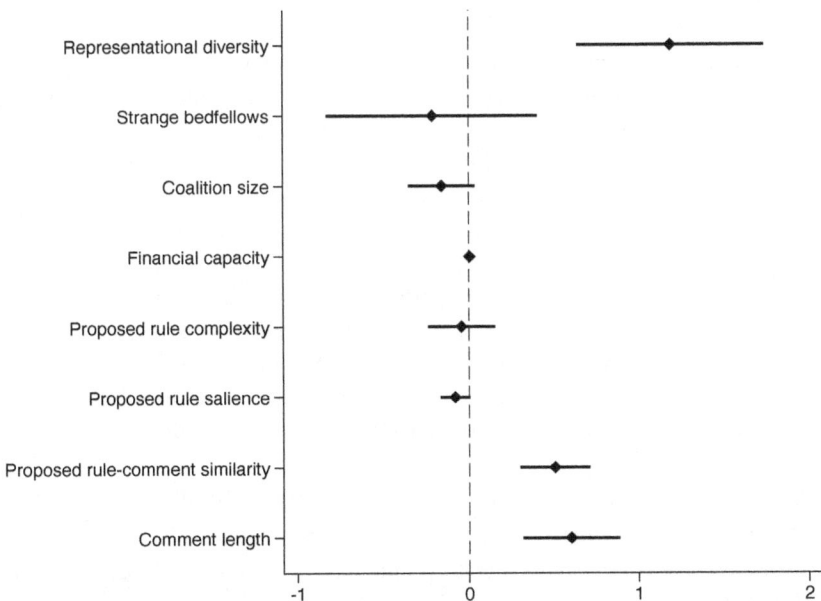

FIGURE 5.2. Formal coalition composition and advocacy influence (Model 4). Ordinary least squares linear regression model with group-clustered standard errors. $N = 127$. Diamonds indicate coefficient values. Lines indicate 95 percent confidence intervals.

have slightly higher financial backings), and often advocate on policies with similar characteristics (i.e., complexity, salience, and length). These patterns, taken in context with the findings of Model 4, may seem puzzling. But they tell an intuitive story. In contrast to their homogenous counterparts, coalitions with partners representing a range of constituent interests have the unique capacity to pool information regarding the many communities they serve. They can deliver the answers to questions that regulators care about, such as, How will this policy affect the population being regulated? How will communities receiving these services react? What are the consequences of making a certain choice (such as setting a standard/establishing a definition) for service providers/service seekers/regulated groups? What are the alternatives? On the other hand, coalitions containing extremely dissimilar partners may have the capacities to answer these questions but struggle to arrive at a common ground because of the very divides that brought them together. Scholars have demonstrated a similar pattern in bipartisan coalition work—which often detracts from advocacy success (Dwidar 2022a). This kind of partnership may thus not allow for the fluid and forward-thinking problem solving that comes naturally to representationally diverse coalitions with greater unity. This story was echoed in my interviews with organizational advocates. A policy director of a racial justice organization, for instance, said to me in an interview,

> Coalitions are a constant [in our work]. We're always needing to form coalitions in order to achieve power . . . by having better positioning to be able to demonstrate who we are, who our friends are, and what we can contribute together. We find partnerships with common ground, where we can say, "We're going to cover these areas and you cover those areas, and together, we'll reach our goal." We ask [ourselves], "Are we working with groups that we trust?" "Are we working with groups that have information in some other space we don't have access to?" We ask [our partners], "Are we thinking about this issue correctly? Are we using the most up-to-date numbers and information?" Through those coalitions, you build power and you build credibility by being able to say, "we are representing these communities en masse." And that's something that's really hard to turn down if you're working on the other side.[20]

In the words of these advocates, there is a link between finding partners that represent a range of constituent communities, collecting well-rounded information, and signaling credibility to policymakers. Not only do these strategists believe that it is vital for their organizations to find coalition partners who can fill informational gaps but also that building these partnerships increases the chances that they will succeed in their advocacy work—a suggestion that

Models 3 and 4 directly support. Like the story this director told, this chapter's analysis suggests that coalitions including partners representing different constituent interests deliver on policymakers' core needs (quality information and wide-ranging consensus) while capitalizing on feelings of trust and unity between partners. Their "strange bedfellow" counterparts, on the other hand, may struggle to successfully capitalize on these capacities because of their extreme compositions.

Last, the main finding of this chapter is also reinforced by existing scholarship. Lorenz (2019), for instance, theorizes that large, homogenous, and well-resourced coalitions of interest groups are unlikely to attract the attention of lawmakers in the US Congress. Instead, he argues that coalitions with interest diversity are far more capable of capturing and sustaining the attention of a critical mass of rank-and-file members. Lorenz suggests that interest-diverse coalitions send unique informational cues about whether a piece of legislation will garner "sustained" support—an important agenda-setting tool for representatives in Congress. Phinney's (2017) analysis of social policy advocacy in Congress similarly contends that lobbying influence is not driven by organizations' choices to collaborate alone, but by the presence of diversity in the interests represented by coalition actors. She argues that these kinds of coalitions address a key source of concern among policymakers: legislative uncertainty. Coalitions that are diverse in this regard, Phinney claims, can more compellingly respond to policy opportunities using their arsenal of greater, more credible information. In the European lobbying context, Junk (2019) and Mahoney (2007) echo these notions. They argue that "not all [. . .] coalitions should be born equal" (Junk 2019, 662). Instead, they suggest that successful coalitions signal "[the] support of a varied group of interests" (Mahoney 2007, 368).

Alternative Explanations

The empirically minded reader may now be wondering a few things. Does the degree, rather than the mere presence, of diversity in coalition work matter? Are social and economic justice groups just more likely to build coalitions with representational diversity when they think they will be influential? Are the results sensitive to the fifty-member coding cut-off? What about agency responses to comments—which are typically embedded in the text of final agency rules? Is this language contributing to overestimation of the observed effect? What about comments that sought to "kill" agency rules, rather than influence their textual content? Before concluding this chapter, I evaluate these, along with other, alternative explanations.[21]

First, the reader may recall that my measure of representational diversity in coalition membership is binary, reflecting the non-zero presence of diversity within coalitions. And the reader may thus wonder whether this measure fails to capture the full effect of a representationally diverse membership—as perhaps greater diversity is associated with greater influence. In chapter 3, I explained that the choice to operationalize this concept in a binary manner was theoretically motivated: scholars have repeatedly demonstrated that the mere entry of diversity to policymaking bodies bears significant influence over its outcomes. Farhang and Wawro (2010), for instance, report that the presence of a single female counterjudge significantly affects case outcomes in sexual harassment cases. Kastellec (2013) and Beim and Kastellec (2014) find, respectively, that the presence of a Black judge on a three-judge panel significantly increases the odds that the remaining non-Black judges will approach an affirmative action case differently, and that the presence of ideological diversity on these panels plays a significant role in judicial decision making. While most of this work has focused on the judicial arena, it is still sensible to extend its findings to other policy-oriented decision-making bodies.

However, to ameliorate lingering concerns regarding the efficacy of this measure, I have reestimated Models 3 and 4 to incorporate an operationalization that captures the *degree* of representational diversity (normalized Shannon's H diversity index, ranging from 0 to 1) along with the original diversity indicator variable (binary).[22] The results of these reestimations are available in appendix E. These model results present a few important takeaways. First, there are insignificant relationships between the diversity indices and advocacy influence, suggesting that a greater degree of representational diversity is not a pivotal condition for organizational influence. Meanwhile, the binary representational diversity variables maintain the same relationships—in both significance and direction—observed in Models 3 and 4. All other variables maintain relationships similar to those observed in Models 3 and 4. These observations lend confidence to the results of previous models and provide potential evidence of a "threshold" effect relating to membership diversity, wherein the entry of at least one representationally diverse partner to organizational coalitions has a significantly greater effect on advocacy influence than that of a greater degree of representational diversity among member organizations.

Next up is the endogeneity question. While it would be impossible to evaluate empirically all circumstances under which advocacy influence might be interrelated with the choice to build certain types of coalitions, there are several obvious and theoretically likely conditions. For instance, as I suggested at the end of chapter 4, coalitions with certain characteristics might form strategically in response to certain kinds of proposed agency rules, such as those with greater levels of complexity or salience. Proposed rules with high levels of complexity or salience necessarily require more complex, or otherwise politically adept, public comments. Comments that reach this standard are typically more difficult to produce; they require drawing on a wider range of informational and tactical expertise, which coalitions with representationally diverse compositions are likely to facilitate. In other words, comments on proposed rules that are more complex or salient might be more likely to be influential when produced by coalitions representing representationally diverse constituencies, and we can reasonably expect coalition partners to be aware of this dynamic.

Starting with policy complexity, if social and economic justice organizations strategically build coalitions with representational diversity under conditions of high policy complexity, then we should seldom observe these types of coalitions occurring in response to less complex policies. But in fact, the opposite is true. Among all representationally diverse coalitions in the *Collaborative Advocacy Dataset*, 34 percent occurred in response to proposed rules with the *lowest possible* degree of complexity (out of six), and 43 percent occurred on the second-lowest level.[23] These statistics should resolve concerns that representationally diverse coalitions predominantly form in response to more complex rules. Next, the case of policy salience: if the reality of coalition strategy is that organizations strategically build representationally diverse partnerships under conditions of high policy salience, then we should seldom observe these coalitions occurring in response to less salient public policies. However, this expectation is also not reflected in the data. Figure 5.3 depicts a summary distribution of proposed regulation salience over the occurrence of representationally diverse coalitions in the *Collaborative Advocacy Dataset*. This distribution demonstrates, plainly, that there is no difference between the levels of salience of proposed agency rules on which coalitions with and without representational diversity advocate.

Now, as the reader may recall from the concluding section of chapter 3, the analyses in this chapter do not include data on coalitions containing more than fifty members. In chapter 3, I explained how this decision was theoretically motivated: since my goal in this book is to understand the outcomes of social and economic justice organizations' *substantive* policy advocacy, I did not code membership-level data on coalitions with greater than fifty members. I established this cut-off in order to control for the appearance of superficial, or symbolic, coalitions, which typically contain hundreds of members and rarely pursue substantive advocacy (Dwidar 2022a; Hojnacki 1997, 1998;

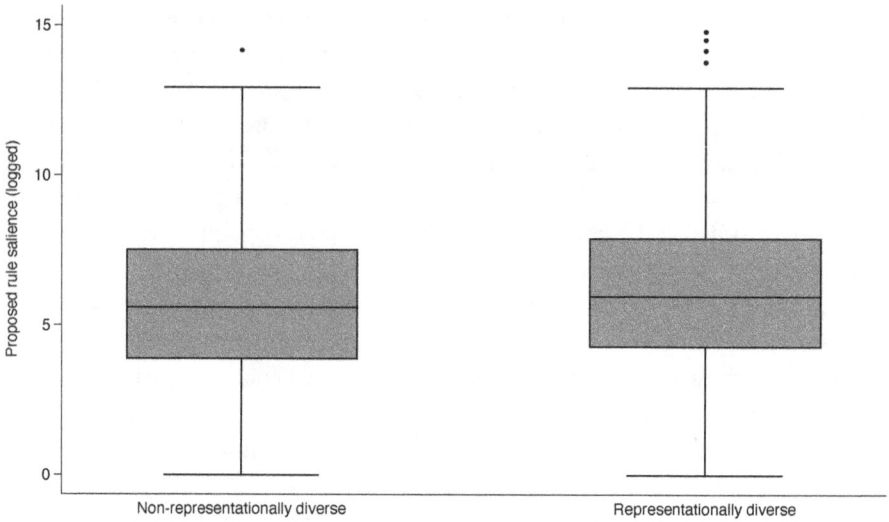

FIGURE 5.3. Distribution of policy salience over representationally diverse coalition building

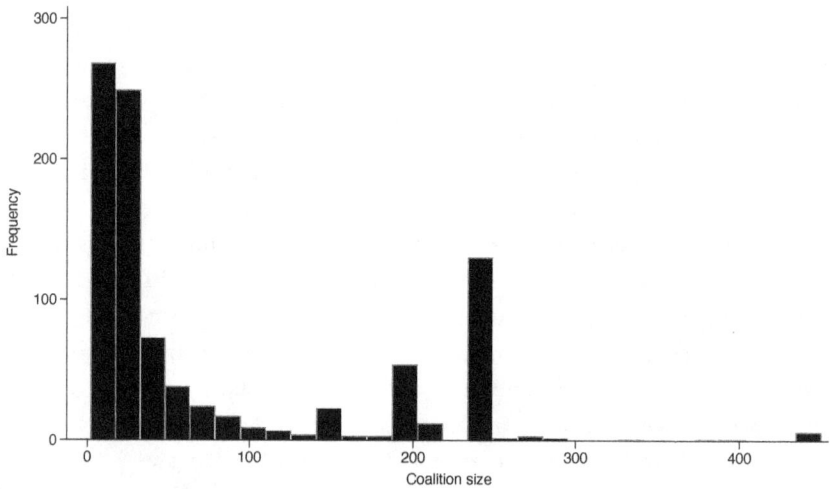

FIGURE 5.4. Distribution of coalition size

Hula 1999). Empirically, however, we have more to discuss. First, according to the *Collaborative Advocacy Dataset*, larger coalitions are less common. In other words, by excluding larger coalitions from my analysis, I omit a limited number of observations. Figure 5.4 illustrates the distribution of the variable *coalition size* in the dataset; it demonstrates that the vast majority of coalitions (65 percent) contain fifty or fewer members.

These trends largely hold true for both formal and ad hoc coalitions—approximately 82 percent of ad hoc coalitions and 50 percent of formal coalitions contain fifty or fewer members. Of course, the difference between these rates may stand out to the reader and may generate some concern about the cut-off. However, recall that formal coalitions are larger, on average, than ad hoc coalitions and that the purpose of the cut-off is to ensure the inclusion of policy-oriented, rather than symbolic, coalitional advocacy. Scholars of interest group politics have repeatedly written that larger coalitions face greater barriers to productivity. They struggle to overcome a classic application of the collective action problem (Hula 1999; Box-Steffensmeier et al. 2018); for larger coalitions, the process of encouraging and separating active members from "seat warmers" poses a significant challenge for coalition leaders and typically leads them to pursue more symbolic advocacy (such as collecting signatures rather than developing more refined lobbying proposals) (Hula 1999). Thus, advocacy by much larger coalitions tends to be symbolic, often consisting of mass email threads, lists of supporters, images of flyers or constituents, and otherwise unsubstantive information with no clear message or recipient (Dwidar 2022a). These trends were echoed in my own qualitative evaluation of the textual data underlying the *Collaborative Advocacy Dataset*.

By nature, however, any cut-off is somewhat arbitrary. Thus, I evaluated several empirical alternatives to validate my choice and ensure that the pertinent analyses presented in this chapter are not sensitive to the fifty-member ceiling. I reestimated the chapters' primary models—Models 3 and 4—varying the membership cut-off at coalitions containing 45 or fewer, 40 or fewer, and 35 or fewer organizations. The corresponding results, available in appendix F (Model 3 reestimations) and appendix G (Model 4 reestimations), maintain support of this chapter's previous findings. These reestimations demonstrate that the results presented earlier in this chapter are not sensitive to the fifty-member cut-off and thus lend confidence to my original measurement choice.

Next, the reader may be aware that federal agencies are required to publish their responses to "significant" comments as a part of each final rule (Potter 2019; West 2004). These responses summarize the key points of the comments and describe the agency's response. They articulate (tersely) whether and why they have chosen to adopt or disregard the comment's recommendations. This communication is important; it reinforces agencies' mandates to carefully evaluate the content of public comments that they receive and establishes a written record for purposes of oversight and judicial review. However, the publication of these responses as a part of final agency rules poses a measurement concern for this project: the inclusion of the agency response—which, in some cases, provides a summary of comments' recommendations—might contribute to an overestimation of the dependent variable. To ameliorate this concern, I manually removed the agency response section from most final rules appearing in the data (63 percent) and reproduced a constrained version of the dependent variable. In the remaining 37 percent, the agency response was interwoven within the final regulatory language (distributed across hundreds—and in some cases thousands—of pages without obvious in-text identifiers), making it impossible to identify and remove each component of the response by hand or using automated tools.

However, within the corpus of rules from which I was able to manually remove the agency response, the correlation between the original and constrained dependent variable was 0.97, suggesting that the results presented in the previous section are not driven by the inclusion of the text of the agency response. Though it is possible that the group of rules from which I was not able to remove the agency response might differ systematically from the group from which I was able to investigate this possibility directly, I did not detect any such differences. Both sets of rules appear similar in complexity, salience, and length.

Finally, because of the operationalization of the dependent variable, my findings do not address cases where a final rule was not issued but where a comment sought to "kill" the rule and thus succeeded in achieving its goal. It is certainly possible that some comments in the corpus successfully urged regulators to shelve the corresponding proposed rules. However, the withdrawal of proposed rules by federal agencies is rare, as they are slowly and carefully developed over long periods of time, typically with the consultation of outside groups (Potter 2019). This trend is reflected in the data, as only 1.2 percent of proposed rules in the full dataset and approximately 3 percent in the dataset of all coalitions containing fewer than fifty-one members were formally withdrawn.

Regardless, this phenomenon is a form of *negative* lobbying power—lobbying against a particular policy proposal in its entirety. Since it is not possible to measure textual similarity without a final rule, these cases are excluded from the data and models presented thus far in this book. However, it is likely that by excluding these instances, the relationships reported are, at worst, understated. A manual textual assessment of the pertinent documents could allow for an analysis of these cases, though it is beyond the scope of the data and analysis used in this book, which are concerned with a form of positive lobbying power—lobbying to refine, rather than eliminate, policy content.

Summary

Social and economic justice organizations build all kinds of coalitions. A program director of a social justice organization said to me in an interview, "[Coalitions] come in different shapes and sizes, but across the board, they contribute to shared power and increase the legitimacy of groups."[24] The analyses of this chapter support this view, in part—coalitions *do* come in all shapes and sizes. According to the *Collaborative Advocacy Dataset*, organizational advocates for social and economic justice organizations build myriad coalition types—from those that are informal and fleeting to long-lasting collaborations with formalized architectures to partnerships with representationally diverse memberships to unions of groups that usually fall on opposite ends of advocacy debates. However, not all of these "shapes and sizes" make for successful coalition work. In this chapter, I demonstrate that the most effective coalitions contain memberships that represent a plurality of interests, rather than memberships that cross significant divides (like social/economic justice–business/industry partnerships). Admittedly, these findings are simple and intuitive. However, they represent a significant step forward for scholarly understandings of collaboration and collective action in social justice advocacy and make several tactical contributions to organizational leaders' and strategists' approaches to coalition work—which I will elaborate on in greater detail in chapter 8.

Moreover, this work also speaks to long-standing debate over the American federal bureaucracy's democratic legitimacy. As the federal bureaucracy has grown in size and scope, the contributions of advocacy organizations to its policymaking have grown increasingly vital. While bureaucratic rulemaking has often been labeled undemocratic—as it lends unelected civil servants a great deal of discretion over the policy process—the findings of this chapter suggest otherwise. If, as the results of this chapter demonstrate, bureaucrats favor the proposals of representationally diverse (i.e., pluralistic) coalitions in the rulemaking process, their rulemaking thus likely considers and represents the interests of a broader public. This conclusion therefore contributes to a storied literature regarding agency responsiveness to public and stakeholder interests, legitimacy in rulemaking, and representative democracy.

In the next chapter, I temporarily turn my focus to a different sample: private professional, and general interest groups. I replicate the analyses of chapters 4 and 5 in an effort to understand whether, and to what degree, there are differences between coalition building and influence by advocates for social and economic justice versus mainstream interest groups. I theorize that,

like their social justice–oriented counterparts, private and professional organizations and general interest groups benefit from coalition work in their
policy advocacy. I argue, however, that we should expect to see differences in
the effects of coalition building across these samples of advocates, and that
the effect of coalition work, and diverse coalition work, should be magnified
for social and economic justice organizations relative to their mainstream
counterparts.

6

Collaboration in Context

Now, to state the obvious. All kinds of organizations, with all kinds of interests, turn to coalition work to achieve their advocacy goals. Even the top spenders in American lobbying, such as the US Chamber of Commerce (founded in 1912, ranked the number two top spender in 2022), the Pharmaceutical Research and Manufacturers of America (formerly the Pharmaceutical Manufacturers Association, founded in 1958, ranked the number three top spender in 2022), and the American Association of Retired Persons (AARP, founded in 1958, ranked the number eleven top spender in 2022) often advocate in partnership with other groups.[1] Unlike the advocates that make up the focus of this book, these well-resourced, comfortably connected, and mainstream interest groups have the money and contacts to advocate alone. But like social and economic justice organizations, they regularly choose to coalesce. They do so because they recognize that the benefits of coalition work go beyond financial considerations. Coalition work is a powerful way for these advocates to signal credibility, consensus, and well-rounded advocacy content. After all, no amount of money or in-house expertise can buy the message that building and sustaining coalitions—especially those that unite different and unfamiliar sectors and communities—sends to policymakers. A former agency official told me, "it's impressive to receive these comments or to see these press conferences [where] all these different groups are together. Because [we know] that something had to bind them together."[2] Like their social and economic justice–oriented counterparts, mainstream interest groups build coalitions because they believe that these partnerships are vital for their success (Heaney 2004; Hula 1999).

Take, for instance, the Regulatory Relief Coalition (RRC), a formal coalition of over thirty medical organizations including the American Medical

Association (AMA, founded in 1847), the American College of Cardiology (ACC, founded in 1949), and the Medical Group Management Association (MGMA, founded in 1926). In early 2023, the RRC began a lobbying campaign in response to a rule issued by the Centers for Medicare and Medicaid Services (CMS). The rule in question proposed a set of prior authorization reforms to Medicare Part C and Medicare Part D coverage. The coalition responded with a series of recommendations designed, in their words, to "protect patients from care interruptions, treatment delays, and unanticipated medical costs."[3] A few years earlier, in 2021, the National Association of Realtors joined a coalition with over a dozen partners, including Bank of America, the Mortgage Bankers Association (MBA), the National Urban League (NUL), and the National Fair Housing Alliance (NFHA), with a single aim: to increase Black homeownership by three million households by the year 2030. Their seven-point plan detailed a series of policy recommendations, tools, and advocacy plans to help reach this goal.[4] Bryan Greene, vice president of policy advocacy for the National Association of Realtors and a member of the coalition's steering committee, described the motivations behind the partnership:

> The legacy of discriminatory practices, as well as official government practices and longstanding harm, has left us with great disparities in wealth and opportunity.[. . .] The goal with [this coalition] is to recognize that [legacy of discrimination] and to try to figure out where we can begin to make more progress. We do need to do something aggressive if we expect to create more homeownership opportunities in this country.[. . .] We have an interest in the housing industry, and I think society at large, to try to find ways to close these gaps, because our economy and our society benefit from more housing opportunities.[5]

As Greene's explanation made clear, the NAR's choice to support these policy goals was not selfless. Their interests in promoting Black homeownership were motivated, at least in part, by financial and economic interests. Still, despite their renowned standing in American lobbying (in 2022, they were ranked the number one top spender),[6] they chose to pursue these interests in partnership with other advocates—including other professional associations, private banks, and nonprofit organizations with experience lobbying for fair housing. In doing so, their collaboration (along with that of the RRC) touched on an important set of dynamics in American interest group politics: that even private and professional interest groups with significant financial advantages seek out lobbying partnerships, build diverse coalitions, and occasionally unite with strange bedfellows. The Mortgage Bankers Association and the National Fair Housing Alliance are, after all, not usually on the same team.

In this chapter, I introduce and assess the second subset of the *Collaborative Advocacy Dataset*, a subset identical to the data I have analyzed in previous chapters but pertaining to a different subject: mainstream interest groups, defined as advocates for communities that are *not* historically marginalized (consisting of general interest, private, and professional organizations).[7] Using these data, I unpack trends in coalition building and composition by these groups and compare them to those of organizational advocates for social and economic justice. I argue that while mainstream interest groups often build coalitions of varying structures and compositions—and benefit from working in these partnerships—the effect of coalition work on advocacy influence is magnified, comparatively, for social and economic justice organizations. In other words, while coalition work benefits all kinds of interest groups, it is *more beneficial* for organizations operating at a systematic disadvantage in the American lobbying landscape. I contend that for these advocates, coalition work levels the playing field.

Connecting to Theory

As I have written in previous chapters, the argument in favor of coalition work for social and economic justice organizations is logical and straightforward. For mainstream interest groups, the argument is just as simple. Most advocacy organizations experience limitations of some kind; even private and professional groups with significant power over policy subsystems face barriers to influence (Baumgartner and Leech 1998; Junk 2019; Lorenz 2019). These barriers—whether financial, social, political, or tactical—lead organizations to encounter difficulties in procuring or producing valuable policy information across multiple issue domains, enjoy close relationships with political elites, or generally possess long-lasting access to formal and informal policymaking venues (Hansen 1991; Hojnacki 1997, 1998). Limitations in social capital—which are usually, but not exclusively, bound to groups that represent stigmatized or marginalized populations—can create even greater constraints to interest group influence (Strolovitch 2007).

Just like their social and economic justice–oriented counterparts, coalition work provides an opportunity for mainstream interest groups to counteract these limitations by increasing their overall lobbying capacity (Hojnacki 1997, 1998; Hula 1999; Nelson and Yackee 2012). Working in partnership with others allows these organizations to not only pool their financial resources (which, alone, might not be a compelling enough sell for some such advocates) but to split lobbying tasks, accumulate expertise, acquire coverage across different tactics and tools, and send cues that their positions are credible and supported by many sectors, industries, and communities (Hojnacki 1997, 1998; Hula 1999). Like the story I have told in previous chapters, policymaker incentives—particularly in the regulatory setting—drive home the value of these partnerships. Agency policymakers, motivated by institutional incentives to seek and react to reasoned, evidence-based, and widely supported advocacy recommendations, place a high premium on public and private reactions to their policy ideas (Nelson and Yackee 2012; Yackee 2006). Thus, as many scholars before me have demonstrated, *all* interest groups, including general interest and private and professional organizations, consider coalition building to be a lobbying strategy that is crucial for their success (Baumgartner and Leech 1998; Hojnacki 1997, 1998; Hula 1999). A former communications director for an industry group, for instance, said to me in an interview, "We always had partner organizations that we worked with. We were always part of some coalition."[8] Thus, I argue that coalition work enhances the advocacy influence of mainstream interest groups.

But again, not all coalitions containing mainstream interests look the same—as illustrated by the two examples with which this chapter began. Mainstream interest groups often build diverse partnerships for the *very same* reasons that drive this manner of coalition work by their social justice–motivated counterparts. For instance, in early 2019, the American Petroleum Institute (API, founded in 1919) came together with the American Fuel and Petrochemical Manufacturers (AFPM, founded in 1902), the National Wildlife Federation (NWF, founded in 1936) and the Clean Air Task Force (CATF, founded in 1996) to oppose an Environmental Protection Agency (EPA) rule. The rule in question proposed a change to existing regulations that would allow for the sale of gasoline with 15 percent Ethanol (E15) year round—an action that had previously been banned by the agency.[9] The NWF and CATF, of course, opposed the rule for environmental reasons. David DeGennaro, a policy specialist with the NWF, said of the rule, "the limits exist in the Clean Air Act for a reason. Ethanol blended in gasoline [produces] more pollutants that lead to smog than gasoline alone [. . .] by increasing the amount from 10 percent to 15 percent, that breaks those limits that are in the Clean Air Act and could potentially lead to more ozone formation." The API and AFPM agreed with the NWF and CATF's opposition to the rule, but for a very different reason: their bottom line. A representative for the AFPM expressed concern for oil companies and fuel refiners' abilities to sell less traditional gasoline—and cause production costs to soar. The EPA eventually rescinded the rule.[10]

Why would oil industry organizations and environmental groups work together? They have polarized positions and their partnerships can lead to significant strife between organizational leaders, members, and donors. The answer is simple and no different from the case I have made previously: building coalitions with diverse compositions helps these groups achieve their advocacy goals. Just like their social and economic justice–oriented counterparts, building diverse coalitions allows mainstream organizations to pool their wide-ranging expertise and produce more informed and carefully targeted policy proposals (Junk 2019; Lorenz 2019). As I have described in previous chapters, developing policy recommendations—particularly in the regulatory setting—is challenging, even for seasoned interest groups (Yackee 2006). The barrier to entry is high; for organizations to break through, their advocacy proposals must incorporate expert knowledge, data, and scholarship along with carefully crafted legal language (Golden 1998; Potter 2019; West 2004; Yackee 2006). Working in a diverse coalition helps these advocates ensure that their policy proposals are strong and supported by a wide and well-rounded range of evidence and expertise. Moreover, the value of gaining credibility through coalition work cannot be underscored enough. As decades of research have demonstrated, reaching consensus in collective action is difficult (Olson 1965). So when coalitions with heterogenous memberships successfully come together, their work sends a strong message of unity in the broader policy subsystem. Together, these phenomena serve as important heuristics for bureaucrats who often rely on external signals to gauge potential responses to their policy decisions (Golden 1998; Workman 2015; Workman and Shafran 2015). Thus, I argue that building diverse coalitions—both those with representational diversity and those uniting strange bedfellows—increases the advocacy influence of mainstream interest groups.

This logic—and these expectations—are nothing new. I've told a similar story before. But in this case, the purpose of these hypotheses is to evaluate the efficacy of coalition work *comparatively* for social and economic justice organizations. As I have described in earlier chapters, unlike their mainstream counterparts, social and economic justice groups face systemic disadvantages in lobbying, both within and beyond their own doors (Han, McKenna, and Oyakawa 2021; Staggenborg 1986; Strolovitch 2006, 2007). To bear influence over public policy, they often go up against groups with ready access and unlimited resources along with processes and institutions designed historically to exclude them (Han, McKenna, and Oyakawa 2021; Martinez 2009; Pinderhughes 1995). The value of coalition work is on full display with these advocates. If they can manage to find and sustain partnerships, they benefit, to the utmost capacity, from the opportunity to conserve their scarce resources, split the difficult work of developing and designing policy recommendations, pool tactical skills and expertise, and garner attention and credibility by advocating en masse. Altogether, these benefits level the playing field for these organizations; gaining legitimacy relative to their mainstream lobbying counterparts is an explicit part of their collaborative calculus. For instance, a program director of an economic justice organization said to me in an interview, "for groups like ours, the coalitions that we convene are very, very important to being perceived as respected and legitimate."[11] Thus, I argue that while coalition work, in its many forms, is a beneficial advocacy tool for all organized interest groups, it is *more beneficial* for the influence of advocates for social and economic justice than that of their mainstream counterparts.

Revisiting the *Collaborative Advocacy Dataset*

In chapter 3, I introduced the quantitative data at the core of this book: the *Collaborative Advocacy Dataset*, which contains information on coalition building by two different samples of nationally active organizations over a seventeen-year period. Together, these two subsets of data detail the collaborative advocacy behaviors of over twenty thousand organizations advocating on approximately 2,800 rules proposed by 116 federal agencies. In previous chapters, my analyses have focused exclusively on the data pertaining to the first of these two samples—social and economic justice groups. In this chapter, I turn my attention to the second sample: mainstream interest groups.

The sample of organizations providing the framework for this second subset of the *Collaborative Advocacy Dataset* contains a range of interest groups. Table 6.1 depicts the advocates in this sample according to their organizational categories. Strikingly, but not surprisingly, the majority of organizations in this sample (56 percent) are professional and occupational groups, such as the American Medical Association and the American Spinal Injury Association (ASIA, founded in 1973). Business groups and citizen groups compose the second most prominent categories of members in this sample, at 18 and 20 percent, respectively. These advocates include groups such as the Bankers Association for Finance and Trade (BAFT, founded in 1921), the National Association of Small Business Investment Companies (NASBIC, founded in 1958), and the Interfaith Alliance (IA, founded in 1994). Unions and governmental associations appear in the sample sparingly, at only 4 and 2 percent, respectively. No charitable foundations, think tanks, or Native American tribes appear in the sample.

Importantly, the organizational composition of this sample differs starkly from that of the sample of social and economic justice organizations (see

TABLE 6.1. Mainstream sample by organizational type

Organizational type	Frequency	Percent
Business or business group	9	18.00
Citizen group	10	20.00
Governmental association	2	4.00
Union	1	2.00
Professional association	28	56.00
Total	50	100%

table 3.1 for a comparison). For instance, while professional and occupational groups make up the most prominent organizational category in the mainstream sample, they compose the smallest category in the sample of advocates for social and economic justice, at only 6 percent. Moreover, while advocates for business and industry interests compose the second most prominent category in the mainstream sample, no such groups appear in the sample under study in earlier chapters. Finally, the sample of social and economic groups is predominantly made up of Native American tribes, at 49 percent of the sample; but as table 6.1 illustrates, no Indian tribes appear in the mainstream sample. These trends reiterate key and expected differences between the organizational compositions of the two samples under study in this book. These sets of advocates are strongly distinct.

The mainstream sample also includes groups specializing in a wide range of policy subjects. Table 6.2 depicts the primary policy foci of the interest groups in the mainstream sample, according to data compiled by the CRP from lobbying disclosure documents. Groups specializing in policy areas relating to finance, insurance, and real estate compose the largest proportion of the sample, at 18 percent. Business policy-oriented groups make up the second-largest contingent, at 10 percent. The remainder of the sample is fairly equally dispersed across all other possible policy foci, ranging from 4 to 8 percent of sample members advocating on policy issues relating to agribusiness, communications and electronics, defense, energy and natural resources, health, labor, and manufacturing and distributing. Only one member of the sample maintained an advocacy focus on education policy. As in table 6.1, the patterns illustrated in table 6.2 strongly juxtapose those relating to the sample of social and economic justice organizations. Importantly, this characteristic occurs by design: as I described in chapter 3, the policy foci appearing in tables 3.2 (social and economic justice sample) and 6.2 (mainstream sample) are the lines along which I established the boundaries of the populations of nationally active social and economic justice organizations and private, professional, and general interest groups.

TABLE 6.2. Mainstream sample by policy focus

Policy focus	Frequency	Percent
Agribusiness	4	8.00
Business	5	10.00
Communications/electronics	4	8.00
Defense	2	4.00
Education	1	2.00
Energy and natural resources	3	6.00
Finance, insurance, and real estate	9	18.00
Health	4	8.00
Ideological/single-issue	4	8.00
Labor	4	8.00
Manufacturing and distributing	3	6.00
Transportation	2	4.00
Unreported	5	10.00
Total	50	100%

Finally, the sample contains interest groups representing several different constituent communities, as illustrated in table 6.3. Eight distinct constituencies are represented by the sample, ranging from business communities to children/youth to constituencies of the whole (general interest); in contrast, as the reader may recall, the sample of social and economic justice organizations covered twelve distinct constituent groups (see table 3.3). The sample is largely composed of groups representing a professional or occupational community, such as professional loggers (e.g., the American Loggers Council, founded in 1994) and officers and sailors of the US Navy (such as the Association of the United States Navy, founded in 1954). Advocates for business communities (such as Alabama businesses—courtesy of the Business Council of Alabama, founded in 1985) and the general interest (such as the separation of church and state—courtesy of Americans United for the Separation of Church and State, founded in 1948) compose the second most prevalent constituent categories in the sample, at 13 and 12 percent, respectively. At roughly equal rates (2 to 4 percent), the remainder of the sample includes advocates for children/youth, people with chronic illnesses/general health care rights, the environment, and religious communities.

As I noted in the previous paragraph, the constituencies represented by organizations in this sample are dwarfed by those covered by the sample of social and economic justice groups; the latter sample covers a range of constituencies that is roughly *30 percent greater* than that of their mainstream counterparts. Further, the samples overlap in their representation of only three constituencies: children and youth, religious communities, and general

TABLE 6.3. Mainstream sample by constituency

Constituency	Frequency	Percent
Business/industry	13	26.00
Children/youth	1	2.00
Environmental rights	2	4.00
General interest	6	12.00
Healthcare rights/chronically ill	2	4.00
Profession/occupation	21	42.00
Religious community	2	4.00
Other	3	6.00
Total	50	100%

interest causes. While the mainstream sample is primarily made up of groups advocating on behalf of industries, professional communities, business interests, and the general interest, the sample of social and economic justice organizations is predominantly composed of advocates for racially minoritized communities. The trends demonstrate, once again, fundamental orientational differences between the two samples under study.

Altogether, members of the mainstream sample submitted 1,849 public comments on 1,674 rules proposed by eighty-six federal agencies during the period under study. Of the proposed rules on which they lobbied, 40 percent corresponded to a published final rule. The agencies appearing in this subset of the data span a range of sizes and policy specializations—from the Department of Health and Human Services (HHS) to the Small Business Administration (SBA) to the National Transportation Safety Board (NTSB)—as well as a mix of executive branch (36 percent) and independent (64 percent) agencies. The proposed rules targeted by this sample also covered a wide array of policy topics. As illustrated by figure 6.1, twenty out of the twenty-one major topics proposed by the Policy Agendas Project's common policy coding scheme are present.[12] These rules are characterized by ranges of complexity and salience. They include straightforward, low-salience proposals, such as an amendment to the Fair Labor Standards Act to allow nursing mothers "reasonable break time," and more technical and salient efforts, such as a revision to the implementation of the Endangered Species Act. Notably, two topics—health and environment—are comparatively prominent in the proposed rules appearing in this subset of the data. However, this prominence likely reflects the national government's growing attention and policy infrastructure relating to health and environmental policy during the period under study (2000–2016).

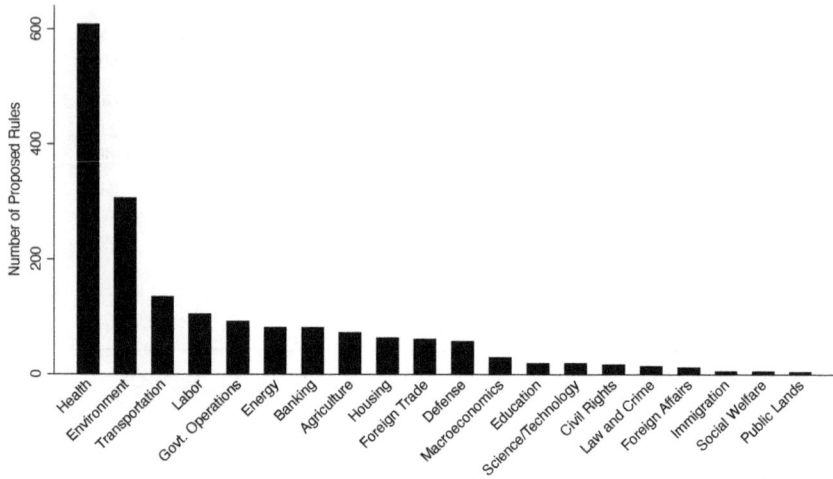

FIGURE 6.1. Proposed rules by policy topic (Mainstream sample)

At a high level, these trends share similarities with the policy contexts and agendas of the sample of social and economic justice organizations. Like the mainstream sample, most proposed agency actions under study in the subset of the *Collaborative Advocacy Dataset* pertaining to advocates for social and economic justice corresponded to a published final agency rule (50 percent). And like the mainstream sample, their targets of regulatory advocacy include a mix of agencies: as I described in chapter 3, 25 percent of regulatory actions by the sample of advocates for social and economic justice were proposed by independent agencies and 75 percent, by executive branch agencies. Both datasets also consist of advocacy efforts targeting a wide range of policy topics; twenty out of the twenty-one major topics proposed by the Policy Agendas Project's common coding scheme are present in the subset of the data analyzed in earlier chapters—a statistic that is identical to that of the data under study in this chapter (see figure 3.1 for a comparison).

But a closer, comparative, examination of these policy trends offers some revealing differences. While both samples engage in substantial advocacy on a number of key policy topics—such as health, labor, and environmental policy, likely due to their unique prominence on the national policy agenda during the period under study—the policy agendas of these sets of advocates are otherwise fairly distinct. For instance, several of the policy topics on the receiving end of the lowest level of advocacy by the mainstream sample—including civil rights, criminal justice, immigration, welfare, and public lands policy—are subject to substantial policy advocacy by the sample of social and economic justice organizations. Conversely, several of the policy topics that receive little advocacy attention by social and economic justice organizations—including science and technology, foreign trade, and energy policy—are frequent targets of advocacy by the sample of mainstream groups. These differences reinforce the core values and orientations of the two samples I explore in this book. As I have described in earlier chapters, organizational advocates for social and economic justice are defined by their origins in historic mass movements for social, racial, and economic equality. As such, they have strong interests in refining and reforming policies addressing social issues, including educational access, criminal justice, public lands, civil rights, social welfare, and more. Mainstream interest groups, on the other hand, have far more majoritarian policy interests.

Contextualizing Collaboration

Patterns of coalition work by mainstream interest groups reflect the theoretical logic I presented earlier in this chapter. According to the *Collaborative Advocacy Dataset*, 42 percent of lobbying efforts by mainstream advocates occur in coalitions. Fifty-two percent of these coalitions are formal in nature—meaning that they retain a formal architecture, with names, fixed memberships, and staff separate from those of their member organizations. These behaviors somewhat parallel those of their social and economic justice-oriented counterparts, which build coalitions at a higher rate (54 percent), but join formalized coalitions at a near-identical rate (51 percent). Across formal and informal coalitions, on average, coalitions built by mainstream interest groups contain thirty-one members (median = 8 groups). Informal coalitions contain about thirty-four members, on average (median = 8 groups); formal coalitions contain twenty-nine members, on average (median = 8 groups). These statistics are in plain contrast to those presented in chapter 4. Across formal and informal collaborations, social and economic justice organizations build much larger coalitions, averaging a membership of seventy-eight (median = 27 groups). Finally, the average financial backing of coalitions observed in the mainstream subset of the data—calculated by summing the total revenue of all coalition members in the year of comment submission for each collaborative advocacy effort—is approximately $221,000,000 (median = $109,000,000). In contrast, the average financial backing of mainstream organizations lobbying alone—calculated using the total revenue of all sample members in years of comment submission for each solo advocacy effort—is approximately $105,000,000 (median = $90,800,000). As the reader may recall, these numbers are significantly larger than those of their social and economic justice–oriented counterparts (see chapter 4).

TABLE 6.4. Coalition building by organizational type (mainstream sample)

Organizational type	Coalitional advocacy (%)
Business or business group	33
Citizen group	56
Governmental association	44
Professional association	40
Union	51

Note: These proportions represent rates of coalitional advocacy within organizational type categories. They were calculated as follows: number of public comments submitted in coalitions by members of the sample in each organizational type divided by the total number of all public comments submitted by members of the sample in each organizational type.

Moreover, across different categories of organizations, mainstream interest groups often rely on coalition work. Table 6.4 illustrates rates of coalition building by mainstream advocates, grouped by organizational type. Across organizational types, most interest groups in the sample build coalitions in nearly half—or more—of their lobbying campaigns. Citizen groups build coalitions at the highest rate, in 56 percent of their advocacy efforts. Unions and governmental associations follow closely, turning to lobbying coalitions in 51 and 44 percent of their campaigns, respectively. Professional associations and business groups build coalitions at the lowest rates, in 40 and 33 percent of cases, respectively. These statistics demonstrate that the trends of coalition work described in the previous paragraph hold true across many different categories of mainstream advocates and parallel the analysis of social and economic justice organizations. Further, they lend support to prevailing research by reiterating that coalition work is a widely prevalent lobbying strategy among mainstream interest groups (Baumgartner and Leech 1998; Baumgartner et al. 2009a; Hojnacki 1997, 1998; Hula 1999; Junk 2019; Lorenz 2019).

These patterns remain consistent even upon evaluating trends in coalition building through a different lens: groups' policy specializations. All thirteen policy specializations present among members of the sample (see table 6.2 for a breakdown of these foci) are subject to coalition work.[13] All but five policy foci are characterized by a high rate of coalition building, ranging from approximately 30 to 60 percent. Interest groups lobbying in the areas of agribusiness, health, and energy/natural resources policy built coalitions at slightly lower rates—13, 20, and 19 percent, respectively, of their advocacy efforts. Groups advocating on issues of defense and labor policy relied more heavily on coalition work, building organizational partnerships in 91 and 90 percent, respectively, of their lobbying campaigns.

Finally, mainstream interest groups with varying financial capacities often rely on collaborative strategy. Table 6.5 depicts rates of coalition building in the mainstream subset of the *Collaborative Advocacy Dataset* by sample groups' total revenue in the year of comment submission. As with the analysis of the subset of social and economic justice organizations (see table 4.3 in chapter 4), for purposes of simplicity, the total revenue data are presented in quartiles, where Quartile 1 corresponds to the lowest level of financial capacity among members of the sample and Quartile 4 corresponds to the highest level. As the table makes clear, mainstream interest groups falling into each quartile *do* build coalitions at a nontrivial rate. However, unlike their social and economic justice–oriented counterparts, mainstream advocates' rates of coalition work appear to decrease a great deal in relation to their financial capacities. Table 6.5, for instance, demonstrates a steadily decreasing rate of collaboration; while organizations with total revenues falling into the first quartile build coalitions in nearly half of their advocacy efforts (46 percent), groups falling into the fourth quartile build coalitions at the lowest rate, in less than a quarter of cases (15 percent).

This finding is fascinating. It may lend support to the theoretical notion that slightly different mechanisms motivate the coalition work of the two samples of organizations examined in this study. For mainstream interest groups, reliance on coalition work decreases substantially for the wealthiest interests, suggesting that moneyed advocates may not view the benefits of coalition work favorably enough to incur the costs. In contrast, for social and economic justice–oriented organizations, rates of coalition work are high and

TABLE 6.5. Coalition building by group total revenue (mainstream sample)

Total revenue	Coalitional advocacy (%)
Quartile 1	46
Quartile 2	38
Quartile 3	36
Quartile 4	15

Note: These proportions represent rates of coalitional advocacy within revenue quartiles. They were calculated as follows: number of public comments submitted in coalitions by members of the sample in each total revenue quartile divided by the total number of all public comments submitted by members of the sample in each total revenue quartile.

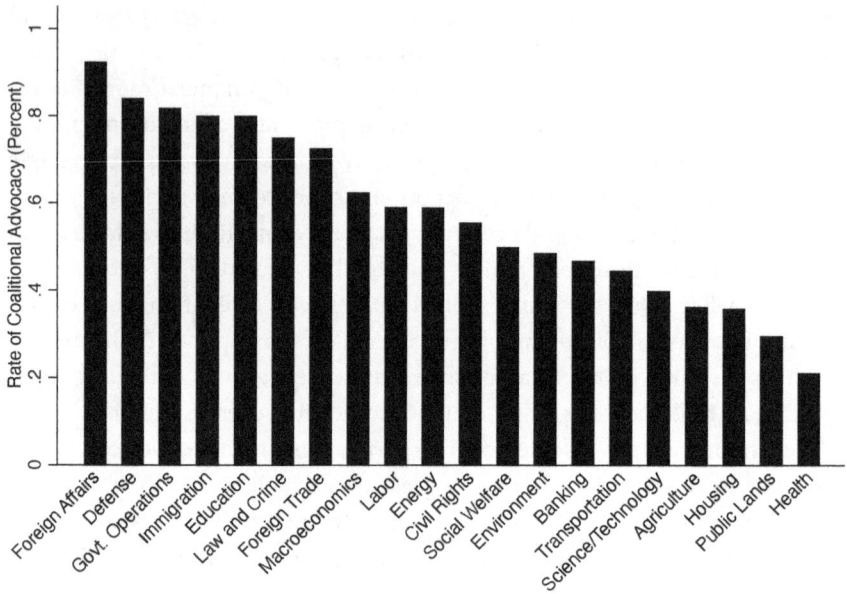

FIGURE 6.2. Coalitional advocacy by proposed rule policy topic (Mainstream sample)

constant across categories of financial capacity (see table 4.3 for a comparison), suggesting that these advocates, regardless of financial backing, believe that they must coalesce in order to effectively counter the capacities of their opposition—which vastly out-resource even their most moneyed allies (see figure 2.2 in chapter 2).

Coalitional lobbying by mainstream interest groups also occurs on nearly every major topic on the national policy agenda. Figure 6.2, which depicts rates of coalitional lobbying by the mainstream sample by policy topic of the targeted proposed rule, illustrates this pattern. Most major policy topics appearing in the data—fourteen out of twenty—are subject to a high rate of coalition building, between 40 and 80 percent. Four topics—agriculture, housing, public lands, and health policy—receive comparatively lower rates of collaborative lobbying, between approximately 20 and 40 percent. Foreign affairs and defense policy are characterized by the highest rate of coalition work; over 80 percent of lobbying efforts on these policy issues occur in coalitions. These trends broadly mirror those of the sample of social and economic justice organizations, in which advocates build coalitions consistently and at high rates across topics on the national policy agenda—in fifteen out of twenty policy topics appearing in the data analyzed in earlier chapters, more than 40 percent of all advocacy efforts occurred in coalitions (see figure 4.1 for a comparison). However, upon closer examination, the policy trends of coalition work by mainstream groups differ systematically, once again, from those of their social and economic justice–oriented counterparts. For instance, several of the policy topics on the receiving end of the lowest level of collaborative advocacy by the mainstream sample—such as housing and health policy—are subject to high rates of coalition work by the sample of social and economic justice organizations. Similarly, several of the policy topics that receive little advocacy by social and economic justice organizations—including foreign affairs and defense policy—are on the receiving end of significant collaborative advocacy by mainstream groups. The takeaway here is simple: that while these sets of advocates build coalitions often and across most policy issues, they are motivated by distinct substantive interests. Policy-level trends in their collaborative advocacy reflect core differences in the interests of the communities that they seek to represent.

Finally, according to the *Collaborative Advocacy Dataset*, 54 percent of all coalitional efforts by mainstream interest groups contain some level of representational diversity. In contrast, only 25 percent of coalitions built by mainstream interest groups unite strange bedfellows—defined, in this chapter, as the unification of mainstream interests (general interest, private, and professional groups) with advocates for social and economic justice (those groups that advocate on issues relating to women, people of color, LGBTQ+ individuals, immigrants, and low-income communities—see table 3.4 for the corresponding coding scheme). Only 6 percent of coalitions with representational diversity also unite strange bedfellows.[14] These rates of diverse coalition work roughly approximate those of their social and economic justice–oriented counterparts, which build representationally diverse and strange bedfellow (uniting with business/industry advocates) partnerships in 58 and 18 percent of their coalitions, respectively.

Table 6.6 depicts mainstream interest groups' rates of building diverse coalitions, grouped by organizational type. All five organizational types build coalitions with some degree of representational diversity, albeit at varying rates. Citizen groups and professional associations build representationally diverse coalitions at the highest rates—in over 50 percent of their coalitional efforts—while unions and business groups do so more sparingly, in 25 and 22 percent of their collaborations, respectively. Like their social and economic justice–oriented counterparts, mainstream interest groups rarely join in coalition with strange bedfellows. Across cases of coalition work by governmental associations and unions, none united with advocates for social/economic justice. Similarly, a small fraction of coalitions built by business and industry groups (11 percent) and professional and occupational groups (8 percent)

TABLE 6.6. Coalition composition by organizational type (mainstream sample)

Organizational type	Representational diversity (%)	Strange bedfellows (%)
Business or business groups	22	11
Citizen group	62	35
Governmental association	33	0
Professional association	56	8
Union	25	0

Note: These proportions represent rates of building representationally diverse and strange bedfellow coalitions, respectively, within organizational type categories. They were calculated as follows: number of diverse/strange bedfellow coalitions formed by members of the sample in each organizational type divided by the total number of all coalitions formed by members of the sample in each organizational type.

united with extremely dissimilar partners. Citizen groups joined coalitions containing strange bedfellows at the highest rate—35 percent—closely mirroring the rate of building such coalitions by citizen groups falling into the social and economic justice–oriented sample of the *Collaborative Advocacy Dataset* (39 percent). Finally, these trends hold true upon examining diverse coalition work through the lens of organizations' policy foci. Across all thirteen policy specializations present among the sample, representationally diverse coalitions are common, composing approximately 30 to 60 percent of collaborative advocacy efforts in each policy specialty. However, across all policy specializations, coalitions that unite strange bedfellows are sparse (occurring in only 3 to 10 percent of partnerships, on average, in each policy focus).

Altogether, these statistics tell an intuitive story. Mainstream interest groups often build coalitions, albeit at lower rates and in slightly different forms than social and economic justice organizations. While mainstream interest groups build coalitions at a high rate (in 42 percent of their lobbying efforts), advocates for social and economic justice collaborate at a rate that is nearly *15 percentage points* higher. Both mainstream and social and economic justice interest groups rely on formal coalition work to similar degrees—in 52 and 51 percent of their collaborative efforts, respectively. Moreover, they build coalitions with diverse memberships at near identical rates, though advocates for social and economic justice join representationally diverse/strange bedfellow coalitions slightly more frequently than mainstream groups. Mainstream interest groups build coalitions that are far smaller than those of their social and economic justice–oriented counterparts; across formal and informal coalitions, their partnerships contain approximately 40 percent fewer members. Both sets of advocates build coalitions at fairly constant rates across different organizational categories, policy specializations, and topics of national policymaking. Financial capacities, however, pose the most striking differ-

ence between these two groups' coalitional behaviors; while coalition building is high and constant across social and economic justice organizations
with varying annual revenues (between 51 and 57 percent of advocacy efforts
across revenue quartiles), mainstream interest groups' reliance on coalition
work appears to drastically decline among the wealthiest groups (dropping
from 46 to 15 percent across revenue quartiles).

Alone, these comparisons offer a significant contribution to existing
scholarship and organizations' strategic capacities. They demonstrate a series
of dynamics previously assumed to be true—but without comprehensive empirical backing—by many scholars and organizers. First, advocacy organizations representing historically marginalized communities rely to a greater degree on coalition work than other, more mainstream interest groups. Second,
while reliance on coalition work by social and economic justice organizations
does not vary across advocates with lesser or greater resources, mainstream
groups with the greatest resources *do* appear to build coalitions more sparingly, suggesting that partnership is a strategic tool designed to boost the
capacities of less resourced groups. Finally, strange bedfellow partnerships
are extremely uncommon—both mainstream interest groups and advocates
for social justice rarely collaborate with extremely dissimilar partners—
occurring in less a quarter of both samples' coalitional efforts. Together, these
findings also offer important context leading into the next section of this
chapter, in which I evaluate the efficacy of coalition work, comparatively, for
these two samples of organizations.

Assessing the Efficacy of Coalition Work

I test the foundational empirical arguments of this chapter—that mainstream
interest groups bear greater influence over public policy when they advocate
in coalitions and in coalitions with diverse memberships—using the second
subset of the *Collaborative Advocacy Dataset*. I do so by once again estimating
a series of generalized linear models (GLM) but largely focus on the results
of Models 5 and 7—models that replicate the primary analyses of chapters 4
and 5. Where appropriate, I refer to the appendixes of this book for models
and tests that evaluate alternative explanations. Like the primary model of
chapter 4 (Model 1)—which evaluates the coalition formation hypothesis—
the dependent variable of Model 5 is the influence of advocacy by mainstream
interest groups (textual similarity between comment–final rule pairs). The
primary predictor variables in Model 5 are binary variables indicating the formation of a coalition and the formation of a formalized coalition. The model
controls for coalition size, financial capacity, characteristics of the targeted

public policy (complexity, salience), and characteristics of the underlying public comment (textual similarity between the public comment and the original proposed rule, public comment length).[15] As with previous models, I account for potential correlations within subpopulations of the data (organizations in the original sample) by clustering the standard errors by group. These relationships (Model 5) can be formally expressed by equation 1 (see chapter 4).

Like the corresponding model in chapter 5 (Model 3), the dependent variable of Model 7—which evaluates the coalition membership hypotheses—is the advocacy influence of mainstream interest groups (once again, textual similarity between comment–final rule pairs). The primary predictor variables of this model are binary indicator variables reflecting the formation of a representationally diverse coalition and a coalition that unites mainstream advocates with advocates for social/economic justice (i.e., strange bedfellows).[16] As with the primary model of chapter 5, this model controls for the formation of a coalition, the formation of a formalized coalition, coalition size, financial capacity, characteristics of the targeted public policy (complexity, salience), and characteristics of the underlying public comment (textual similarity between the public comment and the original proposed rule, public comment length). The model, once again, accounts for potential correlations within subpopulations of the data (groups in the sample) by clustering the standard errors by group. These relationships (Model 7) can be formally expressed by equation 2 (see chapter 5).

Figure 6.3 visualizes the results of Model 5.[17] This model evaluates whether advocacy by mainstream interest groups is more influential when pursued through coalition work. Most prominently, the model results demonstrate a positive, albeit statistically insignificant, relationship between the formation of a coalition and mainstream interest groups' advocacy influence, and a positive and statistically insignificant relationship between the formation of a formalized coalition and mainstream groups' lobbying outcomes. In other words, building coalitions, both with and without formalized structures, does not relate to mainstream groups' advocacy influence. These findings do not lend support to the first component of the argument I have put forth in this chapter, nor do they lend support to existing theoretical expectations or the self-reported beliefs of interest groups themselves (Hojnacki 1997, 1998; Hula 1999). However, as I described in earlier chapters of this book (chapters 1, 2), existing research on the outcomes of coalitional lobbying among mainstream interest groups is fairly mixed. Some scholars report strong, positive relationships between coalition building and lobbying outcomes (see Baumgartner et al. 2009a; McKay and Yackee 2007; Nelson and Yackee 2012),

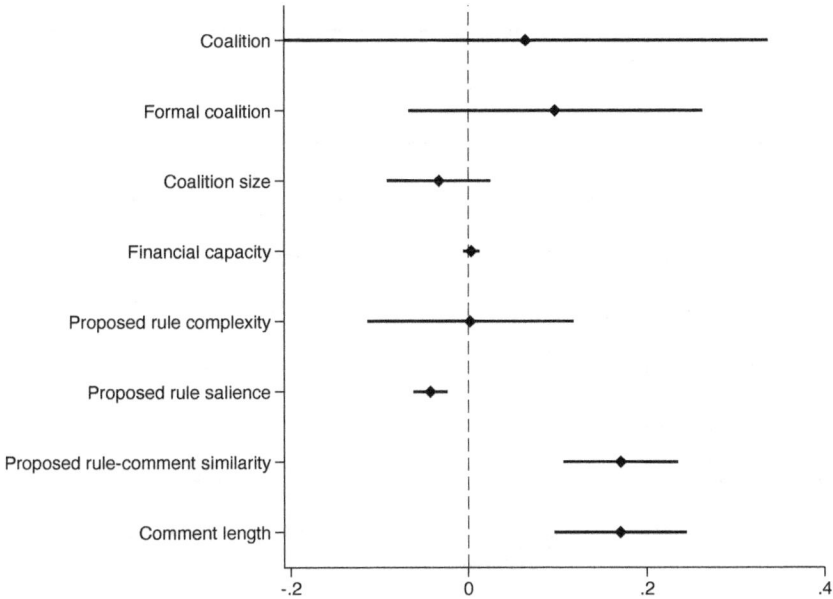

FIGURE 6.3. Coalition building and advocacy influence (Mainstream sample, Model 5). Generalized linear regression model (Gamma family, log link function) with group-clustered standard errors. $N = 739$. Diamonds indicate coefficient values. Lines indicate 95 percent confidence intervals.

while others report inverse or nonexistent relationships (see Gray and Low-ery 1998; Haider-Markel 2006; Heinz et al. 1993; Mahoney and Baumgartner 2004). Thus, a growing body of research—including my own, in this book—has sought to explore the nuance of coalition building by evaluating aspects of coalition composition (see Phinney 2017; Lorenz 2019), which I will return to in a few paragraphs. Finally, as with the analysis of chapter 4, I reestimated this model dropping all non-coalitional observations from the data and repli-cating it in all other respects (see Model 6 in appendix I).[18] The results of this reestimation reiterate the formal coalition relationship observed in Model 5; even within observations of coalitional lobbying, the formation of a coali-tion with a formalized structure does not significantly relate to mainstream groups' advocacy influence.

These findings are partly in contrast to those of chapter 4. While the for-mation of a coalition alone does not benefit either of the two samples I exam-ine in this book, these sets of advocates diverge on the impact of building *for-malized* coalitions. While both samples build formalized coalitions at similar rates—51 percent of social and economic justice organizations' coalitions are formal in nature, while 52 percent of mainstream groups' coalitions retain a formalized structure—formalized coalition work significantly increases the

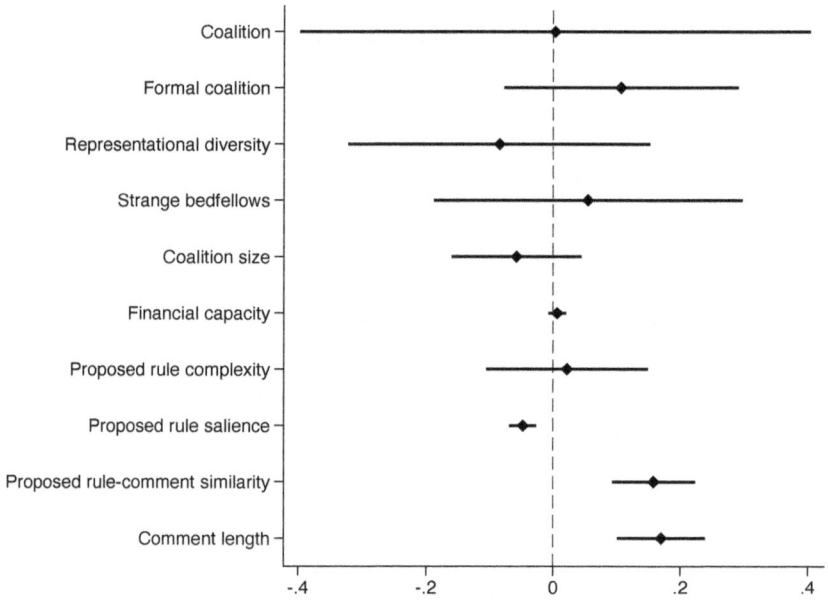

FIGURE 6.4. Coalition composition and advocacy influence (Mainstream sample, Model 7). Generalized linear regression model (Gamma family, log link function) with group-clustered standard errors. $N = 605$. Diamonds indicate coefficient values. Lines indicate 95 percent confidence intervals.

influence of advocates for social and economic justice but not mainstream interest groups. This finding may reflect the differences and realities of these advocates. As I described in chapter 4, the processes and structures inherent to formal coalition work likely enable social and economic justice organizations to surpass the many obstacles to effective advocacy they face—from limited individual capacities to the ability to collectively learn and adapt in a lobbying environment that systematically disadvantages them—a suggestion echoed in my interviews with organizational and coalition leaders. These hurdles are far more expansive than those faced by their mainstream counterparts, as demonstrated by the comparisons in chapter 2. These findings thus reinforce the prevailing point I have sought to make in this chapter: that social and economic justice organizations have more to gain from collaborative advocacy than mainstream interest groups.

Figure 6.4 illustrates the results of Model 7.[19] This model evaluates whether advocacy by mainstream interest groups is more influential when pursued by coalitions with diverse memberships. It illustrates a series of findings: first, there is a positive but statistically insignificant relationship between the formation of a coalition and a formalized coalition, respectively, and mainstream groups' advocacy influence. These findings are consistent with the results of Model 5. Moreover, the primary predictor variables—the formation of a representationally diverse coalition and the formation of a coalition uniting strange bedfellows—share statistically insignificant relationships with the dependent variable. Put differently, these outcomes suggest that mainstream interest groups do not experience significantly greater influence by advocating in coalitions containing membership diversity of either kind. This finding presents a stark contrast to the conclusions of chapter 5—which demonstrate that building coalitions with representational diversity significantly increases the influence of organizational advocates for social and economic justice. The results of Model 7 remain consistent even upon restricting the analyses to observations of coalitions and coalitions with formalized structures (see Models 8 and 9 in appendix I).[20] Finally, several of the models' remaining findings—along with those of Models 3 and 4 in chapter 5—lend support to existing scholarly research. Models 5, 6, and 7, for instance, reflect negative and statistically significant relationships between policy salience and advocacy influence. As I suggested in chapter 3, and as Baumgartner et al. (2009a) report in their foundational work, advocacy influence is heightened when operating in policy contexts with a narrower scope (lower salience). Thus, these reflections of prevailing scholarly consensus should lend confidence to the veracity of these models.

What should you make of these findings? First, these analyses consistently point to the existence of a conditional effect of coalition work and coalition diversity in interest group advocacy. Over the course of more than a dozen models and robustness checks, the analyses of this and earlier chapters demonstrate that coalition building and diversity in coalition membership benefit certain organizations in American lobbying: those representing the most vulnerable communities in American society. Together with the work of chapters 4 and 5, these analyses may help explain decades of conflicting findings on the efficacy of collaborative lobbying in American politics. Upon separating the interest group population along lines of advantage, the results tell a clear story. Coalition work benefits those advocates without the hallmark toolboxes of influential lobbying: ready access to formal and informal policy-making spaces, political connections, endless resources, and the advantage of advocating on the side of dominant groups and the status quo. Advocates *with* these toolboxes—private, professional, and general interest groups—do not experience enhanced policy success though collaborative advocacy in its many variations. Further, while strange bedfellow coalitions might get a great deal of attention, they are not exceptionally influential. For both social and economic justice organizations and mainstream interest groups, building coalitions that cross the proverbial aisle does not move the needle. Rather, for social and economic justice groups, building partnerships that represent a plurality of constituent interests *does*. And policy conditions matter: across the board, when less attention is paid to their advocacy targets, both sets of advocates are significantly more influential.

Alternative Explanations

Now, just as the reader may have wondered at the conclusion of chapter 5, a few questions remain. What about the overall degree of diversity in coalitions? Is the analysis of this subset of the data, unlike the previous one, sensitive to the fifty-member coding cut-off? Similarly, what about the inclusion of the agency response in the text of final rules? Could this language, unlike that of the previous chapters (which evaluate separate text corpora), be contributing to an overestimation of the observed effect? Does the perfect replication of the models in chapters 4 and 5 fully capture the uniqueness of mainstream interest groups—and the ways in which they differ from social and economic justice organizations? Before concluding this chapter, I evaluate these, along with other, alternative explanations.

First, as I discussed at the conclusion of chapter 5, one of the two foundational measures of diversity deployed in my analyses of coalition composition is a binary variable transformed from a discrete measure: the non-zero presence of representational diversity in coalitions. In concluding chapter 5, I demonstrated that the inclusion of a measure capturing the full range of representational diversity in coalitions of social and economic justice organizations bears no weight on the primary outcomes of the chapter's models and, in fact, that this diversity index shares no relationship with the dependent variable. In doing so, I introduced evidence of a potential threshold effect of representational diversity in coalitions—wherein the entry of diversity to a coalition has a significantly greater impact on advocacy outcomes than that of a greater degree of diversity. However, perhaps for the subset of the data under study in this chapter, unlike the previous one, a greater degree of diversity is a pivotal factor for advocacy influence.

While the choice to operationalize representational diversity using a binary measure in this chapter, as with the previous one, was theoretically motivated (see chapters 3 and 5), to ameliorate any lingering concerns, I reestimated Models 7, 8, and 9. These reestimations evaluated the efficacy of a representationally diverse coalition membership by incorporating a measure capturing the overall degree of representational diversity (normalized Shannon's H index, ranging from 0 to 1) along with the original binary predictor variable.[21] These models' findings reiterate those presented in the previous

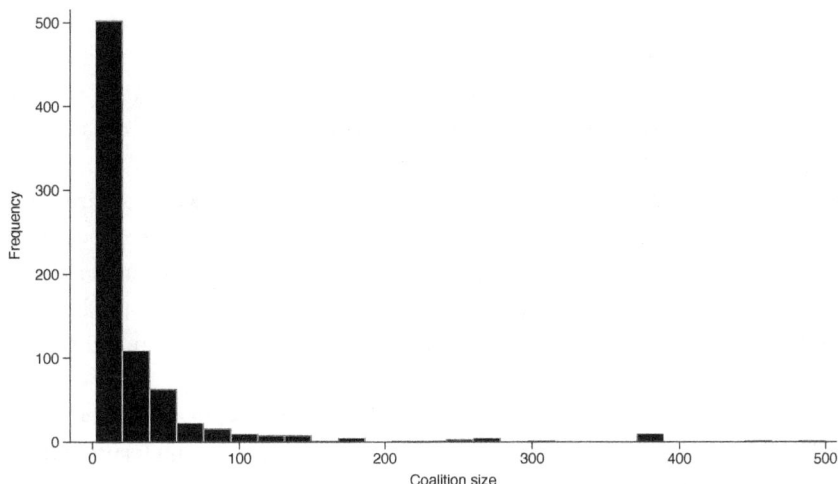

FIGURE 6.5. Distribution of coalition size (Mainstream sample)

section of this chapter—across all three reestimations, neither the original binary indicator variable nor the diversity index share significant relationships with the dependent variable. Meanwhile, the remaining variables maintain relationships similar in direction and significance to those presented earlier in this chapter. These observations should thus lend confidence to my original measurement strategy and to the results of Models 7, 8, and 9.

Second, for the subset of data under study in this chapter, as with that of chapter 5, I did not code data on the memberships of coalitions containing more than fifty member organizations. As I detailed in chapters 3 and 5, this choice was practically and theoretically motivated, designed both to account for feasibility concerns (collecting and coding membership data for all coalitions of fewer than fifty-one members in both subsets of the *Collaborative Advocacy Dataset* required the employment of eighteen research assistants working over a period of seven years to complete) and for the appearance of superficial coalitions, which often include hundreds of members and rarely, if ever, pursue substantive policy advocacy (Box-Steffensmeier et al. 2018; Dwidar 2022a; Hula 1999). However, it is still worth further evaluating this choice.

As with the social and economic justice–oriented subset of the *Collaborative Advocacy Dataset*, very few coalitions in this subset of the data are excluded by way of this measurement choice. As demonstrated by figure 6.5—which depicts the distribution of the variable *coalition size* in this subset of the data—coalition size sharply drops off at approximately the fifty-member mark; the vast majority of coalitions in the data (approximately 82 percent) contain fifty or fewer members. This pattern is consistent across both ad hoc and formal coalitions;

82 percent of ad hoc coalitions and 81 percent of formal coalitions contain fifty or fewer members. However, as I wrote in chapter 5, any cut-off is arbitrary to some degree. Thus, to ameliorate concerns that the results of the previous section are sensitive to this cut-off choice, I reestimated the models evaluating coalition composition—Models 7, 8, and 9—varying the membership cut-off at coalitions containing 45 or fewer, 40 or fewer, and 35 or fewer organizations. The results of these models—available in appendix K (Model 7), appendix L (Model 8), and appendix M (Model 9)—maintain support of this chapter's findings. These reestimations thus demonstrate that the results presented earlier in this chapter are not sensitive to the fifty-member coding cut-off and should lend confidence to my original approach.

Third, as I discussed in chapter 5, all federal agencies are required to publish their responses to "significant" public comments in each final rule (Potter 2019; West 2004). These responses typically offer a brief summary of the key points of the comments and describe the agency's reasoning for including or disregarding their recommendations. As I noted in chapter 5, the inclusion of this language poses a potential measurement concern, as it may lead to an overestimation of the dependent variable. To evaluate this possibility, I replicated the robustness check introduced in chapter 5: I manually removed the agency response from most final rules appearing in the corpus under study in this chapter (58 percent) and reproduced a constrained version of the dependent variable. In the remaining rules, the agency response was interwoven within the final regulatory language (distributed across hundreds—and in some cases thousands—of pages without obvious in-text identifiers), making it impossible to identify and remove each component of the response by hand or using automated tools. However, within the corpus of rules from which I was able to manually remove the agency response, the correlation between the original and constrained dependent variable was 0.98, suggesting that the results presented in the manuscript are not driven by the inclusion of the agency response. It is, of course, possible that the rules from which I was not able to remove the agency response differ systematically from those in which I was able to investigate this possibility directly. However, as with my analysis in chapter 5, I did not detect any significant differences. Both sets of rules are similar in complexity, salience, and length.

Finally, this chapter sought to identically replicate the analyses of chapters 4 and 5 for the purpose of producing comparisons between the two samples under study in this book—a goal that required consistent modeling approaches between the chapters. However, the models of chapters 4 and 5 were specified with advocates for social and economic justice in mind. Scholars seeking to understand the relationship between mainstream interest groups' coalition work and lobbying influence would likely control for additional coalition-level characteristics. Thus, to account for these concerns and the possibility of omitted variable bias, I reestimated the relevant models of this chapter (Models 7, 8, and 9) to include an additional covariate: the proportion of business interests present in a coalition, accounting for research suggesting the outsized influence of business interests in mainstream lobbying (Baumgartner and Leech 1998, 2001; Drutman 2015; Lowery et al. 2015; Nixon et al. 2002).[22] These results of these estimations (available in appendix N) maintain the primary findings reported in the previous section. Additionally, all three models also report a positive and statistically significant relationship between the proportion of business interests present in a coalition and mainstream groups' advocacy influence. In other words, as the degree of business interests in a coalition increases, so too does the influence of mainstream interest groups. This finding is consistent with research that theorizes a connection between business advocates and national policymaking, wherein these advocates—relative to other interest groups in the mainstream lobbying population—experience exceptional influence, particularly in the regulatory context (Carpenter et al. 2022; Drutman 2015; Hojnacki et al. 2015; Lindblom 1977; Lowi 1964; McConnell 1966; McFarland 1987; Nixon, Howard, and DeWitt 2002; Schattschneider 1960; Smith 2000). Thus, this result should also lend confidence to the robust nature of these models.

Summary

Coalitions are fundamental to interest group politics. For decades, scholars and organizational leaders alike have touted the importance of alliances in lobbying. But for just as long, researchers have reported mixed and conflicting findings on the value of building coalitions in American organizational politics (see Baumgartner et al. 2009a; Gray and Lowery 1998; Haider-Markel 2006; Heinz et al. 1993; Mahoney and Baumgartner 2004; Lorenz 2019; McKay and Yackee 2007; Nelson and Yackee 2012; Phinney 2017). Using a variety of study designs, this existing research has largely sought to make claims about the impact of coalitional advocacy across the full range of the interest group population. However, as the analyses of this chapter demonstrate, this choice may have obscured a foundational characteristic of coalition work: that the impact of coalitional lobbying appears conditional, benefiting only certain subsets of nationally active organizations. While all kinds of interest groups regularly build coalitions, private, professional, and general interest advocates do not experience enhanced policy success through coalition work of any form. In contrast, social and economic justice organizations benefit a great deal from coalition work with structures and characteristics that allow them to increase their collective advocacy capacities. In other words, despite their popularity across types of advocates, coalitions appear to be "weapons of the weak" (Mahoney and Baumgartner 2004, 2).

In the next chapter, I switch gears. So far, I have sought to understand whether coalition work increases the ability of social and economic justice organizations to bear influence over public policy. But coalition work has implications that go beyond policy change. Advocates for social and economic justice are not immune from many of the common critiques of interest group politics. Just like their mainstream counterparts, these organizations' representational choices can reinforce or mediate the oppressions faced by their constituencies. For instance, because of intra- and extra-organizational limitations, many social and economic justice–oriented groups often choose to advocate on behalf of their most privileged constituencies. A women's organization, for example, is most likely to take up the interests of their white women constituents at the expense of those of women of color (Kitchener 2020; Strolovitch 2006, 2007). These agenda-setting choices have significant implications, sidelining the needs of these groups' most vulnerable constituencies: those with intersectional disadvantage. In chapter 7, I make the case that coalition work is an important moderator for the occurrence and outcomes of intersectional advocacy—advocacy on behalf of multiply disadvantaged subgroups of already marginalized groups.

7

Collaboration and Intersectional Representation

In late July 2020, on the heels of a nationwide racial reckoning, three of the oldest women's organizations in the United States came under fire. The call had come from inside the house: twenty former staffers of the National Organization for Women (NOW), the Feminist Majority Foundation (FMF), and the American Association of University Women (AAUW) went on the record with the *Washington Post* to describe systemic biases in their former employers' agenda-setting choices. These staffers, mainly young women of color, all expressed variations of the same sentiment: that while these storied organizations "see themselves as feminist pioneers, fighting for the equality of all women, . . . [i]n practice, they really only fight for white women." At the AAUW, for instance, former staffers recalled that they would often propose policy initiatives that centered the experiences and needs of women of color, but organizational leaders "always chose to focus its major initiatives on issues most relevant to white women" (Kitchener 2020). At NOW, staffers said, "they don't want to truly engage with young women of color [. . .] they want complacent young women of color bodies in the room because it is trendy to be inclusive" (Shugerman 2020). Across all three organizations, staffers described feeling "baffled by the amount of time and money their organizations still devote to legislation that feels 'obsolete' and irrelevant to [. . .] women who are not white, straight, cisgender, highly educated and upper-middle class" (Kitchener 2020). Raina Nelson, who worked for the AAUW from 2017 to 2019, said of these dynamics, "my understanding was that the folks that were funding us were [. . .] more interested in more quote-unquote 'neutral' topics" (Kitchener 2020).

These staffers' allegations touch on an important facet of the work of social and economic justice organizations which I have yet to discuss in this book, along with a growing body of research on a phenomenon called "intersectional advocacy." This phenomenon, as its name suggests, derives from theories of intersectionality that were introduced by Black feminists in the mid-nineteenth century (see Truth 1851; Combahee River Collective 1977) and officially coined by Kimberlé Crenshaw in the last decade of the twentieth century. As I described in chapter 2, these theories were born out of the frustrations felt by women of color with first- and second-wave feminist movements that prioritized the experiences, positions, and needs of white women—while framing them as those of "all women"—along with a civil rights movement that centered the experiences and positions of Black men (Collins 1990; Crenshaw 1989; Davis 1981; hooks 1981). The intersectional framework is simple. It describes something we all know, implicitly, to be true: that different social categorizations—such as gender, race, class, and sexuality—intersect to create compounding systems of discrimination and disadvantage. Women of color, for instance, are marginalized on the basis of their race and gender; together, these two categories manifest in simultaneous, interlocking oppressions. Intersectionality is inescapable, structuring every facet of an individual's life experiences.

Intersectional *advocacy*, then, refers to the choice by advocacy organizations to promote the interests of their constituents who experience intersectional disadvantage—those who fall into multiply disadvantaged subgroups of broader marginalized groups, such as disabled women, children living in poverty, or transgender people of color (Strolovitch 2006, 2007). Unsurprisingly, the choices that these organizations make regarding which issues and interests to promote can either reinforce or work to mediate the oppressions faced by their intersectionally marginalized constituencies (English 2019, 2020; Marchetti 2014). Most of the time, these organizations make the tactical choice to reinforce these oppressions—though not necessarily out of ill will. As I described in earlier chapters, despite the importance of their work (recall that they often provide the sole source of political representation for their constituent communities), social and economic justice organizations are vastly outpaced by other, more mainstream advocates in the interest group population, such as the private, professional, and general interest groups I discussed in chapter 6. Meanwhile, they operate in crowded political environments, often competing with many other interests to gain access to a limited national policy agenda. So, like many other political actors, they "satisfice"— they do the best they can with what they have. They prioritize their interests and, in doing so, their constituencies.

The outcome of these intersecting dynamics is precisely the trend described by the former staffers of the AAUW, FMF, and NOW. Despite claims that intersectional advocacy is central to their goals, social and economic justice organizations largely neglect the needs of their most vulnerable constituents—those with intersectional disadvantage. They label intersectional advocacy as "narrow" and "controversial" (Staggenborg 1986; Strolovitch 2007). They devote the vast majority of their time and resources to more expedient and "winnable" policy work—which, as it turns out, often reflects the interests of their most advantaged constituents (see English 2019, 2020; Marchetti 2014, 2019)—just as the former staffers of the AAUW, FMF, and NOW alleged.

This chapter is dedicated to unpacking this dynamic. In the coming pages, I describe trends in social and economic justice organizations' treatment of intersectional advocacy and evaluate the structural conditions that might rectify bias against this sort of work. I argue that coalition building offers a strategic solution to the challenges of intersectional advocacy. I reiterate the importance of intersectional work to the missions of many social and economic justice organizations and make the case that coalition work offers "cover" for these advocates to engage with intersectional policy issues. I link this argument to the dynamics that compel social and economic justice–oriented groups to sideline their intersectionally marginalized constituencies: scarce resources and disapproval by patrons and members on whom these organizations are heavily dependent to survive. Together with the analyses of chapters 4 and 5, I seek to demonstrate that coalition building not only benefits the advocacy influence of social and economic justice organizations but also enables them to promote more equitable, *intersectionally minded*, advocacy.

Connecting to Theory

Chapter 4 began with the question, When do historically marginalized communities receive political representation? In this chapter, I take this question one step further: When do *intersectionally marginalized* communities receive political representation? While scholars have historically devoted little attention to the representation of historically marginalized communities in national politics, even less attention has been paid to the representational experiences of multiply marginalized groups. Existing research has considered the impact of grassroots power building, social movements, and the work of elected officials (Brown et al. 2017; Gershon et al. 2019; Laperrière and Lépinard 2016; Purdie-Vaughns and Eibach 2008; Reingold, Widner, and Harmon 2019; Skrentny 2002), but a great deal more remains to be understood. A growing body of research has recently highlighted the importance of advocacy organizations to understanding trends and biases in intersectional representation (Brower 2024; English 2019, 2020; Marchetti 2014, 2019; Strolovitch 2006, 2007). A consistent theme emerges from this research: that coalition work might offer strategic incentives for the pursuit of intersectional advocacy (Strolovitch 2007).

As I described in chapters 1 and 2, and as the case of the women's organizations at the outset of this chapter demonstrated, social and economic justice organizations face significant disadvantages in American lobbying. They have fewer members, smaller budgets, and more limited issue agendas than many of their competitors (Schlozman, Verba, and Brady 2012; Strolovitch 2007). They are often funded by government grant programs, charitable foundations, and membership dues, leaving them vulnerable to the preferences of political actors, patrons, and active members—many of whom are both influential in shaping these groups' advocacy agendas and often represent the identities and priorities of the groups' most advantaged constituents (Imig 1996). For instance, at both the AAUW and NOW, most members are white women. Kimberly Churches, former executive director of the AAUW, described that such a homogenous membership posed challenges to inclusive policy agenda setting at the organization: "[AAUW] has historically had a predominantly white membership [. . .] and faces challenges when it comes to diversity and inclusion" (Kitchener 2020). The author of the *Washington Post* article I discussed at the start of this chapter describes,

> NOW and AAUW are built around a membership model, with approximately 500,000 and 60,000 members, respectively, scattered in state and local chapters across the country. At both NOW and AAUW, the membership helps determine the organization's mission and focus, voting on certain policy and leadership decisions. While neither organization conducts demographic surveys of their membership today, eight former staffers at NOW and four at AAUW say the vast majority are white. In 1974, when NOW conducted its last known demographic membership survey, white women made up 90 percent of NOW's membership. (Kitchener 2020)

Together, these structural limitations—limited resources, constrained agenda space, and dependence on members and patrons who reflect more advantaged subgroups of their constituents—have direct implications for the intersectional advocacy strategies of social and economic justice organizations. For instance, existing research has demonstrated that these advocates systematically prioritize broad-reaching issues at the expense of intersectional issues in their lobbying and overrepresent class-based issues while underrepresenting gender-based issues relative to the proportions of poor and female members of their constituencies (English 2019a, 2020; Marchetti 2014; Strolovitch 2006, 2007). In other words, these organizations most often represent the interests of their most advantaged constituents at the expense of constituents with intersectional disadvantage. For instance, an LGBTQ+ organization is more likely to advocate on behalf of the interests of economically advantaged members of the LGBTQ+ community than those of lower-income members of the community. As a result, intersectional advocacy typically composes a small minority of social and economic justice groups' policy agendas. The Human Rights Campaign (HRC), for example, promoted intersectional policy recommendations in less than one third of the public comments they submitted during the period under study in this book.

Scholars have thus theorized that intersectional advocacy is governed by organizational priorities and political environments, wherein social and economic justice organizations—strapped for resources and thirsty for political wins—prioritize broad-ranging, palatable issues (English 2019a, 2020; Marchetti 2014, 2019). However, these trends do not mean that these advocates cannot or do not want to address intersectional issues among their constituencies, only that it is unlikely for this advocacy to make up a large proportion of their work (Marchetti 2014; Strolovitch 2007). Many of these organizations, in fact, report interests in intersectional policy work and dedicate considerable effort to remedying inequalities in their advocacy agendas (Strolovitch 2007).[1]

The argument I make in this chapter is premised on several notions developed by this burgeoning scholarship. First, as I hope I have convinced the reader by now, coalitions provide significant benefits to advocacy organizations that represent historically marginalized communities. These groups have limited institutional resources relative to their mainstream counterparts. For instance, as I described in chapter 1, social and economic justice organizations are significantly less likely than mainstream advocates to retain a legal staff, employ lobbyists, and maintain political action committees (PACs) (Strolovitch 2007). Moreover, they operate in competitive and costly lobbying contexts and are vastly outnumbered and out-resourced by their competitors (Baumgartner et al. 2009a; Hojnacki 1997; Strolovitch 2007; Walker 1991). Thus, they *compensate by collaborating*, and as I demonstrated in the analyses of chapters 4, 5, and 6, coalition work is a popular and uniquely effective strategy for these advocates.

But coalition work likely offers another distinct benefit to these organizations: a lower-profile opportunity to engage with "controversial"—intersectional— policy issues. As I described earlier in this section, social and economic justice organizations seldom pursue intersectional advocacy (Brower 2024; English 2019a, 2020; Marchetti 2014; Strolovitch 2006, 2007). Existing research

has suggested that together with their intra- and extra-organizational resource constraints, these advocates' unique dependence on their funders
and members facilitates this trend, just as the women's organizations' staffers
I described at the start of this chapter alleged (Imig 1996; Kitchener 2020).
These key actors play outsized roles in determining the direction and scope
of social and economic justice organizations' advocacy agendas (Imig 1996;
Staggenborg 1986). Because of the nature and requirement of the roles, they
typically reflect the identities and priorities of the groups' most advantaged
constituencies (see Strolovitch 2007) and often express ambivalence, disinter-
est, or disapproval toward intersectional advocacy (Imig 1996; Staggenborg
1986; Strolovitch 2007). This dynamic is not much different from that in electoral representation. Organizations, like elected officials, have strong incentives to respond to the interests of donors and constituents who contribute
time, money, and labor to their efforts (Dwidar, Marchetti, and Strolovitch,
forthcoming).

As an example, consider the National Organization for Women's (NOW's)
advocacy surrounding the Equal Rights Amendment (ERA). As is the case
with many women's organizations, the ERA has been central to NOW's policy
agenda since its introduction in 1923. The amendment seeks "legal equality of
the sexes"; however, it has been historically critiqued for its erasure of wom-
en's intersectional identities and needs (Kitchener 2020). So, in 2017, NOW
was asked to support a new version of the ERA, the "Intersectional ERA," an
alternative that was to be introduced to Congress by Congresswoman Pra-
mila Jayapal. To many, support for this alternative from NOW would seem
obvious. However, NOW's leaders, members, and patrons were extremely
hesitant to support the policy. In their view, its "narrower" focus and explicit
protection of a wide range of intersecting identities, including women of
color and women marginalized "on the basis of faith," posed a distraction
from the broader goals of their feminist advocacy (Kitchener 2020).

NOW's internal debates on the topic caused significant strife and were
later the subject of a series of exposés, one of which I cited at the outset of
this chapter (Kitchener 2020; Shugerman 2020). And while the Intersectional
ERA ultimately never entered the congressional agenda, NOW's treatment of
it since—particularly relative to that of the original ERA—has been telling.
For instance, a keyword search in public comment records suggests that since
its failure, NOW has since referenced the content of the Intersectional ERA
on only one occasion, as a part of a broader collaboration (the ERA Coalition) in 2020.[2] In contrast, in the same year, NOW submitted *twelve* comments as an individual organization referencing the content of the original
ERA—which, like the Intersectional ERA, has yet to reach fruition.

This example encapsulates my argument in this chapter, that coalition work can allow social and economic justice organizations to advocate on behalf of important but internally controversial issues without expending scarce resources *and* without drawing the ire of members and patrons. To put it simply, coalition work provides much-needed "cover" for intersectional advocacy. In the case of NOW, organizational leaders and patrons were hesitant to promote the Intersectional ERA because of conflict surrounding its scope but *did* ultimately do so—albeit fleetingly—through a collaborative effort. NOW's selective advocacy on the Intersectional ERA and its broader counterpart suggests that participating in the ERA Coalition offered the organization a strategic, lower-profile opportunity ("cover") for intersectional advocacy. In other words, the deliberate use of coalitions by these organizations signals to disapproving key actors that intersectional policy work is not occurring at the expense of broader organizational priorities (Strolovitch 2007). Thus, I argue that social and economic justice organizations are more likely to pursue intersectional advocacy through coalitions.

Patterns of Intersectional Advocacy

To evaluate this claim, I return, for the last time, to the *Collaborative Advocacy Dataset*. Existing scholarship suggests that while intersectional advocacy should appear on social and economic justice organizations' policy agendas, it should make up a minority of their work. The data support this consensus: according to the *Collaborative Advocacy Dataset*, 39 percent of social and economic justice organizations' regulatory advocacy is intersectional in nature. Rates of intersectional advocacy by these organizations have also grown exponentially over time. As figure 7.1 illustrates, advocates for social and economic justice have increasingly adopted intersectionally oriented items into their policy agendas. This trend is likely attributable to the growing salience of the concept and practice of intersectionality in both popular and organizing circles over the last decades (Coaston 2019).

Moreover, 73 percent of social and economic justice groups' intersectional advocacy efforts were pursued through coalition work. Eleven percent were pursued by organizations with exclusively intersectional missions (which compose a small minority of the sample—only 13 percent), such as Immigration Equality (founded in 1994), an advocate for LGBTQ and HIV-positive immigrants and the National American Indian Housing Council (NAIHC, founded in 1974), an advocate for low-income and chronically unhoused American Indians. Table 7.1 depicts the rate of intersectional advocacy among the members of the sample of social and economic justice organizations,

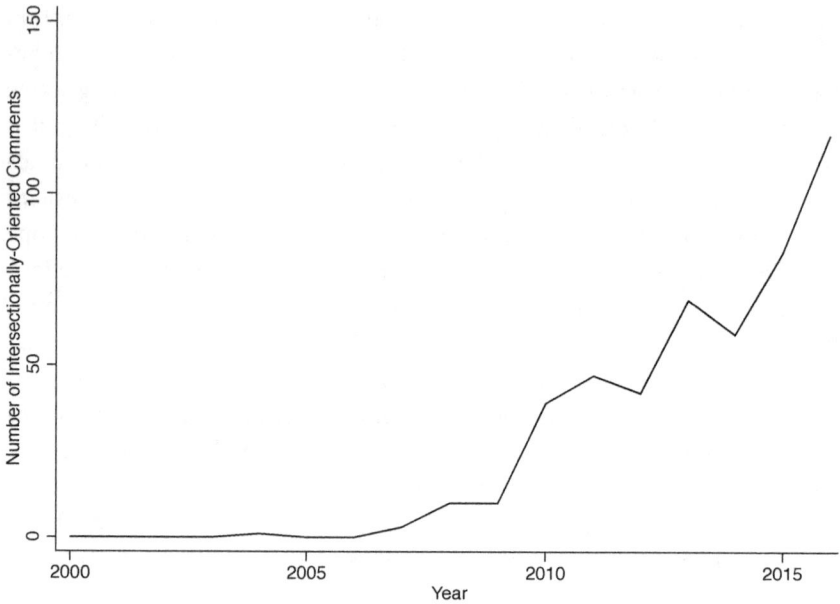

FIGURE 7.1. Intersectional advocacy over time (2000–2016)

TABLE 7.1. Intersectional advocacy by organizational type

Organizational type	Intersectional advocacy (%)
Charitable foundation/think tank	18
Citizen group	33
Native American tribe	20
Professional association	19

Note: These proportions represent rates of intersectional advocacy within organizational type categories. They were calculated as follows: number of intersectional advocacy efforts by members of the sample in each organizational type divided by the total number of all advocacy efforts (comments submitted) by members of the sample in each organizational type.

grouped by organizational type. As illustrated in the table, across organizational categories, intersectional advocacy takes up a small proportion of the policy agendas of advocates in the sample, ranging from roughly 20 to 30 percent. Citizen groups pursue intersectional advocacy at the highest rate—33 percent. Native American tribes follow closely, engaging in intersectional policy work in 20 percent of their advocacy efforts. Professional associations and charitable foundations/think tanks promote intersectional advocacy at the lowest rates—19 and 18 percent, respectively.

Table 7.2 illustrates patterns of intersectional advocacy among the members of the sample of social and economic justice organizations, grouped by policy foci. These trends mirror those of table 7.1. Across all possible policy specializations, intersectional advocacy takes up, once again, a minority of social and economic justice groups' advocacy agendas. Organizational advocates for racial justice (racial/ethnic minority) engage in intersectional advocacy at the highest rate, in 36 percent of their lobbying efforts. Groups advocating on anti-poverty, LGBTQ+, and women's issues pursue intersectional policy work at the second-highest rates, ranging from 29 to 31 percent of their advocacy efforts. Advocates for Indigenous policy issues (Native American) pursued intersectional advocacy at the lowest rate, in only 21 percent of cases.

Table 7.3 depicts rates of intersectional advocacy in the data by sample groups' total revenue in the year of comment submission. As with previous analyses, for purposes of simplicity, the total revenue data are presented in

TABLE 7.2. Intersectional advocacy by group policy focus

Policy focus	Intersectional advocacy (%)
Anti-poverty	31
LGBTQ+ issues	31
Native American	21
Racial/ethnic minority	36
Women's issues	29

Note: These proportions represent rates of intersectional advocacy within policy foci. They were calculated as follows: number intersectional advocacy efforts pursued by members of the sample in each policy focus divided by the total number of all advocacy efforts (comments submitted) pursued by members of the sample in each policy focus.

TABLE 7.3. Intersectional advocacy by group total revenue

Total revenue	Intersectional advocacy (%)
Quartile 1	20
Quartile 2	31
Quartile 3	30
Quartile 4	31

Note: These proportions represent rates of intersectional advocacy within revenue quartiles. They were calculated as follows: number of intersectional advocacy efforts pursued by members of the sample in each total revenue quartile divided by the total number of all advocacy efforts (comments submitted) pursued by members of the sample in each total revenue quartile.

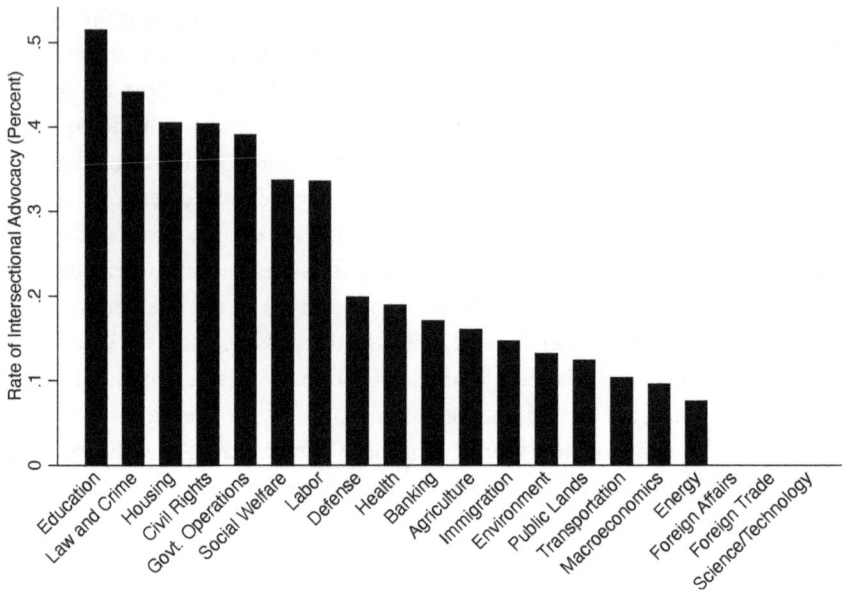

FIGURE 7.2. Intersectional advocacy by proposed rule policy topic

quartiles, where Quartile 1 corresponds to the lowest level of financial capacity among members of the sample and Quartile 4 corresponds to the highest level. These trends are particularly telling. While rates of intersectional advocacy are roughly constant across the second, third, and fourth revenue quartiles (ranging from 30 to 31 percent), rates of intersectional policy work are significantly lower for organizations falling into the first (lowest) quartile of financial capacity (20 percent). In other words, social and economic justice organizations with the most limited financial resources are, comparatively, the *least likely* to promote intersectional advocacy. This trend lends support to an important aspect of my theoretical narrative in this chapter—that resource limitations may relate to organizations' abilities to engage with intersectional policy issues.

Finally, social and economic justice organizations promote intersectional advocacy regularly across a wide range of topics appearing on the national governmental agenda. Figure 7.2 depicts rates of intersectional advocacy in the *Collaborative Advocacy Dataset*, broken down by the major policy topic of the targeted proposed agency rules. The vast majority of national policy topics—17 out of 21—are subject to intersectionally oriented advocacy by the organizations under study in this book. This coverage is slightly narrower than the range of policy topics subject to advocacy, broadly speaking, by organizational advocates for social and economic justice (as I explored earlier in this book—see figure 3.1 for a comparison); nearly all policy topics subject to the attention of social and economic justice organizations received some level of intersectionally oriented advocacy. Only three policy topics present in the broader dataset were not subject to intersectional advocacy: foreign affairs, foreign trade, and science/technology policy. However, because of the domestic and social justice–oriented focus of the organizations I examine in this book, this trend is not surprising. For instance, as I reported in chapters 3 and 4, these three topics are the policy areas subject to the lowest level of advocacy by social and economic justice organizations. Moreover, foreign affairs policy and science/technology policy were the only two topics appearing in the data that were subject to no coalitional advocacy (see figure 4.1 for a comparison).

Altogether, these descriptive statistics reiterate the findings of existing scholarship and lend support to key tenets of this chapter's theoretical argument. Like the works of Brower (2024), English (2019, 2020), Marchetti (2014, 2019), and Strolovitch (2006, 2007), the *Collaborative Advocacy Dataset* reveals that intersectional advocacy composes a small portion of social and economic justice organizations' policy agendas. Across organizational categories, policy specializations, and financial capacities, these advocates spend a minority of their time promoting the needs of their most vulnerable constituencies. Intuitively, the least resourced organizations engage in intersectional work at a rate more than 10 percentage points lower than their more moneyed counterparts. Finally, when social and economic justice organizations *do* choose to promote intersectional advocacy, they predominantly do so through coalition work—as the data demonstrate, 73 percent of intersectional advocacy efforts by these groups occur in coalitions.

Predicting Intersectional Advocacy

I evaluate the central claim of this chapter—that intersectional advocacy by social and economic justice organizations is more likely to occur in coalitions—using the first subset of the *Collaborative Advocacy Dataset*.[3] In this section, I estimate a series of logistic regression models but focus my discussion on the results of Model 10. Where needed, I refer to the appendix section of this book for models that evaluate alternative explanations. Model 10's dependent variable is a binary variable indicating the presence of intersectional advocacy within a given public comment. Its primary predictor variable is a binary indicator of the formation of a coalition. The model controls for coalition size, financial capacity, the presence of an organization with an intersectionally oriented mission among advocates in the sample, and characteristics of

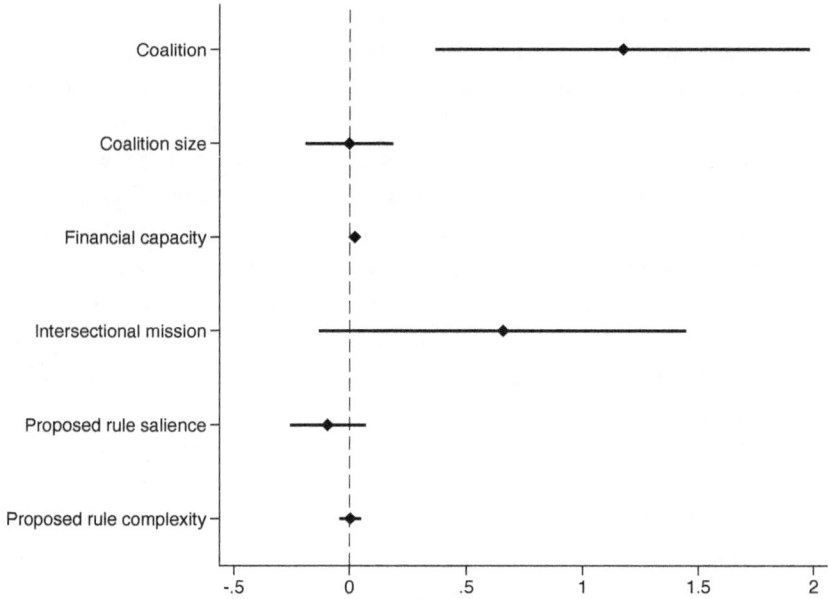

FIGURE 7.3. Intersectional advocacy and coalition building (Model 10). Logistic regression model with group-clustered standard errors. $N = 1,731$. Diamonds indicate coefficient values. Lines indicate 95% confidence intervals.

the targeted public policy (complexity, salience).[4] I also account for potential correlations within the data by clustering the standard errors by group. The relationships of interest can be expressed by the following equation (eq. 3):

$$
\ln\left[\frac{\pi_i}{1-\pi_i}\right] = \alpha + \beta_1 \text{Coalition}_i \\
+ \beta_2 \text{CoalitionSize}_i \\
+ \beta_3 \text{FinancialCapacity}_i \\
+ \beta_4 \text{IntersectionalMission}_i \\
+ \beta_5 \text{ProposedRuleComplexity}_i \\
+ \beta_6 \text{ProposedRuleSalience}_i
$$

Figure 7.3 depicts the results of Model 10.[5] This model assesses whether intersectional advocacy is more likely to occur in coalitions. It illustrates a number of findings. First, there is a positive and statistically significant relationship between the formation of a coalition and the presence of intersectional advocacy in public comments, suggesting that social and economic justice organizations are more likely to pursue intersectional advocacy when lobbying in partnership with other groups. More specifically, holding all other independent variables at their means, the model results indicate that a shift from advocating alone to advocating in a coalition more than doubles the predicted probability of intersectional advocacy, moving from 0.16 to 0.38. This result strongly supports the argument that organizational advocates for social and economic justice strategically coalesce to pursue intersectional advocacy.

Second, there is a positive and statistically significant relationship between organizations' financial capacity and the occurrence of intersectional advocacy in public comments. In other words, as organizations' financial capacities increase, so too does their likelihood of pursuing intersectional policy work. More specifically, holding all other independent variables at their means, the model results indicate that, for example, an increase in financial capacity from the twenty-fifth to the seventy-fifth percentile yields an increase in the predicted probability of intersectional advocacy from 0.21 to 0.39. This result thus suggests that resources moderate social and economic justice organizations' choice to pursue intersectional advocacy—lending support to a key theoretical tenet of my argument. This result is also consistent with existing empirical research on the importance of financial resources to intersectional advocacy (Marchetti 2014, 2019; Strolovitch 2007).

This model's key finding—a positive and statistically significant relationship between the occurrence of intersectional advocacy and coalition work—has powerful implications. It suggests that organizational strategy plays a large and important role in social and economic justice groups' agenda-setting choices. By their own admission, these advocates care about intersectional policy issues but struggle to incorporate them into their work (Strolovitch 2007). Their unique intra-organizational constraints drive them, instead, to promote broad-reaching advocacy that reflects the interests of their most advantaged constituents while reinforcing the marginalizations faced by their intersectionally disadvantaged constituents. But the results of this chapter's analysis reveal that these organizations have not abandoned these issues. As scholars have suggested, they leverage a strategic tool—collaboration—to attend to and promote the intersectional interests of their constituent communities. The takeaway here is simple: coalition building is not merely a tool for achieving greater influence over public policy; it also offers a strategic avenue through which social and economic justice organizations can rectify representational inequalities in their advocacy agendas. The results of this chapter demonstrate that coalition building enables these advocates to promote more equitable, widely representative, administrative policy proposals.

This key finding makes a significant contribution to existing scholarly research. By empirically establishing a link between intersectional advocacy and organizational alliances—a relationship that has only been theorized by previous scholarship—it establishes the centrality of lobbying strategy to the study of organizational agendas. Most research on organizational advocacy has focused on outputs, such as the degree to which advocacy organizations achieve influence over governmental agendas and policy outcomes. My work in this chapter, however, demonstrates the importance of an added dimension to this line of research: *intra*-organizational agenda setting. By focusing on the political and policy outcomes of organizational advocacy, an earlier, and especially important, stage of the lobbying process is obscured—the stage at which organizations decide which issues to take up. As the analyses of this chapter have demonstrated, decisions made at this stage have potent policy implications with downstream consequences for "who wins, who loses, and why" (Baumgartner et al. 2009a, 1). As such, my work in this chapter has important implications for our scholarly understanding of organizational strategy, agendas, and representation as well as the possibilities of representative democracy more generally.

Alternative Explanations

Now, for the last time, I turn to alternative explanations. A few possibilities may stand out to the reader based on the previous section, such as whether it might be the case that intersectional advocacy just so happens to occur on policies where coalition work is likely to be more attractive to social and economic justice groups—for example, more complicated or salient proposed rules. And what about the role of a critical organizational condition I described at the start of this chapter—the presence of a paying membership? Perhaps strategically building coalitions to promote intersectional advocacy is simply a tool of organizations with dues-paying members and, upon accounting for this condition, the findings of the previous section no longer persist. In this section, I evaluate these, along with other alternative explanations.

First, what about the possibility that intersectional advocacy just so happens to co-occur on highly complex and salient public policies? If this is the case, then perhaps coalition building by social and economic justice organizations is a strategic response to the nature of these policies rather than the nature of the target population. If true, the data should reflect this dynamic. However, they do not. In fact, according to the *Collaborative Advocacy Dataset*, 41 percent of observations of intersectional advocacy in the data occur in response to proposed rules with the lowest possible level of complexity (out of six).[6] Moreover, 45 percent occur in response to proposed rules with the second-lowest possible level of complexity. Figure 7.4 evaluates the second of

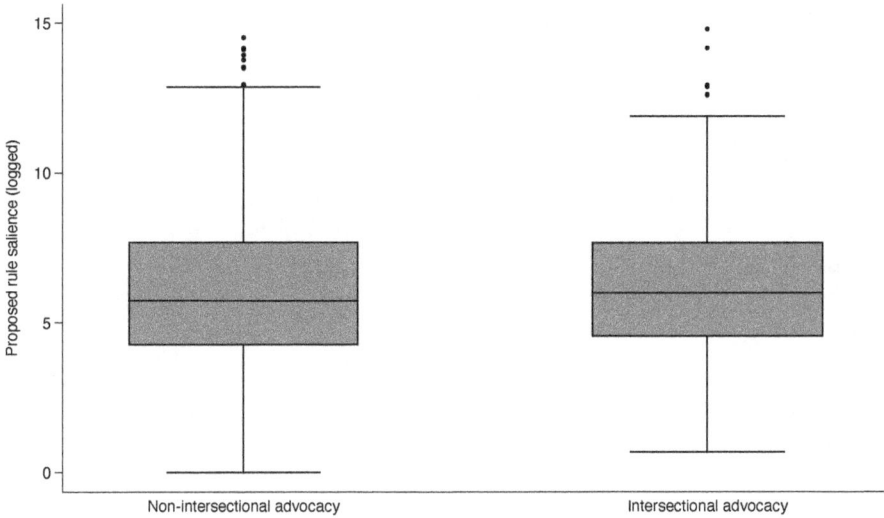

FIGURE 7.4. Distribution of proposed rule salience over intersectional advocacy

these two possibilities. It depicts a summary distribution of proposed rule salience (logged) over the occurrence of intersectional advocacy in the *Collaborative Advocacy Dataset*. This distribution demonstrates, with great clarity, that there is no difference between the salience of public policies targeted by intersectional advocacy and those targeted by non-intersectional advocacy. This simple illustration should ameliorate the concern that intersectional advocacy simply conceals the effect of policy salience.

Next, I tackle the question of organizations with dues-paying memberships. As I described earlier in this chapter, one of the explanations that scholars have posed regarding the scarcity of intersectional advocacy is related to pressure by the members of these organizations. The AAUW, FMF, and NOW, for instance, operate based on membership models; women across the nation pay monthly or yearly dues to these organizations. These dues help fund the work of these groups, but at a cost: in exchange for their dues, these members expect to be involved in the organizations' decisions, ranging from which priorities to take up each quarter to who is chosen to helm the group. Different social and economic justice organizations approach and engage with their membership bases in widely variable ways. However, what largely holds true is that the people who can afford to make a regular financial commitment to an organization are typically not the people who most need its advocacy. For instance, the former women's organizations' staffers I described earlier in this chapter speculated that their memberships were largely composed of white women (Kitchener 2020).

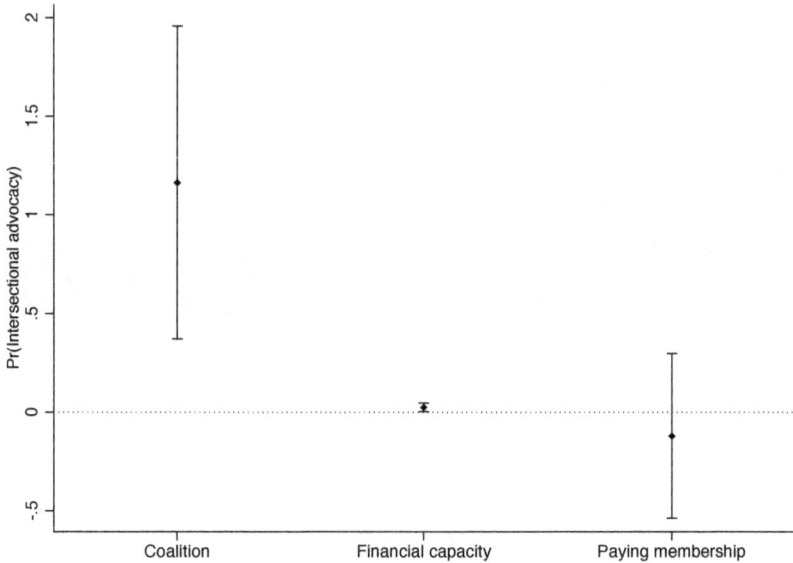

FIGURE 7.5. Intersectional advocacy and paying membership (Model 11). Logistic regression model with group-clustered standard errors. $N = 1,731$. Diamonds indicate coefficient values. Lines indicate 95% confidence intervals.

However, not all social and economic groups rely on this model. While many such organizations maintain paying memberships, plenty of other advocates (such as Community Change Action, NumbersUSA, and the National LGBTQ Task Force) do not. In fact, only 18 percent of the social and economic justice organizations in the sample under study in this book maintain a membership model. And while my argument in this chapter makes the case that the link between intersectional advocacy and coalitional strategy holds true for all kinds of social and economic justice organizations, it could be the case that the results of Model 10 are sensitive to omitted variable bias driven by the exclusion of a variable accounting for the presence of a paying membership model. Thus, to account for this possibility, I have reestimated Model 10 to include a binary variable reflecting whether or not each organization in my sample of social and economic justice groups maintained a paying membership in the year of comment submission.[7] Figure 7.5 depicts the results of this model.[8]

As the figure demonstrates, even upon the inclusion of a covariate accounting for the presence of an organization with a paying membership, the relationship between intersectional advocacy and coalition work remains positive and statistically significant. So, too, does the relationship between intersectional advocacy and financial capacity. Moreover, there is a negative but statistically insignificant relationship between the presence of a paying membership and the occurrence of intersectional advocacy. In other words, this reestimation reiterates the key relationship observed in Model 10: that coalition building positively and significantly increases the likelihood of intersectional advocacy by social and economic justice groups.

Summary

In this chapter, I have sought to make a simple point. Through a series of empirical analyses, I have demonstrated that social and economic justice organizations are significantly more likely to pursue intersectional advocacy when collaborating with other groups. This finding makes a number of theoretical and practical contributions. It is among the first analyses of organizational advocacy—along with English (2019, 2020)—to evaluate the conditions that might ameliorate agenda-setting bias by organizations advocating for historically vulnerable and marginalized communities in American politics. Together with the analyses of chapters 4, 5, and 6, this finding carries with it important implications for our scholarly understanding of the interconnectedness of organizational agendas, representational inequality, lobbying strategy, and policy outcomes.

This work, of course, is not the last word on this topic. As I will discuss in the final chapter, the concept and practice of intersectionality have recently gained popular and cultural salience (Coaston 2019). Organizational leaders have begun facing greater public pressure to contend with both the intersectional identities of their constituents and their historic and systemic neglect of these constituents' needs. For instance, in the months and years that followed the racial reckoning of the summer of 2020, many social and economic justice organizations pledged to do better by their constituencies. UnidosUS, the nation's largest Hispanic civil rights organization, promptly acknowledged the need for a more intersectional approach to their advocacy with regard to their Afro-Latino members—a multiply marginalized subgroup of their constituency.[9] Soon after, Sunrise Movement, a fast-growing environmental justice group, centered the importance of intersectional environmentalism. In an op-ed penned on behalf of the group, Sunrise organizer Nikayla Jefferson wrote, "this isn't just the white climate kids' movement anymore—this is an intersectional movement for justice."[10] And three years later, in the midst of a historic labor movement in the summer and fall of 2023, a coalition of labor unions in the Pacific Northwest—the Coalition of Independent Unions (CIU), established with an explicit mission of intersectional solidarity—organized its first "Trans Day of Solidarity." An organizer with the coalition reflected on their mission by speaking to the importance of organized and intersectional advocacy: "we believe [that] in the current political climate, organizations such as unions can be a beacon of hope for trans individuals against employers who are increasingly turning their backs on LGBTQ+ peoples.[. . .] The future is going to be more intersectional."[11]

While some organizations—such as UnidosUS, Sunrise, and CIU—have responded to these pressures, others have been decried for their silence or the disparity between their public claims to support intersectional work and their lack of substantive intersectional advocacy (see Kitchener 2020; Shugerman 2020). However, scholars have yet to systematically explore the effects of this trend on organizations' advocacy choices. While the work of this chapter offers a critical foundational understanding of social and economic justice organizations' general treatment of intersectional policy work—along with an exploration of the linkage between organizational strategy and intersectional advocacy—much more remains to be understood. In particular, as our cultural context continues to shift, understanding the relationship between public and organizational attention to intersectionally minded public policy is an essential next step for this body of scholarship.

In the final chapter, I draw connections between the four analytic chapters of this book. I describe that while social and economic justice organizations have historically received little scholarly attention, their agendas and strategies have profound consequences for the content and evolution of American policymaking. I offer a series of recommendations for organizational leaders, staffers, and organizers seeking to adopt or improve coalition strategies, and I supplement these takeaways with insights from the organizational leaders and policymakers I interviewed for this project. Finally, I conclude with a discussion of future areas for research.

8

Conclusion

On a brisk February morning in Washington, DC, I sat down for a cup of coffee with a veteran political organizer. He had built a career working for the kinds of advocacy organizations at the heart of this book—advocates for social and economic justice. No stranger to canvassing or policy work, he described his experiences working for state- and local-level advocacy groups and grassroots campaigns in Texas and Wisconsin, along with his time with large, national-level membership organizations in Washington, DC. When I asked him about the histories and missions of the organizations he had worked for, he spoke with passion,

> I've worked for several advocacy groups. The one I work with right now was founded out of the civil rights movement by people who worked with Dr. Martin Luther King Jr. and Senator Robert F. Kennedy to try to lift up the voices of people of color and marginalized people who are impacted by political issues. I think a lot of these organizations come from . . . that purpose of understanding that these communities, these Black, Brown, immigrant, and poor communities just don't have the same access that white and wealthy communities have. Their mission is to advance their political opportunities . . . to attain greater access and equity for them. That's really what drives the work that these organizations do.[1]

Many of the other organizational leaders and staffers that I spoke with while conducting research for this book shared this perspective. As the organizer from the previous quote alluded, and as I described in chapters 1 and 2, the organizations they work for were born out of historic movements for women's rights and civil rights for communities of color in the mid- to late twentieth century, and which persist today to realize the goals of these movements: equity for historically marginalized, vulnerable, and excluded communities in American society. Through the organizations they sustain, these leaders and staffers recognize the great burden they bear, are deeply committed to their work, and are enormously proud of their accomplishments, however incremental. But they are quick to acknowledge the challenges they face, from limited or short-term funding to the politics of membership bases to political realities.

Across two years of conversations with current and former organizational leaders and staffers—for advocates large and small—the power of *coalition work* came up time and time again. Every individual I spoke with brought up the importance of building and sustaining organizational partnerships to their work as a resolution to the unique challenges faced by their groups. One said, "frankly, the assumption is that [we're] going to work in coalition."[2] Another said, "coalitions bring so much power to the work that [we] do."[3] And a third said, "[coalitions] offer a kind of credibility that is hard for us to come by otherwise."[4] Each of them qualified, too, that successful coalitions require hard work. The organizer I shared coffee with, for instance, pointed to the importance of a united front, "where there isn't unity in a coalition . . . things break off or [you] lose on what [you're] trying to achieve." He described that "coalitions that do really well . . . have a forward-thinking mindset.[. . .] They convene after the fact and talk about what went well, what didn't, and what they can do better next time." These observations are reflected in this book. Over the course of the last seven chapters, using a novel dataset containing information on the characteristics, behaviors, and outcomes of over 1,700 coalitions in American national politics, I demonstrated that partnership *is* powerful—and uniquely so for social and economic justice groups. But just as my interviewees suggested, I found evidence that only certain kinds of coalitions enable successful advocacy outcomes: those that bring together member organizations with diverse backgrounds and specialties and with structural characteristics that encourage collective learning and adaptability.

In this final chapter, I reflect on the implications of these findings. I describe their contributions to existing research by drawing connections to broader scholarship on organizational structures, partnerships, and agenda setting and suggest areas for future work. I emphasize the consequences of this study for the nature and outcomes of administrative policymaking—a frequent but understudied target of organizational advocacy. Finally, I offer a series of best practices for organizational leaders and staffers who seek to improve or implement coalition strategies.

Implications and Contributions: Organizational Politics

At the start of this book, I told the story of Kansans for Constitutional Freedom (KCF), a bipartisan coalition of advocacy organizations that came together in 2022 to fight a proposed constitutional amendment that would have allowed lawmakers to ban abortion in the state of Kansas. Despite insurmountable odds, KCF succeeded, and in the months that followed their victory, strategists, scholars, and organizers in other parts of the country puzzled over how they managed to pull it off. In this book, I have argued that a key part of their success—and others like it—was coalition work. But not just any kind of coalition work. I have made the case that organizational coalitions that intentionally and strategically unite a plurality of voices are most effective at achieving their goals.

In the case of KCF, this dynamic could not be clearer: coalition leaders joined together religious groups, civil rights groups, and advocates for reproductive rights, along with organizations of different ideological affinities. With these many perspectives, connections, and constituencies in tow, KCF could more credibly and compellingly make their case to a wide range of Kansas voters. In the words of Ashley All, KCF's communications director, "Coalition building is absolutely critical. No matter where you live, whatever state you're in—I don't care if you're in New York, California, Montana, or Kentucky—coalition building is critical. You've got to bring a lot of different voices to the table."[5] And while this case was situated in a particular context—state-level political organizing—as this book has demonstrated, its lessons transcend this boundary. More than a year later, for example, many of KCF's member organizations are hard at work in a strikingly similar coalition, spanning advocates for reproductive rights, consumer protection, and the health care industry.[6] Their target? A 2023 rule proposed by the Department of Health and Human Services (HHS) banning providers covered by the Health Insurance Portability and Accountability Act (HIPAA) from sharing medical records that could be used to investigate abortions—a response by the Biden Administration to the *Dobbs* decision.[7]

If I am to leave the reader with a single point, it is that coalitions are foundational to social justice advocacy. My work here has focused on a particular political institution and policy process—notice-and-comment rulemaking by the American federal bureaucracy. But the implications of my work go far beyond this setting. While this book represents the first comprehensive empirical study of lobbying coalitions in American national politics, it stands on the shoulders of dozens of scholars who have explored the merits of this ubiquitous advocacy strategy across political and policy contexts. In fact, existing research has demonstrated the value of this tool for organizations targeting the legislative process (Phinney 2017), social movements (Davies 2023; Levi and Murphy 2006; Staggenborg 1986; Woodly 2015, 2021), and electoral politics (Mahoney 2007).

But several aspects of my conclusions cause this book to stand out from this scholarship. By leveraging an original dataset containing information on the coalition behaviors and outcomes of a nationally representative sample of social and economic justice organizations—the first of its kind—I have been able to both test my central arguments *and* uncover new findings regarding the efficacy and limitations of coalition work. The first such finding, as the reader may recall, pertains to the importance of coalition architecture. In chapter 4, I demonstrated that among advocates for social and economic justice, coalition building alone is not a sufficient condition for policy influence. Instead, I showed that within and beyond collaborative efforts, building coalitions with *formalized structures* significantly increases the policy influence of these organized interest groups.

This conclusion connects with a growing and interdisciplinary body of research on coalition structures—within and beyond the field of political science. For instance, writing for an audience of practitioners, Zack and colleagues argue that successful coalitions should contain "good coalition architecture" (Zack et al. 2023, 2). Synthesizing the work of other scholars, they contend that "good" architecture requires the presence of practices and processes that distribute power and define mechanisms for accountability within coalitions (e.g., democratic governance); the ability to learn, change, and adapt (e.g., learning feedback loops); clarity around roles (e.g., who is and is not in the coalition and understandings of the responsibilities of each coalition partner); and even separate (sometimes paid) staff that facilitate coordinating the coalition (Nilsson 2019; Tattersall 2020; Szulecki, Pattberg, and Biermann 2011; Wolff 2001). My work in chapter 4 demonstrates that coalitions with these features do, in fact, systematically enable greater success rates. In doing so, it significantly advances this literature—and, I hope, it will encourage future scholars of organizational politics to continue to explore the causes, consequences, and features of coalition architecture.

The second such finding pertains to the importance of coalition membership. In chapter 5, I explored the consequences of coalition composition for advocacy outcomes. I focused on two facets of coalition composition: representational diversity and "strange bedfellow" partnerships. I demonstrated that partnerships uniting advocates with *crosscutting constituent interests*—that is, representational diversity—are significantly more influential than their homogenous counterparts or than advocates working alone. Moreover, I showed that despite popular opinion and scholarly speculation, coalitions of strange bedfellows do not experience exceptional success.

These parallel conclusions connect with and advance a burgeoning body of research on coalition composition in interest group politics. Recent work by Phinney, Junk, Lorenz, and Mahoney has established a link between diverse partners and coalition outcomes in the case of social welfare reform (Phinney 2017), congressional committee agenda setting (Lorenz 2019), and European Union politics (Junk 2019; Mahoney 2007). My conclusions support these researchers' arguments that membership diversity is important to the success of collaborative lobbying. However, my conclusions take this literature one step further by demonstrating that not all diverse coalitions are created equally. In the case of social and economic justice organizations, the most consequential coalitions are those that unite crosscutting constituent interests—enabling the coalition, as a collective, to advance more informed and well-rounded advocacy—and not necessarily those coalitions that are so striking they make the evening news.

My third overarching finding illuminated the conditional value of coalition work. In chapter 6, I investigated whether coalitions are, as some scholars have speculated, "weapons of the weak" (Mahoney and Baumgartner 2004, 2). And while I object to the characterization of the organizations I focus on in this book as "weak"—they are, in my view, unflinchingly resolute—I found evidence to support this claim. By comparing the coalition behaviors and outcomes of two representative samples of nationally active interest groups (the first representing the population of social and economic justice groups and the second, the population of private, professional, and general interest groups), I discovered that coalition building uniquely benefits organizational advocates for historically marginalized communities. More specifically, while formalized and representationally diverse coalition work lend significant benefits to the advocacy efforts of social and economic justice organizations, neither coalition building (ad hoc or formal) nor diverse coalition building significantly enhance the advocacy efforts of their mainstream counterparts.

This particular finding may offer a resolution to decades of conflicting research on the efficacy of lobbying coalitions in American politics. Since the late 1990s, scholars of interest group politics have debated the merits of organizational alliances in policy advocacy. As I described in earlier chapters, some scholars have reported positive, significant effects (see McKay and Yackee 2007; Nelson and Yackee 2012; Phinney 2017; Lorenz 2019), while others have reported negative or null relationships between coalitional strategy and lobbying outcomes (see Baumgartner et al. 2009a; Heinz et al. 1993; Gray and Lowery 1998; Mahoney and Baumgartner 2004; Haider-Markel 2006). These mixed findings have led researchers to suggest that coalition work may be of value only to certain kinds of organizations, such as those at a systematic disadvantage in the lobbying environment (Mahoney and Baumgartner 2004; Whitford 2003). Whitford, for instance, proposes that coalition work may uniquely benefit "minority interests" seeking to "assemble into more powerful blocs" (45). However, until now, these theories have gone untested. My approach in this book—which separated the lobbying population along the very lines that scholars have theorized may govern the value of coalition work—may thus help put speculation on this subject to rest.

Finally, I arrived at my final contribution by turning the lens of the book inward to evaluate whether collaborative strategy enables social and economic justice organizations to rectify biases in their advocacy agendas. Drawing on research on the challenges and scarcity of intersectional advocacy, I contended and found that coalition work also provides a critical avenue through which advocates for social and economic justice can elevate the needs of their most vulnerable constituents—those with intersectional disadvantage. This finding comes with powerful implications. Practically speaking, it uncovers a key means by which advocacy organizations can, despite their intra-organizational limitations, nonetheless advance more widely representative policy agendas. Theoretically speaking, this finding lends empirical support to a notion that has gone previously untested: that coalitional advocacy is, by definition, intersectional advocacy (Strolovitch 2006, 2007). Moreover, this work should encourage scholars to dedicate greater attention to organizations' internal agenda-setting choices. The second face of power, after all, is just as consequential as the first (Bachrach and Baratz 1962).

Together, these conclusions paint an optimistic picture. They suggest that while social and economic justice organizations *are* at a disadvantage—financially, tactically, and politically—coalition tactics can help ameliorate these disparities. Building and sustaining alliances uniquely allows these groups not only to advocate more effectively, but also more equitably. Investing in coalitions with structures, processes, and memberships that facilitate clarity, accountability, collective learning, and diverse perspectives is a feasible means by which these advocates can make a mark on American public policy.

Implications and Contributions: Bureaucratic Politics

A parallel set of implications from this work pertains to the role of information and legitimacy in bureaucratic policymaking. Like other stages of the policymaking process, agency rulemaking is complex and consequential.

However, unlike other stages, it offers a formal platform for private citizens and organized interest groups to voice their opinions: the public comment period.[8] This platform is equal opportunity; while some groups are more equipped to write persuasive comments than others, any advocate can contribute, with or without an invitation. Moreover, the recommendations made by advocates in this setting are highly sought by rulemaking-oriented civil servants. For example, an agency official said to me in an interview,

> Within [my agency's] four walls, we can only do so much. We write rules based on our own knowledge, experience, and histories. Information from public comments is extremely helpful to us—[commenters] can point out things that we missed, or possible negative consequences. They always have some information that we don't.[9]

Another said to me, "We have just one perspective, and it's based on our experiences and knowledge. Public comments expose us to other perspectives. They point out areas where we fell short, where we could be more aggressive. They're extremely important to the work that we do."[10] Other agency officials who chose to speak with me off the record shared similar outlooks. In my conversations with them, these agency officials repeatedly highlighted the importance of information in their work. They reiterated that their agencies, more than anything else, care about "getting it right."[11] One described how in her decades-long career as a civil servant, her teams have guided their work around implementing durable and justifiable rules that adhere to their statutes. In her view, the notice-and-comment process serves to facilitate this: "*Information* is what matters.[. . .] The comments we receive can be anywhere between 1 and 100 pages, but the ones that are most helpful don't just say that they don't like our rule, they explain why they agree or disagree, and use evidence to back up their argument."[12] The theoretical foundations of this book—that agencies are likely to favor public comments by partnerships that facilitate high informational content—very much reflect her assessment, as well as those of many other off-the-record agency officials.

Thus, a key contribution of this work is its advancement of scholarship on information processing by the American federal bureaucracy. Researchers have long debated the presence and consequences of informational asymmetries across political institutions in American government. The federal bureaucracy, with its large and expansive body of experts, enjoys a great informational advantage (see Abermach and Rockman 2006; Baumgartner and Jones 2005; Goodnow 1900; Niskanen 1971; Simon 1972; Meier and O'Toole 2006; Wilson 1989; Workman 2015). Its agencies often strategically deploy this advantage by insulating their activity from political scrutiny by other branches of government (see Carpenter 2002; Gailmard 2002; Potter 2019). Comparatively little attention, however, has been paid to how federal agencies process and respond to information received in the notice-and-comment context. The conclusions of this book suggest that public comments by organized interest groups *can* be consequential for policy outcomes, just as other scholars have reported (see Cropper et al. 1992; Yackee 2006; MacKay and Yackee 2007). They are an important, much-needed source of information for federal agencies working to promulgate provisions of the law (Croley 1998; Golden 1998; Kerwin, Furlong, and West 2011; West 2004).

By exploring the policy outcomes of different organizational approaches to notice-and-comment lobbying, my work advances this literature in a timely and practical direction. I have shown that—as the agency officials from earlier in this section suggest—comments submitted under conditions allowing for a greater exchange of substantive knowledge, perspectives, and experiences by their coauthors (i.e., formalized and representationally diverse coalitions) can produce recommendations that approximate the high level of informational content sought out by civil servants, and therefore best serve agency interests. This conclusion further solidifies the value of public perspectives in agency policymaking and suggests a simple prescription for organizations seeking to contribute more effectively to notice-and-comment rulemaking: in the eyes of agency officials, informational content reigns supreme. For organizational advocates who cannot develop this content alone—such as the advocates I focus on in this book—the secondary lesson is just as straightforward: building coalitions that facilitate well-rounded, informed, and evidence-based policy recommendations is critical for success.

Finally, these conclusions offer a more optimistic picture than previous research on regulatory lobbying—that of a legitimate and deliberate federal bureaucracy. Specifically, my discovery of a link between advocacy by representationally diverse coalitions and policy outcomes has direct consequences for our understanding, as scholars, of the democratic nature of bureaucratic policymaking. Bureaucratic policymaking is often viewed as unsavory and undemocratic; some scholars have gone so far as labeling it "imperialist" in modern American politics (Crepelle 2021; Holden 2014). And while this characterization might seem hyperbolic, it stems from an uncomfortable reality: unelected and insulated civil servants serving in federal agencies have a great deal of discretion over the American political process (Brierly et al. 2023; Potter 2019). As the US Congress has lost institutional capacity—and thus has ceased to write clear and detailed legislation—the taxing work of interpreting, positioning, and writing public policies now falls to these unassuming, often unaccountable, individuals (Potter 2019; Warren 2018). This trend should be a source of great concern. But a silver lining is that my work indicates that these bureaucrats typically favor policy recommendations from representationally diverse coalitions of advocacy organizations rather than those coming from elite or moneyed interests (see Dwidar 2022a). This relationship suggests that bureaucratic decision making likely considers and represents the interests of a broader public. While questions about the representative nature of diverse coalitions should be assessed more directly in future work, these findings nonetheless hold significant implications for scholarship regarding agency responsiveness to public and stakeholder interests and democratic legitimacy in the administrative policy process.

Best Practices of Coalition Work

Now, to the organizational leader or staffer: What should you make of all this? This book's findings, while captured through a mass of measurement and statistical jargon, are fairly direct. They resonate with the experiences and stories of many of your colleagues—and I hope with your own. Their takeaways for building successful coalitions can be broken down into three lessons: the importance of a forward-thinking mindset, facilitating complementary capacities, and encouraging less restrictive funding strategies.

A FORWARD-THINKING MINDSET

In one of my last conversations for this project, a program manager for an economic justice advocacy organization almost perfectly summarized this book's first lesson of coalition building: the importance of a forward-thinking mindset.

> I think the [coalitions] that do well [. . .] convene after the fact and talk about what went well, what didn't, and what they can do better next time. Not every coalition does that. Not every coalition keeps on the staff to be able to do that and has that forward-thinking mindset.[. . .] Those kinds of debriefs and analyses are important and to be honest, they don't happen enough. You can't just convene a coalition without thinking about what went wrong before and how you can try to avoid those mistakes next time.[13]

According to my research, coalitions that are successful tend to have structures that allow for member organizations to have these very conversations about "what went well, what didn't, and what they can do better next time." These structures can take many forms. In my work, I focused on three structural characteristics: the presence of a coalition name and staff separate from that of member organizations, and the presence of a fixed membership roll. For instance, Voces Verdes—a coalition of Latinx community organizations and businesses advocating for racial and environmental justice—maintains three paid staff: an executive director, a partnership and constituency advocate, and a research and outreach associate. Their membership consists of more than forty partners, all listed on their website, including Mujeres de la Tierra (MDLT, founded in 2004), the National Black and Latino Council (NBLC, founded in 2008), and the League of United Latin American Citizens. Moreover, the coalition *itself* has a mission, an advisory board, and a steering committee to guide and facilitate its advocacy work.

These structures, of course, are not easy to develop. They require time, effort, and funds—all of which entail each member organization to make a costly commitment (Gelbman 2021; Schroering and Staggenborg 2022). I do not want to minimize this reality. Some organizations simply might not be able to invest in partnerships like these. But other groups, which might be looking to understand how they can more effectively build partnerships, should take note. These structures are incredibly consequential. They are not just aesthetic. They enable their partners to develop the capacity to plan over long periods of time and learn from each iteration of advocacy, as well as generally clear up the kinds of ambiguities that tend to cause coalitions to break—from confusion about how to make decisions to who is or is not in the coalition to the role of each partner.

Thus, *lesson number one* is to develop long-lasting coalitions with architectures that govern membership, leadership, and decision making. In other words, you should have difficult conversations about who is in the coalition and who is in charge of it. Decide what the leadership structure will look like and whether leadership will rotate among member organizations. Existing research, for instance, suggests that in coalitions where there are large power differences between members, attempting to represent all groups across leadership roles can help enhance unity (Levine 2022). Consider who the best leader(s) might be: typically, they should be "organic," influential, trusted, and well respected by their collaborators (McAlevey 2016; Zack et al. 2023). Sketch out how you plan to make decisions and how you plan to resolve disagreements. There is no single answer here—simply establishing a clear and consistent process is the mechanism for success. Common systems for decision making in coalitions include requiring unanimous consent to make a decision (100 percent of all members agreeing), majority rule (50 percent or more of members agreeing), supermajority rule (two-thirds of members agreeing), or even "consent-based" decision making, where a delegate (such as a coalition leader) is responsible for the final decision but works with each partner to ensure that the final outcome is within their "range of tolerance" (Dentoni, Bitzer, and Schouten 2018; Foster-Fishman et al. 2001; Levine 2022; Zack et al. 2023; Zack and Smithson-Stanley 2024). Finally, create regular venues for information sharing, like a monthly or bimonthly meeting. Adopt norms about taking and sharing meeting minutes and receiving updates or reactions from each partner. These practices enable transparency, which facilitates more informed decision making (Ansell and Gash 2007; Bäckstrand 2006; Mena and Palazzo 2012; Ostrom 1990; Zack et al. 2023; Zack and Smithson-Stanley 2024).

COMPLEMENTARY CAPACITIES

About halfway through this project, I had a conversation with a colleague of mine. In a previous life, she had been an organizer in the environmental justice movement. She'd designed advocacy strategies, spearheaded fundraising campaigns, and led coalitions. When I asked her about the challenges that accompany coalition work, she said,

> [We] need to be able to come together and have very real, candid conversations about complementary capacities. There is this very real tension. You feel like you have to have everything. You have to have a membership that acts, you have to have legal staff, you have to have policy know-how. It seems to me that the healthier, more effective coalitions have recognized that those skills and capacities are unequally distributed across organizations and then are brave enough to actually have conversations about how we do this together.[14]

Her response touched on something I had been thinking about for years, though she put it far more succinctly than I ever had: the notion and importance of "complementary capacities" in coalition work. Earlier that year, another interviewee had said something to me to the same effect: "In my experience, in successful coalitions, every partner is brought to the table for a reason. Because they can bring the constituents, they have the connections in Congress, or they have the money. It's important to recognize each organization's strengths."[15] And a third interviewee said, "Every organization has their specialty, what they can contribute.[. . .] That's why they were chosen for the coalition."[16]

According to my research, coalitions with complementary capacities *are* more successful. In my work, I defined this characteristic as coalitions that unite representationally diverse memberships, bringing together partners that represent different constituencies and thus that "complement" each other through the distinct experiences, perspectives, and specialties they bring to the table. Doing so enables coalitions to position themselves more strategically.

Some of the organizational leaders and staffers looking to improve their co-alition strategies might already think (or know) this to be true. For them, this lesson might be more validating than it is groundbreaking. For others, who tend to turn to partnerships with groups that are similar to their own, this lesson is more tangible. Coalition work is hard. It is even harder when it requires conversations and negotiations that cross divides—whether in missions, constituencies, policy priorities, or theories of change. Thus, returning to comfortable, homogenous alliances is perfectly understandable. But for social and economic justice organizations, it is not conducive to achieving policy change.

Lesson number two is thus to develop coalitions with representationally diverse memberships—that is, with complementary capacities. I acknowledge that this recommendation is a tall order. Doing so can lead to strain, conflict, and greater disagreement within coalitions (Levi and Murphy 2006; Staggenborg 1998). Diverse coalitions are also more likely to magnify uneven power dynamics, which can cause friction and compound feelings of discomfort or distrust among partners (Ansell and Gash 2007; Cheyns and Riisgaard 2014; Levine 2022). For instance, researchers have found that organizations that enter coalitions with greater resources and legitimacy are more likely to hold leadership positions and exert greater power over coalition decisions. Thus, in diverse coalitions, less powerful groups—advocates with fewer resources—can be excluded from or marginalized in conversations and decisions about key issues (Agranoff and Mcguire 2001).

However, as my research demonstrates, these kinds of partnerships are vital for advocacy influence. Uniting partners with many different constituent interests assembles the kinds of complementary capacities that facilitate better, more well-rounded advocacy content—from information that is otherwise inaccessible to a certain class of organization to experience implementing certain tactics, such as writing a public comment or organizing a protest. Thus, I encourage organizational leaders and staffers working toward social justice advocacy to carefully consider the company of the coalitions they build and join. To resolve the difficulties of diverse coalition work—and the power dynamics inherent within them—this second lesson should be taken in parallel with *lesson number one*. Researchers have demonstrated that clarity and structures in coalition work can help ameliorate power imbalances and foster greater trust between coalition partners. Unaddressed, these imbalances can manifest in conflict and reduced commitment to the coalition (Gray 1989; Huxham and Vangen 2004; Fox and Gersham 2000). But structures that balance power—such as establishing practices that allow for equitable participation, equal roles for partners in key decision-making bodies (like working groups or committees), and rotating leadership responsibility—can reduce this risk and help a diverse coalition realize its full potential (Bryson, Crosby, and Stone 2006; Gray and Stites 2013; Foster-Fishman et al. 2001).

My final word of advice is directed to the philanthropists funding the work of advocacy organizations. One of the most pervasive and consequential trends of social and economic justice advocacy is its systemic neglect of the people who are most in need—those experiencing intersectional disadvantage. Take, for instance, the not-so-hypothetical case of chronically unhoused women: if women's organizations seldom advocate for unhoused women because their policy needs are too "controversial" and economic justice organizations seldom advocate for these women because their policy needs are too "narrow," then who will? The answer is no one; save for the work of a small number of exclusively intersectionally oriented groups, the vast majority of advocacy by social and economic justice organizations maintains a majoritarian focus (Brower 2024; English 2019, 2020; Marchetti 2014; Strolovitch 2006, 2007). This trend is no accident. In fact, it is most directly motivated by the challenge that *funding* poses to advocacy organizations. The executive director of a social justice organization explained,

> There [are] tons of challenges. Funding is a major one.[. . .] Some organizations work on grants that are tied to specific initiatives. Some of them are short-term, some can be longer-term. I think . . . organizations really appreciate the longer-term investments because they know they can keep specific staff and commit to working in certain communities for a period of time. Some of that funding means that you get to open up an office in a new community that you previously didn't access . . . or you can hire someone who's from a [certain] space that has expertise that you need.[17]

As my research demonstrates, social and economic justice organizations compensate for this dynamic of limited—and often short-term—funding by building coalitions. A coalition leader said to me in an interview, "funding incentives are a big part of [coalitions]."[18] Coalition work, moreover, is a driving factor in organizations' choices to pursue intersectional advocacy. But better funding practices could reduce the pressure on these groups to prioritize certain agenda items and compensate for their neglect of others through collaboration. One coalition leader remarked, "I think donors could do a lot more . . . and there's always a standing invitation [for them] to participate in a more authentic way."[19] My findings support this coalition leader's suggestion.

I demonstrate that a second key predictor of intersectional advocacy is *funding*. Social and economic justice groups with greater financial resources are far more likely to promote the interests of their intersectionally disadvantaged constituents than their less resourced counterparts.

The implication for philanthropists, then, is to establish funding practices that enable more equitable and consistent advocacy. *Lesson number three* is thus to commit to longer-term, less restrictive funding. Stable funding and longer timelines will empower social and economic justice organizations to expand their advocacy agendas to include issues that are not just "broad" and "winnable" but that are responsive to the evolving needs of their constituencies, however divisive or complex. Moreover, less restrictive funding will reduce internal debates stemming from resource scarcity and competition over a limited organizational agenda (Tattersall 2020). This simple reform can offer social and economic justice organizations the very flexibility enjoyed by their private and professional counterparts. Reducing resource constraints will lower barriers to expanding organizations' strategic capacity and allow them, over time, to invest in specialized staff and develop initiatives that advance wider—and more equitable—advocacy agendas.

Future Directions

The subject of advocacy organizations in social justice movements is rife with opportunities for future research. First, while I have discussed the importance of coalition structure at length, there is much more to understand regarding the dynamics of *organizational* structure and how different internal structures might facilitate different organizational behaviors and outcomes, from lesser or greater agenda diversity to degrees of long-term durability in policy successes—both individually and within coalitions. For instance, what about the characteristics of who, exactly, leads social and economic justice organizations? The story of the AAUW, NOW, and FMF from chapter 7, along with a growing body of research (see Andrews, Caren, and Lu 2020; Baggetta, Han, and Andrews 2013; Dwidar, Marchetti, and Strolovitch, forthcoming), might suggest that as in the case of elected officials, descriptive representation in leadership positions within advocacy organizations matters—both in terms of who sits at the helm and who composes organizations' boards of directors. And what about staff? As the former women's organizations' staffers recounted, the small number of women of color on staff were largely relegated to junior positions. Perhaps greater degrees of diversity among staff, as well as congruence between the identities of leaders and junior staffers, is consequential for the above-mentioned, as well as other, outcomes.

Second, there is much more to unpack regarding the relationship between donors and the advocacy organizations they support. In the previous section, I discussed some of the ways in which donors can more consciously distribute funds. But should they choose, donors can also play a more direct role in guiding advocacy organizations and encouraging "healthier" coalition strategies. Donors can, for instance, take a bottom-up approach by encouraging organizations to develop partnerships with "buy-in, commitment, trust, and agency" rather than a top-down approach that dictates which partnerships to build (Zack et al. 2023, 25). They can also help coalition leaders develop technical capacities (such as developing data infrastructure) and create spaces where partners and leaders can invest in building their relationships (such as semiannual retreats) (Zack et al. 2023; Zack and Smithson-Stanley 2024). To that end, how can funders facilitate architecture, learning, and long-term investments in coalition work? And what are the consequences of different funding models? These questions deserve further study.

Third, representationally diverse coalitions, as effective as they might be, come with a host of difficulties. One of the most salient such difficulties is the presence of power imbalances among partners. By bringing together advocates representing many distinct interests operating in different contexts, they are likely to encounter many of the same challenges their members face in the broader lobbying environment: uneven resources, competition for attention to their core issues, and unequal perceptions of legitimacy. These conditions are likely to cause some organizations to be sidelined or feel tokenized in coalition negotiations. How, exactly, does this play out? To what degree might these imbalances affect coalition membership, durability, and advocacy? Similarly, are diverse coalitions that implement democratic leadership and decision-making structures more likely to be long lasting and facilitate more long-lasting policy change? These questions, too, represent important avenues for future research.

Finally, advocacy organizations often engage in "dual advocacy"—the practice of advocating on the same issue both individually and in coalition. Scholars have documented the prevalence of this behavior in the legislative setting (Baumgartner et al. 2009a; Mahoney and Baumgartner 2004). Dual advocacy is similarly common in the regulatory venue. For instance, more than 90 percent of the organizations under study in this book engaged in some level of dual advocacy—across nearly all major policy topics appearing in both subsets of the data and across agency rules with varying characteristics. Coupled with qualitative evidence from elite interviews conducted for this project, these trends suggest that dual advocacy is a necessary accompaniment to coalition work. Many of the organizational leaders and staffers that I spoke with emphasized the agenda limitations of coalitions; coalitions form around areas of shared interest, but many coalition members hold separate areas of interests beyond those that are addressed through their coalition work. Thus, organizations often advocate individually, expressing recommendations that are beyond the purview of their coalitional advocacy targeting the same policy. This dynamic represents an important and interesting pattern that should be explored in future research.

Closing Thought

For decades, scholars of organizational politics have decried bias in the "pressure group" system. In the famed words of E. E. Schattschneider, "the flaw in the pluralist heaven is that the heavenly chorus sings with a strong upper-class accent" (1960, 35). Schattschneider, of course, was—and still is—correct. Most policy change is incremental and favors the status quo: wealthy, elite interests (Baumgartner et al. 2009a). Groups that can afford to invest in repeated, consistent advocacy reign supreme (Drutman 2015). Each year, the amount of money spent on lobbying the American government increases exponentially—the vast majority of which comes from advocates for big business, industries, and general interest causes.[20]

But there is hope. In response to historic movements and greater investments in political organizing, the number of organizations advocating for historically marginalized communities is growing. Meanwhile, many policymakers *do* care about accounting for these communities' interests. One of the last agency officials I spoke with ended our conversation by asking me to encourage these organizations to submit more public comments: "We want to hear from them. We want to hear what they think we should do. Industry, they have our number. The more that the smaller groups talk to us, the more we can act to serve more people."[21] While existing research has reported that try as they might, these advocates rarely win, the story of this book offers a new and encouraging perspective. For those groups that often get the short end of the stick, building coalitions can help level the playing field. By building alliances, especially those that ascribe to the best practices of coalition work, social and economic justice organizations can reduce their individual limitations and expand their collective capacities, achieving credibility that they do not otherwise enjoy and championing more well-rounded and well-informed policy ideas. By working together, they can overcome many of the barriers to successful policy advocacy. Partnership is, indeed, powerful.

Acknowledgments

My first internship was with a civil rights organization. It was staffed by only two people. Each year, at its annual fundraiser, it raised a little over $150,000—most of its operating budget for the next twelve months. The executive director worked evenings and weekends to make sure that every community member who called their office received careful attention. They spent months preparing for their yearly trip to Washington—scheduling meetings with policy-makers, potential partners, and funders. At the time, I thought their efforts were futile. How could such a small operation make a difference? But it *did*. By offering voting guides, "Know Your Rights" workshops, and free legal aid, it helped its constituents become more politically aware and feel more safe and secure. And its consistent political advocacy, together with that of its allies, slowly chipped away at harmful policies that infringed on the civil rights of a newly marginalized community in the United States: Muslim Americans. Years later, as a graduate student, I decided to start a project that would help organizations like it learn which of its tactics were most effective, and why. This book is the culmination of that work and before beginning, I owe enormous thanks to the superwomen who ran that organization—who showed me, firsthand, just how much their work mattered and who helped my own family when we were in need.

My second and greatest debt of gratitude is to my graduate adviser, the inimitable Bryan Jones. Bryan took a chance on me many years ago. I struggled in my early years of graduate school; I was asked to leave my PhD program not once, but twice! But Bryan fought for me. Each week, he told me that he believed in me and encouraged me to keep working hard. He pushed me to think big, take on challenging tasks (like reading and hand coding tens of thousands of regulatory documents), and celebrate each win. His mantra, "one paper, one point" is the driving force behind each of my projects—particularly this one. We spent years debating the theory and measurement behind each claim and concept I present in this book. Those conversations shaped my thinking, and I am extraordinarily thankful for his guidance. Most importantly, Bryan taught me to work to live—and not the other way around. He rarely worked on evenings or weekends and, twice a year, dragged his graduate students out to his hill country ranch (the Rock n' Cedar) for a much-needed break. Some of my fondest memories are sitting by the creek on his property, surrounded by friends. I am grateful to have the greatest teacher and mentor a student could ask for.

I also owe thanks to many other incredible people: Amber Boydstun, whose spring 2012 undergraduate Policy Agenda-Setting class sparked my love for research; Rhonda Evans and David Leal, whose generosity helped sustain this project at critical points; Shana Gadarian, who shepherded my transition to the tenure track and guided me through the early stages of writing this book with infinite patience and care; Hahrie Han, who welcomed me into her P3 Lab and offered invaluable comments—and unfailing support—in the final stages of my writing process; Beth Leech, who read many early drafts of this work and offered valuable advice; Eric McDaniel, who first encouraged me to collect the pilot data that transformed, over more than seven years, into the backbone of this book—and who has been my cheerleader and sounding board every step of the way; Brian Roberts, who spent years helping me hone the theories driving this book (by staring me down and refusing to accept my many half-baked ideas); Dara Strolovitch, whose work inspired this project and helped me find my place in this discipline—and whose encouragement to write the book I wanted to write (and not the one I thought I *should* write) is the reason this book exists; and Chris Wlezien, who helped me develop and validate many of the empirical strategies I put forth in this book.

While writing this book, I have been lucky to have the most kind and generous colleagues and friends. I won the lottery with my first academic position at Syracuse University. Writing this book would have been an infinitely more difficult task if not for the support of my colleagues and students at 'Cuse: Lamis Abdelaaty, Mark Brockway, Devin Caramma, Elizabeth Cohen, Adam Cucchiara, Nicholas D'Amico, Curtis Edmonds, Chris Faricy, Shana Gadarian, Liwu Gan, Ryan Griffiths, Seth Jolly, Sarah Jones, Minju Kim, Kaia Kirk, Dan McDowell, Jacquie Meyer, Sarah Pralle, Dennis Rasmussen, Grant Reeher, Brian Taylor, Emily Thorson, Brock Titlow, Greg Smith, Simon Weschle, Steven White, and Yael Zeira. And if winning the lottery once was not enough, my colleagues at Georgetown University made crossing the finish line of this book far less daunting. I am extraordinarily grateful to Tony

Arend, Mike Bailey, Laia Balcells, Chantal Berman, Nadia Brown, Amanda d'Urso, John Griffin, Alana Hendy, Jon Ladd, David Myles, Hans Noel, Mark Richardson, Jamil Scott, Joel Simmons, Lahra Smith, Michele Swers, and Tiago Ventura.

I am immensely thankful to the team at the University of Chicago Press, especially Sara Doskow, for her editorial guidance; Erika Barrios and Rosemary Frehe, for their editorial assistance; Beth Ina and Michaela Luckey, for shepherding my book through production and promotion; and the three anonymous reviewers of this book, whose thoughtful and thorough comments helped strengthen and polish this work in more ways than I can count (though any remaining errors are, of course, my own). I am also grateful to Cambridge University Press and Wiley Periodicals LLC for allowing me to reuse portions of the following materials, which have been reprinted with permission in this book:

Dwidar, Maraam A. 2022. "Coalitional Lobbying and Intersectional Representation in American Rulemaking." *American Political Science Review* 116 (1): 301–21.

Dwidar, Maraam A. 2022. "Diverse Lobbying Coalitions and Influence in Notice-and-Comment Rulemaking." *Policy Studies Journal* 50 (1): 199–240.

I am thankful, too, to Abe Barranca, Jane Booth-Tobin, Ross Buchanan, Alice Cavalieri, Alvaro Corral, Jordie Davies, Megan Dias, Alex Dildine, Lindsay Dun, Connor Dye, EJ Fagan, Klara Fredriksson, Guy Freeman, Iasmin Goes, Devin Green, Jae Yeon Kim, Chris Koski, Mary Kroeger, Neeley Lawrence, Stella Lee, Katie Madel, Katie Marchetti, Jereny Mendoza, Carolina Moehlecke, Philip Moniz, Rachel Navarre, God'swill Osa, Brooke Shannon, Kyle Shen, Lynsy Smithson-Stanley, JoBeth Surface-Shafran, Joe Tafoya, Laura Quaglia, Daniel Weitzel, Michelle Wolfe, Sam Workman, and Lizzy Zack for their many thoughtful comments, words of encouragement, and sanity checks over the years. I am especially grateful to Clare Brock, Calla Hummel, Jon Lewallen, and Trey Thomas, who have counseled me on the "hidden curriculum" of academia since my first day as a graduate student—and who helped me close the chapter on this book by offering advice on everything from reviewer comments to time management to indexing. I can only hope to pay their kindness forward. Audiences at Boston University; Johns Hopkins University; the University of California, Riverside; the University of California, Santa Barbara; the University of Maryland, College Park; the University of Texas at Arlington; Vanderbilt University; Virginia Commonwealth University; and West Virginia University asked insightful questions and offered instructive feedback that helped develop this book at critical points. I am grateful for their generosity. And most importantly, this book would not exist if not for the research assistance of eighteen truly amazing people: Lindsey Asis, Natalee Ball, Molly Beker, Hannah Bevers, Catherine Blair, Travis Clark, Bria Dononhue, John Flattery, Sreya Gandra, Devin Green, Sydney Gold, Mia Juliano, Bailey Klemm, Kris McDermott, Sydney Mike-Mayer, Tarika Nath, Emily Nguyen, and Stephanie Ward. Their meticulous work hand coding the data underlying this book began in 2015 and took more than seven years to complete. I am immensely appreciative of their time, effort, and dedication— and I am forever in their debt.

My friends and family have been ever patient throughout my journey of writing this book. For better or for worse, writing a book is hard, and over the years, my feelings toward this project oscillated between excitement, panic, pride, and absolute despondence. I am so very thankful to Kristina Black, Hilary Brennan-Marquez, James Burchill, Sarah Campbell, Alyssa DeForest, Sam Gass, Zainab Ghwari, Rawiya Kameir, Benjamin Laughlin, Nate Moyer, Alex Olsen, Jocelyn Perry, Nicky Pinko, Lauren Pinson, and Amelia Watts for humoring me, distracting me, and encouraging me to keep at it. My younger siblings, Yara, Rami, and Sundus Dwidar are the greatest gift I've ever received. Thank you for putting up with me. My parents, Azza Fahmi and Ahmed Dwidar encouraged me, from a very young age, to invest in my education. My achievements, however slight, are a testament to their determination. *Jazakum Allahu Khairan.* And through many long walks on the beach, early mornings at the dining table, and everything in between, Louise Whitaker and Brad Shaffer have been stalwart pillars of support. I am lucky to call them my family.

Finally, words cannot convey my love and gratitude for my husband, Robert Shaffer. I had the misfortune of writing most of this book in the middle of an uncertain global pandemic. But I had the great fortune of being with my favorite person while doing so. Each time I flopped down on the kitchen floor and insisted that I would never finish this book (which happened at least three or four times a week), Robert would sit down next to me and encourage me to keep my eyes on the prize. For the two years it took to write and revise this book, he kept me grounded with his infinite patience and optimism, made sure I ate my daily serving of leafy greens, and helped debug many a Python script. Robert, you're simply the best.

Appendixes

Appendix A: Perfectly Matching Phrase Example

The text below presents an example of a perfectly matching phrase identified between a public comment submitted by the Coalition Against Religious
Discrimination (CARD) and a final rule promulgated by the Department of
Veterans Affairs (VA) using the methodology described in chapter 3. The text
that appears is preprocessed; the perfectly matching phrase is underlined for
readability purposes.

Public Comment from CARD

shall not provid services <u>discrimin program beneficiari prospect program
beneficiari basi religion religi belief refus hold religi belief refus attend particip religi practice</u>.

Final Rule by VA

shall not, provid servic outreach activ relat services <u>discrimin program beneficiari prospect program beneficiari basi religion religi belief refus hold religi
belief refus attend particip religi practice</u>.

Appendix B: Intersectional Advocacy Example

The text below offers an example of intersectional advocacy observed in the *Collaborative Advocacy Dataset*. The comment, submitted by Federally Employed Women, advocates for a change to a proposed rule issued by the Small Business Administration. Portions of the comment that reference the intersectionally marginalized target population and the policy recommendation (both required for a value of 1 under the *intersectional advocacy* variable) are underlined for readability.

Public Comment from Federally Employed Women

The proposed regulations set forth a mechanism to determine whether women-owned businesses are underrepresented in a specific four-digit NAICS code in terms of contracts awarded and dollars of contracts awarded. If there is underrepresentation as determined by either calculation, the NAICS code becomes one in which a contracting officer, if other criteria are met, <u>may limit the competition by those small businesses owned by socially and economically disadvantaged women.</u> . . .

As the NPRM notes, the Central Contractor Registration (CCR) data used to make the determinations of underrepresentation and substantial underrepresentation, is, in all likelihood, incomplete, in that it only includes those women-owned businesses that choose to register in it. <u>Therefore, we recommend that SBA use in its disparity calculations, in addition to CCR data, other data sources that will allow for a more complete picture of the availability of women-owned businesses for competition.</u>

Appendix C: Summary Statistics, Chapters 3–5 and 7

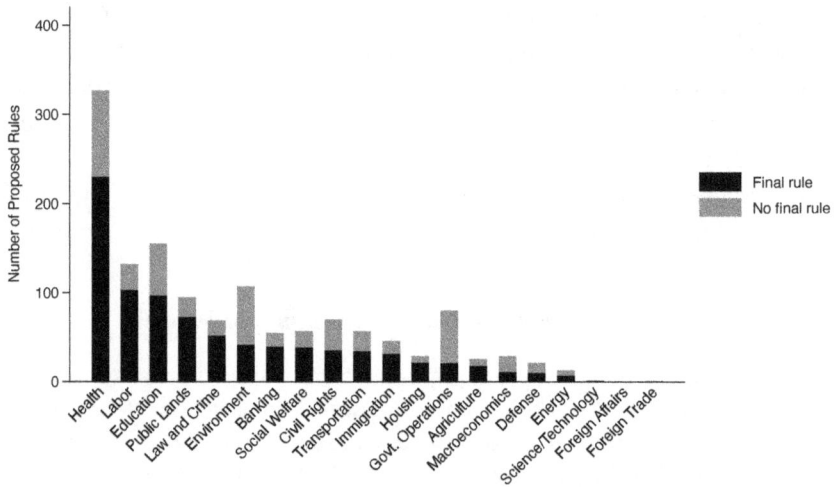

FIGURE A.1. Policy breakdown of proposed rules by final rule status (SEJ sample)

TABLE A.1A. Summary statistics, chapters 4, 5, and 7

Variable	Mean	Min.	Max.	Std. dev.	Obs.
Advocacy influence[a]	3.32	0	7.91	1.86	869
Representational diversity (Shannon's H)	0.68	0	1.00	0.35	1,545
Coalition size[a]	1.91	0	6.11	2.05	1,731
Financial capacity[a]	12.73	0	23.03	7.62	1,731
Proposed rule complexity	1.78	1	6.00	0.77	1,731
Proposed rule salience[a]	6.21	0	14.80	2.81	1,731
Proposed rule–comment similarity[a]	3.41	0	7.72	1.71	869
Comment length[a]	7.26	3.22	12.22	0.98	1,731

Note: The number of observations in the final column varies because of data limitations and coding procedures; the variables *advocacy influence* and *proposed rule–comment similarity* received values only in cases where a final rule was issued, and the variable *representational diversity* received a value only in cases of coalitions with fewer than 51 members. See chapter 3 for greater detail.
[a] Logged transformation of original variable. Importantly, because the variables *advocacy influence, financial capacity,* and *proposed rule–comment similarity* have observations with values of 0, simply taking their natural log would result in undefined observations. Thus, an $\ln(x + 1)$ transformation was applied to these variables. Table A.1b presents summary statistics for the original forms of these variables.

TABLE A.1B. Summary statistics, chapters 4, 5 and 7 (original forms)

Variable	Mean	Min.	Max.	Std. dev.	Obs.
Advocacy influence	98.09	0	2,710	194.61	869
Coalition size	42.99	1	450	78.07	1,731
Financial capacity	108,000,000	0	10,000,000,000	357,000,000	1,731
Proposed rule salience	33,317.14	1	2,682,626	171,096.80	1,731
Proposed rule–comment similarity	96.01	0	2,268	206.32	869
Comment length	2,830.11	25	202,594	9,465.45	1,731

Note: The number of observations in the final column varies because of data limitations and coding procedures; the variables *advocacy influence* and *proposed rule–comment similarity* received values only in cases where a final rule was issued. See chapter 3 for greater detail.

Appendix D: Models 1–2 Regression Table

TABLE A.2. Models 1–2 regression table

Dependent variable: advocacy influence	1	2
Coalition	0.029	
	(0.131)	
Formal coalition	0.251*	0.223*
	(0.073)	(0.072)
Coalition size	−0.006	−0.009
	(0.031)	(0.030)
Financial capacity	0.006	0.002
	(0.003)	(0.003)
Proposed rule complexity	−0.046	−0.084
	(0.040)	(0.043)
Proposed rule salience	−0.027*	−0.016
	(0.011)	(0.012)
Proposed rule–comment similarity	0.353*	0.313*
	(0.041)	(0.051)
Comment length	−0.009	0.008
	(0.052)	(0.066)
Intercept	0.032	0.144
	(0.246)	(0.304)
N	869	428

Note: Models 1 and 2 are generalized linear regression models (Gamma family, log link function) with group-clustered standard errors. The dependent variable is advocacy influence (see chapter 3). The observations appearing in Model 1 are all advocacy efforts corresponding to a published final rule (see chapter 3). The observations appearing in Model 2 are all advocacy efforts corresponding to a published final rule submitted by all coalitions.

*$p < .05$

Appendix E: Models 3–4 Regression Table

TABLE A.3. Models 3–4 regression table

Dependent variable: advocacy influence	3	4	3b	4b
Coalition	0.247		0.075	
	(0.163)		(0.217)	
Formal coalition	0.238*		0.203*	
	(0.094)		(0.095)	
Representational diversity (binary)	0.334*	1.167*	0.371*	1.150*
	(0.118)	(0.266)	(0.135)	(0.254)
Representational diversity (Shannon's H)			−0.188	0.095
			(0.217)	(0.408)
Strange bedfellows	−0.056	−0.170	−0.053	−0.155
	(0.105)	(0.304)	(0.107)	(0.300)
Coalition size	−0.069	−0.065	−0.052	−0.058
	(0.049)	(0.099)	(0.044)	(0.100)
Financial capacity	0.004	0.004	0.005	0.003
	(0.003)	(0.007)	(0.004)	(0.010)
Proposed rule complexity	−0.049	−0.048	−0.053	−0.045
	(0.048)	(0.095)	(0.050)	(0.096)
Proposed rule salience	−0.028	−0.087*	−0.029*	−0.086
	(0.014)	(0.042)	(0.014)	(0.043)
Proposed rule–comment similarity	0.349*	0.504*	0.349*	0.504*
	(0.047)	(0.100)	(0.047)	(0.101)

(*continues*)

Dependent variable: advocacy influence	3	4	3b	4b
Comment length	−0.008	0.562*	−0.006	0.556*
	(0.058)	(0.136)	(0.058)	(0.142)
Intercept	−0.259	−2.289	−0.121	−2.267
	(0.308)	(0.864)	(0.322)	(0.887)
N	623	127	623	127

Note: Models 3 and 4 are generalized linear regression models (Gamma family, log link function) with group-clustered standard errors. Models 3b and 4b are ordinary least squares linear regression models with group-clustered standard errors. In all four models, the dependent variable is advocacy influence (see chapter 3). The observations appearing in Model 3 and 3b are all advocacy efforts corresponding to a published final rule and, in cases of coalitions, all coalitions with fewer than fifty-one members (see chapter 3). The observations appearing in Models 4 and 4b are all advocacy efforts corresponding to a published final rule submitted by formalized coalitions with fewer than fifty-one members. Importantly, Models 3b and 4b do not satisfy the minimum conditions for maximum likelihood estimation (MLE) (sample size of two hundred or greater, at least twenty observations per parameter). Their sample sizes (in both cases, $N = 127$) are considerably smaller than those of other models in this table. Thus, I have estimated these models using ordinary least squares (OLS) linear regression—an approach that is considered similar and superior to MLE in cases of small samples (Long 1997).

Appendix F: Model 3 Membership Cut-off Reestimation

TABLE A.4. Model 3 membership cut-off reestimation

Dependent variable: advocacy influence	45	40	35
Coalition	0.220	0.165	0.147
	(0.162)	(0.162)	(0.160)
Formal coalition	0.245*	0.202*	0.207*
	(0.093)	(0.085)	(0.082)
Representational diversity	0.298*	0.285*	0.281*
	(0.115)	(0.117)	(0.119)
Strange bedfellows	−0.060	−0.048	−0.051
	(0.103)	(0.094)	(0.085)
Coalition size	−0.063	−0.033	−0.024
	(0.049)	(0.046)	(0.046)
Financial capacity	0.004	0.005	0.005
	(0.003)	(0.003)	(0.003)
Proposed rule complexity	−0.042	−0.023	−0.021
	(0.046)	(0.044)	(0.044)
Proposed rule salience	−0.026	−0.026	−0.024
	(0.014)	(0.014)	(0.014)
Proposed rule–comment similarity	0.344*	0.328*	0.325*
	(0.046)	(0.044)	(0.043)
Comment length	−0.002	0.005	0.002
	(0.057)	(0.058)	(0.059)
Intercept	−0.277	−0.306	0.292
	(0.306)	(0.322)	(0.324)
N	621	610	603

Note: Generalized linear regression models (Gamma family, log link function) with group-clustered standard errors. The dependent variable is advocacy influence (see chapter 3). The observations appearing in these reestimations of Model 3 are all advocacy efforts corresponding to a published final rule and, in cases of coalitions, all coalitions with fewer than forty-five, forty, and thirty-five members, respectively.
*$p < .05$

Appendix G: Model 4 Membership Cut-off Reestimation

TABLE A.5. Model 4 membership cut-off reestimation

Dependent variable: advocacy influence	45	40	35
Representational diversity	1.108*	1.182*	1.227*
	(0.257)	(0.266)	(0.269)
Strange bedfellows	−0.188	−0.182	−0.144
	(0.295)	(0.301)	(0.304)
Coalition size	−0.050	−0.086	−0.045
	(0.102)	(0.114)	(0.120)
Financial capacity	0.006	0.008	0.011
	(0.007)	(0.007)	(0.008)
Proposed rule complexity	−0.024	−0.025	−0.033
	(0.092)	(0.095)	(0.089)
Proposed rule salience	−0.079	−0.084	−0.068
	(0.042)	(0.042)	(0.044)
Proposed rule–comment similarity	0.476*	0.456*	0.447*
	(0.103)	(0.105)	(0.104)
Comment length	0.598*	0.644*	0.619*
	(0.139)	(0.150)	(0.150)
Intercept	−2.543*	−2.775*	−2.806*
	(0.881)	(0.914)	(0.932)
N	126	120	117

Note: Ordinary least squares linear regression models with group-clustered standard errors. The dependent variable is advocacy influence (see chapter 3). The observations appearing in these reestimations of Model 4 are all advocacy efforts corresponding to a published final rule submitted by formalized coalitions with fewer than forty-five, forty, and thirty-five members, respectively. Importantly, these models do not satisfy the minimum conditions for maximum likelihood estimation (MLE) (sample size of two hundred or greater, at least twenty observations per parameter). Their sample sizes (ranging from 117 to 126) are considerably smaller than those of previous models. Thus, I have estimated these models using ordinary least squares (OLS) linear regression—an approach that is considered similar and superior to MLE in cases of small samples (Long 1997).
*$p < .05$

Appendix H: Summary Statistics, Chapter 6

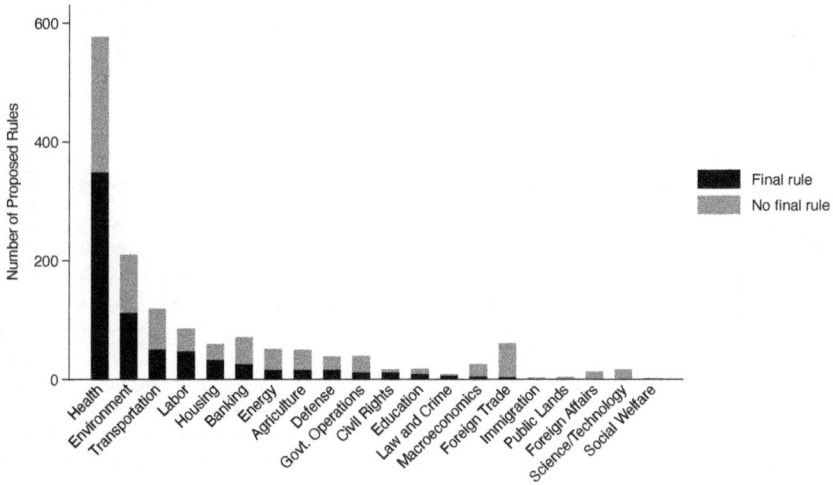

FIGURE A.2. Policy breakdown of proposed rules by final rule status (Mainstream sample)

TABLE A.6A. Summary statistics, chapter 6

Variable	Mean	Min.	Max.	Std. dev.	Obs.
Advocacy influence[a]	3.79	0	8.75	1.82	739
Representational diversity (Shannon's H)	0.66	0	1.00	0.43	1,671
Coalition size[a]	1.09	0	6.21	1.50	1,849
Financial capacity[a]	6.48	0	23.06	8.94	1,849
Proportion business	0.02	0	1.00	0.09	1,671
Proposed rule complexity	1.29	1	4.00	0.52	1,849
Proposed rule salience[a]	5.54	0	15.28	3.04	1,849
Proposed rule–comment similarity[a]	3.27	0	8.74	2.02	739
Comment length[a]	7.27	3.71	12.42	1.16	1,849

Note: The number of observations in the final column varies because of data limitations and coding procedures. The variables *advocacy influence* and *proposed rule–comment similarity* received values only in cases where a final rule was issued, and the variables *representational diversity* and *proportion business* received values only in cases of coalitions with fewer than fifty-one members. See chapter 3 for greater detail.
[a] Logged transformation of original variable. Importantly, because the variables *advocacy influence, financial capacity,* and *proposed rule–comment similarity* have observations with values of 0, simply taking their natural log would result in undefined observations. Thus, an $\ln(x + 1)$ transformation was applied to these variables. Table A.6b presents summary statistics for the original forms of these variables.

TABLE A.6B. Summary statistics, chapter 6 (original forms)

Variable	Mean	Min.	Max.	Std. dev.	Obs.
Advocacy influence	177.77	0	6,286	492.91	739
Coalition size	14.07	1	500	42.79	1,849
Financial capacity	93,900,000	0	10,300,000,000	339,000,000.00	1,849
Proposed rule salience	61,437.84	0	4,343,039	376,635.60	1,849
Proposed rule-comment similarity	131.54	0	6,294	392.88	739
Comment length	3,711.03	41	249,742	13,306.34	1,849

Note: The number of observations in the final column varies because of data limitations and coding procedures; the variables *advocacy influence* and *proposed rule–comment similarity* received values only in cases where a final rule was issued. See chapter 3 for greater detail.

Appendix I: Models 5–9 Regression Table

TABLE A.7. Models 5–9 regression table

Dependent variable: advocacy influence	5	6	7	8	9
Coalition	0.083		0.003		
	(0.137)		(0.204)		
Formal coalition	0.077	0.050	0.107	0.056	
	(0.087)	(0.090)	(0.094)	(0.109)	
Representational diversity			−0.084	−0.082	−0.884
			(0.121)	(0.110)	(0.548)
Strange bedfellows			0.054	0.080	0.084
			(0.123)	(0.125)	(0.522)
Coalition size	−0.036	−0.015	−0.057	−0.028	0.033
	(0.029)	(0.029)	(0.052)	(0.046)	(0.229)
Financial capacity	0.002	0.002	0.006	0.005	0.315
	(0.004)	(0.004)	(0.007)	(0.008)	(0.242)
Proposed rule complexity	0.017	0.000	0.021	0.012	0.399
	(0.061)	(0.106)	(0.065)	(0.140)	(0.312)
Proposed rule salience	−0.044*	−0.043*	−0.047*	−0.053*	−0.186*
	(0.009)	(0.009)	(0.010)	(0.012)	(0.056)
Proposed rule–comment similarity	0.169*	0.126*	0.158*	0.104*	0.123
	(0.033)	(0.040)	(0.033)	(0.037)	(0.172)

(continues)

Dependent variable: advocacy influence	5	6	7	8	9
Comment length	0.169*	0.199*	0.170*	0.189*	1.031*
	(0.038)	(0.045)	(0.035)	(0.044)	(0.287)
Intercept	−0.382	−0.414	−0.242	−0.221	−9.275
	(0.257)	(0.321)	(0.250)	(0.309)	(5.059)
N	739	279	605	221	106

Note: Models 5, 6, 7, and 8 are generalized linear regression models (Gamma family, log link function) with group-clustered standard errors. Model 9 is an ordinary least squares linear regression model with group-clustered standard errors. In all five models, the dependent variable is advocacy influence (see Chapter 3). The observations appearing in Model 5 are all advocacy efforts corresponding to a published final rule. The observations appearing in Model 6 are all advocacy efforts corresponding to a published final rule submitted by coalitions. The observations appearing in Model 7 are all advocacy efforts corresponding to a published final rule and, in cases of coalitions, all coalitions with fewer than fifty-one members (see chapter 3). The observations appearing in Model 8 are all advocacy efforts corresponding to a published final rule submitted by coalitions of fewer than fifty-one members. The observations appearing in Model 9 are all advocacy efforts corresponding to a published final rule submitted by formalized coalitions of fewer than fifty-one members. Importantly, Model 9 does not satisfy the minimum conditions for maximum likelihood estimation (MLE) (sample size of two hundred or greater, at least twenty observations per parameter). Its sample size (N=106) is considerably smaller than those of previous models. Thus, I have estimated this model using ordinary least squares (OLS) linear regression—an approach that is considered similar and superior to MLE in cases of small samples (Long 1997).

*$p < .05$

Appendix J: Models 7–9 Regression Table (Diversity Indices Included)

TABLE A.8. Models 7–9 regression table (diversity indices included)

Dependent variable: advocacy influence	7	8	9
Coalition	−0.218		
	(0.365)		
Formal coalition	0.093	0.044	
	(0.097)	(0.113)	
Representational diversity (binary)	−0.040	−0.042	−0.919
	(0.120)	(0.116)	(0.521)
Representational diversity (Shannon's H)	−0.260	−0.234	0.242
	(0.383)	(0.418)	(1.325)
Strange bedfellows	0.113	0.136	0.042
	(0.198)	(0.217)	(0.641)
Coalition size	−0.058	−0.028	0.031
	(0.052)	(0.047)	(0.224)
Financial capacity	0.007	0.006	0.315
	(0.006)	(0.008)	(0.241)
Proposed rule complexity	0.018	0.002	0.396
	(0.068)	(0.150)	(0.322)
Proposed rule salience	−0.047*	−0.053*	−0.185*
	(0.011)	(0.012)	(0.059)
Proposed rule-comment similarity	0.158*	0.105*	0.120
	(0.033)	(0.038)	(0.177)

(*continues*)

TABLE A.8. (continued)

Dependent variable: advocacy influence	7	8	9
Comment length	0.170*	0.189*	1.023*
	(0.035)	(0.044)	(0.291)
Intercept	−0.022	−0.214	−9.215
	(0.477)	(0.315)	(5.103)
N	605	221	106

Note: Models 7 and 8 are generalized linear regression models (Gamma family, log link function) with group-clustered standard errors. Model 9 is an ordinary least squares linear regression model with group-clustered standard errors. In all three models, the dependent variable is advocacy influence (see Chapter 3). The observations appearing in Model 7 are all advocacy efforts corresponding to a published final rule and, in cases of coalitions, all coalitions with fewer than fifty-one members (see chapter 3). The observations appearing in Model 8 are all advocacy efforts corresponding to a published final rule submitted by coalitions of fewer than fifty-one members. The observations appearing in Model 9 are all advocacy efforts corresponding to a published final rule submitted by formalized coalitions of fewer than fifty-one members. Importantly, Model 9 does not satisfy the minimum conditions for maximum likelihood estimation (MLE) (sample size of two hundred or greater, at least twenty observations per parameter). Its sample size ($N = 106$) is considerably smaller than those of previous models. Thus, I have estimated this model using ordinary least squares (OLS) linear regression—an approach that is considered similar and superior to MLE in cases of small samples (Long 1997).

*$p < .05$

Appendix K: Model 7 Membership Cut-off Reestimation

TABLE A.9. Model 7 membership cut-off reestimation

Dependent variable: advocacy influence	45	40	35
Coalition	0.000	−0.006	0.003
	(0.205)	(0.205)	(0.210)
Formal coalition	0.107	0.118	0.112
	(0.099)	(0.103)	(0.110)
Representational diversity	−0.084	−0.090	−0.080
	(0.121)	(0.121)	(0.124)
Strange bedfellows	0.053	0.063	−0.014
	(0.147)	(0.153)	(0.166)
Coalition size	−0.057	−0.071	−0.067
	(0.064)	(0.072)	(0.072)
Financial capacity	0.006	0.008	0.008
	(0.007)	(0.007)	(0.007)
Proposed rule complexity	0.021	0.026	0.022
	(0.065)	(0.065)	(0.067)
Proposed rule salience	−0.048*	−0.048*	−0.048*
	(0.011)	(0.011)	(0.011)
Proposed rule–comment similarity	0.158*	0.159*	0.161*
	(0.033)	(0.033)	(0.035)
Comment length	0.170*	−0.170*	0.169*
	(0.035)	(0.035)	(0.035)
Intercept	−0.247	−0.243	−0.255
	(0.248)	(0.246)	(0.259)
N	597	593	586

Note: Generalized linear regression models (Gamma family, log link function) with group-clustered standard errors. The dependent variable is advocacy influence (see chapter 3). The observations appearing in these reestimations of Model 7 are all advocacy efforts corresponding to a published final rule and, in cases of coalitions, all coalitions with forty-five, forty, and thirty-five members or fewer, respectively.
$*p < .05$

Appendix L: Model 8 Membership Cut-off Reestimation

TABLE A.10. Model 8 membership cut-off reestimation

Dependent variable: advocacy influence	45	40	35
Formal coalition	0.048	0.058	0.057
	(0.116)	(0.120)	(0.125)
Representational diversity	−0.081	−0.084	−0.079
	(0.109)	(0.109)	(0.111)
Strange bedfellows	0.092	0.098	0.038
	(0.134)	(0.138)	(0.150)
Coalition size	−0.036	−0.050	−0.040
	(0.053)	(0.059)	(0.061)
Financial capacity	0.006	0.007	0.007
	(0.008)	(0.008)	(0.008)
Proposed rule complexity	0.020*	0.032	0.018
	(0.147)	(0.149)	(0.160)
Proposed rule salience	−0.054*	−0.054*	−0.053*
	(0.012)	(0.012)	(0.013)
Proposed rule–comment similarity	0.104*	0.104*	0.105*
	(0.038)	(0.038)	(0.042)
Comment length	0.191*	0.190*	0.191*
	(0.044)	(0.044)	(0.045)
Intercept	−0.234	−0.241	−0.247
	(0.312)	(0.315)	(0.337)
N	213	209	202

Note: Generalized linear regression models (Gamma family, log link function) with group-clustered standard errors. The dependent variable is advocacy influence (see chapter 3). The observations appearing in these reestimations of Model 8 are all advocacy efforts corresponding to a published final rule submitted by coalitions with forty-five, forty, and thirty-five members or fewer, respectively.
*$p < .05$

Appendix M: Model 9 Membership Cut-off Reestimation

TABLE A.11. Model 9 membership cut-off reestimation

Dependent variable: advocacy influence	45	40	35
Representational diversity	−0.801	−0.801	−0.835
	(0.509)	(0.509)	(0.517)
Strange bedfellows	0.246	0.246	0.249
	(0.817)	(0.817)	(0.820)
Coalition size	−0.139	−0.139	−0.117
	(0.555)	(0.555)	(0.587)
Financial capacity	0.316	0.316	0.314
	(0.243)	(0.243)	(0.249)
Proposed rule complexity	0.542	0.542	0.481
	(0.450)	(0.450)	(0.540)
Proposed rule salience	−0.194*	−0.194*	−0.195*
	(0.055)	(0.055)	(0.055)
Proposed rule–comment similarity	0.104	0.104	0.113
	(0.177)	(0.177)	(0.206)
Comment length	1.042*	1.042*	1.025*
	(0.293)	(0.293)	(0.302)
Intercept	−9.204	−9.204	−8.998
	(5.042)	(5.042)	(5.282)
N	98	98	94

Note: Ordinary least squares linear regression models with group-clustered standard errors. The dependent variable is advocacy influence (see chapter 3). The observations appearing in these reestimations of Model 9 are all advocacy efforts corresponding to a published final rule submitted by formalized coalitions with forty-five, forty, and thirty-five members or fewer, respectively. Importantly, these models do not satisfy the minimum conditions for maximum likelihood estimation (MLE) (sample size of two hundred or greater, at least twenty observations per parameter). Its sample size ($N = 106$) is considerably smaller than those of previous models. Thus, I have estimated this model using ordinary least squares (OLS) linear regression—an approach that is considered similar and superior to MLE in cases of small samples (Long 1997).
*$p < .05$

Appendix N: Models 7–9 Regression Table (Proportion Business)

TABLE A.12. Models 7–9 regression table (proportion business)

Dependent variable: advocacy influence	7	8	9
Coalition	−0.001		
	(0.209)		
Formal coalition	0.041	−0.005	
	(0.099)	(0.115)	
Representational diversity	−0.133	−0.125	−1.145
	(0.127)	(0.118)	(0.661)
Strange bedfellows	0.135	0.157	0.323
	(0.144)	(0.156)	(0.668)
Proportion business	0.566*	0.519*	1.190*
	(0.220)	(0.247)	(0.929)
Coalition size	−0.070	−0.042	−0.032
	(0.056)	(0.050)	(0.278)
Financial capacity	0.006	0.005	0.326
	(0.007)	(0.008)	(0.252)
Proposed rule complexity	0.027	0.022	0.386
	(0.064)	(0.140)	(0.307)
Proposed rule salience	−0.048*	−0.053*	−0.182*
	(0.010)	(0.012)	(0.052)
Proposed rule–comment similarity	0.159*	0.106*	0.140
	(0.033)	(0.038)	(0.182)

(*continues*)

Dependent variable: advocacy influence	7	8	9
Comment length	0.174*	0.201*	1.060*
	(0.035)	(0.044)	(0.281)
Intercept	−0.234	−0.284	−9.605
	(0.260)	(0.297)	(5.183)
N	605	221	106

Note: Models 7 and 8 are generalized linear regression models (Gamma family, log link function) with group-clustered standard errors. Model 9 is an ordinary least squares linear regression model with group-clustered standard errors. In all three models, the dependent variable is advocacy influence (see chapter 3). The observations appearing in Model 7 are all advocacy efforts corresponding to a published final rule and, in cases of coalitions, all coalitions with fewer than fifty-one members (see chapter 3). The observations appearing in Model 8 are all advocacy efforts corresponding to a published final rule submitted by coalitions of fewer than fifty-one members. The observations appearing in Model 9 are all advocacy efforts corresponding to a published final rule submitted by formalized coalitions of fewer than fifty-one members. Importantly, Model 9 does not satisfy the minimum conditions for maximum likelihood estimation (MLE) (sample size of two hundred or greater, at least twenty observations per parameter). Its sample size ($N = 106$) is considerably smaller than those of previous models. Thus, I have estimated this model using ordinary least squares (OLS) linear regression—an approach that is considered similar and superior to MLE in cases of small samples (Long 1997).

*$p < .05$

Appendix O: Models 10–11 Regression Table

TABLE A.13. Models 10–11 regression table

Dependent variable: intersectional advocacy	10	11
Coalition	1.174*	1.163*
	(0.410)	(0.404)
Coalition size	−0.001	0.003
	(0.095)	(0.094)
Financial capacity	0.021*	0.024*
	(0.010)	(0.011)
Intersectional mission	0.657	0.625
	(0.400)	(0.417)
Paying membership		−0.120
		(0.213)
Proposed rule complexity	−0.093	−0.096
	(0.082)	(0.081)
Proposed rule salience	0.003	0.002
	(0.023)	(0.024)
Intercept	−1.820*	−1.792*
	(0.288)	(0.292)
N	1,731	1,731

Note: Generalized linear regression models (Gamma family, log link function) with group-clustered standard errors. The dependent variable is the occurrence of intersectional advocacy (see chapter 3). The observations appearing in Models 10 and 11 are all advocacy efforts in the SEJ data (see chapter 3).
$^*p < .05$

Appendix P: Models 1–3 Regression Table (Tribes Excluded)

TABLE A.14. Models 1–3 regression table (tribes excluded)

Dependent variable: advocacy influence	1	2	3
Coalition	−0.016		0.272
	(0.161)		(0.188)
Formal coalition	0.206*	0.209*	0.116*
	(0.072)	(0.079)	(0.115)
Representational diversity			0.356*
			(0.180)
Strange bedfellows			−0.030
			(0.118)
Coalition size	0.007	0.006	−0.098
	(0.038)	(0.040)	(0.064)
Financial capacity	0.007	0.012	0.010
	(0.010)	(0.011)	(0.012)
Proposed rule complexity	−0.050	−0.070	−0.055
	(0.049)	(0.059)	(0.056)
Proposed rule salience	−0.031*	−0.026	−0.034*
	(0.012)	(0.016)	(0.016)
Proposed rule–comment similarity	0.374*	0.362*	0.377*
	(0.055)	(0.064)	(0.069)
Comment length	−0.049	−0.044	−0.060
	(0.063)	(0.085)	(0.074)
Intercept	0.281	0.200	−0.023
	(0.272)	(0.340)	(0.331)
N	562	336	445

Note: Generalized linear regression models (Gamma family, log link function) with group-clustered standard errors. The dependent variable is advocacy influence (see chapter 3). The observations appearing in Model 1 are all advocacy efforts corresponding to a published final rule, excluding observations by Native American tribes. The observations appearing in Model 2 are all advocacy efforts corresponding to a published final rule submitted by coalitions, excluding observations by Native American tribes. The observations appearing in Model 3 are all advocacy efforts corresponding to a published final rule and, in cases of coalitions, all coalitions with fewer than fifty-one members (see chapter 3), excluding Native American tribes.
*$p < .05$

Appendix Q: Model 4 Means Comparison

TABLE A.15. Model 4 means comparison

Data	Mean of advocacy influence
All data	3.32
Tribes excluded	3.44

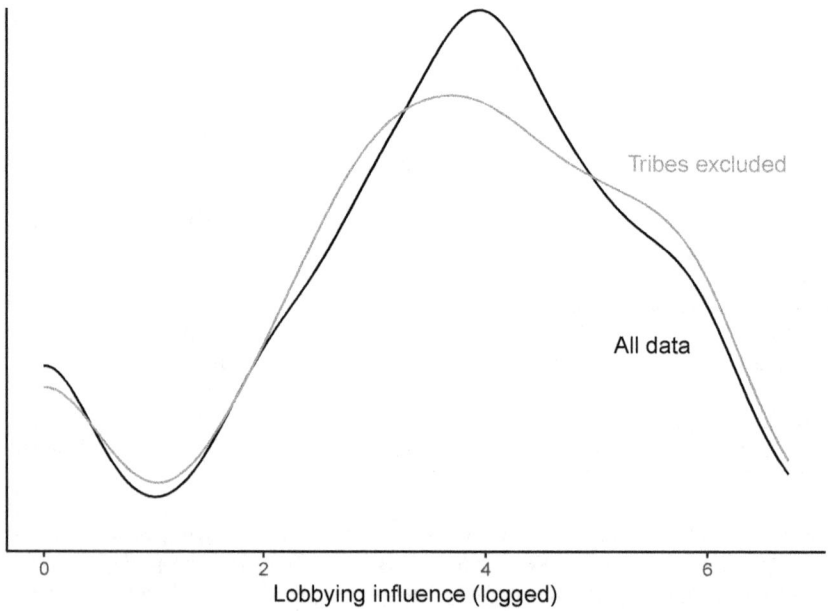

FIGURE A.3. Density of advocacy influence

Appendix R: Model 10 Regression Table (Tribes Excluded)

TABLE A.16. Model 10 regression table (tribes excluded)

Dependent variable: Intersectional Advocacy	10
Coalition	1.167*
	(0.482)
Coalition size	−0.001
	(0.108)
Financial capacity	0.012
	(0.202)
Intersectional mission	0.601
	(0.408)
Proposed rule complexity	−0.176
	(0.101)
Proposed rule salience	0.018
	(0.024)
Intercept	−1.577*
	(0.403)
N	1,269

Note: Generalized linear regression model (Gamma family, log link function) with group-clustered standard errors. The dependent variable is the occurrence of intersectional advocacy (see chapter 3). The observations appearing in Model 10 are all advocacy efforts in the SEJ data (see chapter 3), excluding Native American tribes.

$^*p < .05$

Notes

Chapter One

1. Peter Slevin, "Blueprinting the Kansas Abortion-Rights Victory," *New Yorker*, August 7. 2022, https://www.newyorker.com/news/news-desk/blueprinting-the-kansas-abortion-rights-victory.

2. https://thehill.com/policy/energy-environment/410675-oil-industry-green-groups-join-to-oppose-trumps-ethanol-plan/.

3. Rick Rojas, "As the Flag Comes Down, 'Looking for a New Mississippi," *New York Times*, July 10, 2020, https://www.nytimes.com/2020/07/10/us/mississippi-confederate-flag.html.

4. "Congress Votes to Lift Ban on Pell Grants for People in Prison," Vera Institute of Justice, https://www.vera.org/newsroom/congress-votes-to-lift-ban-on-pell-grants-for-people-in-prison.

5. I define "social and economic justice organizations" as organizational advocates for historically marginalized communities, that is, those marginalized on the basis of gender, race, class, sexual orientation, or intersections thereof—a definition that is consistent with that of other scholars of social justice advocacy (Marchetti 2014; Strolovitch 2006, 2007).

6. Students Learn Students Vote, https://slsvcoalition.org.

7. Erin Fitzgerald, "Dangerous Loopholes Allow Facilities to Release Toxic, Unchecked Air Pollutants," Earthjustice, September 13, 2022, https://earthjustice.org/press/2022/dangerous-loopholes-allow-facilities-to-release-toxic-unchecked-air-pollutants; "Housing and Civil Rights Leaders Announce National Initiative to Increase Black Homeownership," National Fair Housing Alliance, June 18, 2021, https://nationalfairhousing.org/housing-and-civil-rights-leaders-announce-national-initiative-to-increase-black-homeownership/.

8. Marc Cooper, "Teamsters and Turtles: They're Together at Last," *Los Angeles Times*, December 2, 1999, https://www.latimes.com/archives/la-xpm-1999-dec-02-me-39707-story.html.

9. https://fee.org/articles/greens-and-big-industry-are-the-baptists-and-bootleggers-of-climate-policy/.

10. Data compiled by the author from LexisNexis records, https://www.lexisnexis.com.

11. https://www.prnewswire.com/news-releases/georgia-power-and-coalition-of-georgia-businesses-urge-passage-of-hate-crimes-legislation-301072159.html.

12. https://www.washingtonpost.com/gender-identity/how-many-women-of-color-have-to-cry-top-feminist-organizations-are-plagued-by-racism-20-former-staffers-say/.

13. Pew Research Center Report, July 22, 2019, https://www.pewresearch.org/politics/2019/07/22/how-americans-see-problems-of-trust/.

14. Elizabeth Rush, "I Would Never Have Bought This Home If I Knew It Flooded," *New York Times*, April 11, 2022, https://www.nytimes.com/2022/04/11/opinion/climate-change-flooding.html.

Chapter Two

1. Peter Slevin, "Blueprinting the Kansas Abortion-Rights Victory,"1. https://www.civisana lytics.com/wp content/uploads/2020/06/Public_Opinion_Data_BLM_CombinedCrosstabs_ALL. pdf https://www.nytimes.com/interactive/2020/07/03/us/george-floyd-protests-crowd-size.html.

2. "The Movement for Black Lives Celebrates BREATHE Act Anniversary," M4BL, July 7, 2021, https://m4bl.org/press/the-movement-for-black-lives-celebrates-breathe-act-anniversary/.

3. Lori Villarosa, Muhammed Lamin Saidykhan, Tynesha McHarris, and Fernanda Lopes, "Two Years after 2020's Global Movement for Racial Justice, Where Are We Now?," *Alliance*, May 24, 2022, https://www.alliancemagazine.org/analysis/racial-justice-after-2020-where-are-we-now/

4. https://www.pewresearch.org/short-reads/2021/01/28/racial-ethnic-diversity-increases-yet -again-with-the-117th-congress/.

5. Data compiled by the author from CRP records, https://www.opensecrets.org.

6. As I described in chapter 1, social and economic justice groups are significantly less likely than their private and professional counterparts to employ lobbyists or a legal staff or have affiliated PACs. Scholars have suggested that this latter disparity in particular has been exacerbated by the Supreme Court's 2010 decision in *Citizens United v. FEC*, which overturned previous efforts to limit PAC money in electoral politics (Hertel-Fernandez and Skocpol 2015; Strolovitch and Forrest 2010).

7. https://about.bgov.com/news/staff-departures-hit-two-decade-high-as-congress-seeks-re medies/.

8. Nixon et al.'s "privileged" interest groups refer to Self-Regulating Organizations (SROs)— private organizations explicitly formed to regulate certain industries or professions and thought to enjoy special influence over bureaucratic policymaking.

9. https://home.treasury.gov/news/press-releases/Treasury-and-IRS-Announce-Families-of -Nearly-60-Million-Children-Receive-%2415-Billion-Dollars-in-First-Payments-of-Expanded -and-Newly-Advanceable-Child-Tax-Credit.

10. "Federal Rulemaking: Agencies Could Take Steps to Respond to Public Comments," GAO 13-21, December 2012, https://www.gao.gov/assets/660/651052.pdf.

11. Source: Executive Order 12866.

12. Soraya Nadia McDonald, "John Olivers Net Neutrality Rant May Have Caused FCC Site Crash," Washington Post, June 4, 2014, https://www.washingtonpost.com/news/morning-mix /wp/2014/06/04/john-olivers-net-neutrality-rant-may-have-caused-fcc-site-crash/.

13. Interview with an agency official with rulemaking duties, November 2022.

Chapter Three

1. "About the eRulemaking Initiative," Regulations.gov, https://www.regulations.gov/about.

2. These data (de-identified) and accompanying research documentation can be made avail- able to others upon reasonable request.

3. Historically marginalized communities in the United States are commonly defined as those that experience marginalizations on the bases of race, gender, class, sexual orientation, and intersections thereof (see chapter 1) (Marchetti 2014; Strolovitch 2006, 2007).

4. Importantly, in this work, I make a syntactic choice to refer to the name of two category codes marginally differently from the CRP. I term the CRP category code "welfare & social work" *anti-poverty* and the code "gay & lesbian rights & issues" *LGBTQ+ issues* in the pages to come.

5. Regrettably, the CRP's coding guide is not publicly available; these procedures were confirmed through direct correspondence with their research team.

6. "Interest Groups by Sector," Open Secrets, https://www.opensecrets.org/industries/slist.

7. The CRP's Bulk Data entry point is available at https://www.opensecrets.org/bulk-data. The codebook may be accessed by creating a Bulk Data account, navigating to the heading "Reference Data," and downloading the file titled "CRP_Categories.txt."

8. To ensure that the CRP's complete codebook remains available in its current form for future inquiries and replication efforts, an archived copy is available for direct download on my website: https://www.maraamdwidar.com/power-to-the-partners.html.

9. In total, the sampling frame for this sample consisted of approximately 1,400 groups. Duplicate observations were dropped before establishing the sampling frame.

10. The nature of the sampling procedure (based on CRP category codes, which are assigned consistently across registrants) prevents organizations in the social and economic justice–oriented sampling frame from appearing in the mainstream sampling frame, and vice versa.

11. In total, the sampling frame for this sample consisted of approximately 40,500 groups. Duplicate observations were dropped before establishing the sampling frame.

12. These sample sizes were chosen strategically, for practical reasons. To generate data for these samples of groups and corresponding text corpora, over nineteen thousand public comments were read and over twenty thousand coalition members were hand coded across seven attributes (producing approximately one hundred forty thousand observations). These sample sizes therefore represent a reasonable compromise between practical limitations and inferential strength.

13. Data compiled by the author from records provided by the Office of the Clerk, US House of Representatives, https://lobbyingdisclosure.house.gov.

14. In 2021, this threshold was raised to $14,000 in response to changes in the Consumer Price Index.

15. The organizational type coding scheme underlying these statistics is available in table 3.5.

16. The constituency coding scheme underlying these statistics is available in table 3.4.

17. Source: OpenSecrets, https://www.opensecrets.org.

18. The term *contender* refers to Schneider and Ingram's (1993) "emergent contenders"—groups that have been historically compromised in American politics but have steadily gained degrees of power and influence resembling those of mainstream lobbying organizations.

19. This API allows users to search for documents containing specific terms while controlling for submission dates, document types, and agencies.

20. The API only allows for free-text searches rather than searches by author or cosignatory. As a result, the search I describe yielded all public comments in which a given interest group was mentioned, rather than all comments authored by a given interest group. For reference, the initial searches for the 150 groups examined for this project returned roughly nineteen thousand comments, of which approximately 2,800 had been submitted by the organizations in my samples.

21. A "stem" is the root of a word that remains after suffixes are removed. For example, the words "eating," "eats," and "eaten" all share the same stem: "eat." Stemming words in a corpus allows for the grouping of words that share a common meaning but are superficially different (Porter 1980; Grimmer and Stewart 2013).

22. A "stop word" is a word that primarily serves a grammatical purpose and otherwise does not convey meaning (Grimmer and Stewart 2013). Examples include "a," "and," "but," "how," "or," and "what."

23. Data on the social and economic justice sample (SEJ) contained information on 1,731 public comments submitted on 1,243 proposed rules issued by seventy-three federal agencies. Of these proposed agency actions, as of September 2022, 869 corresponded to a published final rule. Data on the mainstream sample contained information on 1,849 comments submitted on 1,674 proposed rules issued by eighty-six federal agencies. Of these proposed agency actions, as of September 2022, 739 corresponded to a published final rule. Additionally, approximately three thousand rules are published yearly in the *Federal Register*, the official publication for activities of the federal bureaucracy, and there are between 250 and four hundred federal agencies in existence.

24. David E. Lewis and Jennifer L. Selin, *Sourcebook of United States Executive Agencies* (Washington, DC: Administrative Conference of the United States, 2012).

25. A figure depicting the policy breakdown of these proposed rules by the status of the corresponding final rule—as of September 2022—is available in appendix C.

26. The reader may be aware that federal agencies are required to publish their responses to "significant" comments as a part of each final rule (Potter 2019; West 2004). These responses tersely summarize the key points of the comments and describe whether and why they have chosen to adopt or disregard the comment's recommendations. Critically, the publication of these responses as a part of final agency rules poses a measurement concern for this variable, as the inclusion of the agency response—which in some cases provides a summary of comments' recommendations—could potentially contribute to an overestimation of the dependent variable. To ameliorate this concern, I execute a series of robustness checks evaluating this possibility in chapters 5 and 6. Their outcomes demonstrate that there is little cause for concern regarding the possibility of this language contributing to an overestimation of this variable. Additionally, because of my chosen operationalization, my analyses will not capture cases where a final rule was not issued but where a comment sought to "kill" the rule and thus succeeded in achieving its goal. I elaborate on this dynamic at greater length in the coming chapters.

27. These decision rules are straightforward to implement and existing research reports that they are reliable for detecting text reuse in policy documents (Lyon, Malcolm, and Dickerson 2001; Clough and Stevenson 2011; Kroeger 2016).

28. This is the minimum string length considered to be a match.

29. This is the maximum number of nonmatches allowed between perfectly matching portions of a phrase.

30. This is the minimum percentage of perfect matches that a phrase can contain and be considered a match. Setting this value at 100 percent limits WCopyfind to returning only perfect matches.

31. These are words containing any characters other than letters, except for internal hyphens and apostrophes.

32. These are often nontextual items, including file names, URLs, or image data.

33. See appendix A for an example of a perfectly matching phrase identified using this methodology.

34. These examples derive from a public comment submitted by Federally Employed Women to the Small Business Association.

35. See appendix B for examples of intersectional policy recommendations observed in the data.

36. It is worth noting that coalitions may recur in the data; the same coalition can recur by offering public comment on multiple proposed rules.

37. This classification scheme was informed by the work of Strolovitch (2006, 2007). Additionally, these codes were assigned on the basis of the primary target population (i.e., constituency) served by each organization—not on the basis of organizational categories. For instance, a professional association serving women (such as the AAUW) would receive the constituency code "women." In ambiguous cases—that is, those in which multiple constituencies received equal weight in an organization's mission statement—the numerically lower constituency code was assigned. This "numerically lower constituency code" refers to the category with the lower numeric value, as each constituency category corresponded to a randomly assigned number code. This decision rule is a replication of the Policy Agendas Project's guidelines for common coding schema.

38. Alternative diversity indices include the non-normalized Shannon's H or the Herfindahl index. I selected normalized Shannon's H over these alternatives because of its greater sensitivity to changes in diversity (Boydstun, Bevan, and Thomas, 2014).

39. In this context, "attention" refers to the degree of representation of the ith constituency type among a coalition's membership.

40. Comments submitted by a single author were recorded as having no representational diversity. Additionally, it is worth noting that I chose to measure the presence of diversity—rather than the degree of diversity—because of existing research reporting a threshold effect relating to the entry of diversity to decision-making bodies (see Kastellec 2013), particularly in the context of lobbying coalitions (see Dwidar 2022a). However, as a robustness check, in all analyses to come, I will estimate models accounting for both the binary presence of diversity and the overall degree of diversity in coalition membership.

41. This coding scheme was informed by the work of Baumgartner et al. (2009a) and Hojnacki et al. (2015).

42. https://projects.propublica.org/nonprofits/.

43. In keeping with existing research (see Hojnacki et al. 2015), professional and occupational interests are classified under the category "professional association." Corporate and industry interests are classified under the category "business or business group."

44. Comments submitted by a single author received a value of 0.

45. Scholars have also evaluated interest groups' financial capacity through lobbying spending, often by way of independent expenditures. However, not all organizations choose to dedicate resources to lobbying or maintain Political Action Committees (PACs), and research on campaign finance has demonstrated that it is the threat of independent expenditures, rather than the expenditures themselves, that often drives lobbying influence (Werner and Coleman 2014). Total revenue reflects the scale of potential lobbying spending and is thus a more precise and direct measure of organizations' financial capacity.

46. Comments not submitted in coalitions were recorded as having one member.

47. As with my secondary dependent variable, I defined an "intersectionally marginalized population" as any population that included multiply disadvantaged subgroups of marginalized groups. In keeping with existing research, this definition included any combination of populations marginalized on the basis of gender, race, income, age, sexual orientation or identity, ability, and immigration/citizenship status (see Marchetti 2014; Strolovitch 2006, 2007).

48. This is according to the Policy Agendas Project's common policy coding scheme and determined by reading the summary of each rule.

Chapter Four

1. Amanda Seitz, "Monkeypox Cases Dropping, but Racial Disparities Growing," AP, September 7, 2022, https://apnews.com/article/monkeypox-health-government-and-politics-7343de5a b515b9f09a5862ca284b6ea2.

2. Jared Todd, "Human Rights Campaign Calls for Equitable Monkeypox (MPV) Response amidst Disturbing Report of Vaccine Disparities," Human Rights Campaign, August 12, 2022, https://www.hrc.org/press-releases/human-rights-campaign-calls-for-equitable-monkeypox -mpv-response-amidst-disturbing-reports-of-vaccine-disparities.

3. "NCDHHS Releases Monkeypox Case, Vaccine and Testing Demographic Report," North Carolina Department of Health and Human Services, August 10, 2022, https://www.ncdhhs .gov/news/press-releases/2022/08/10/ncdhhs-releases-monkeypox-case-vaccine-and-testing -demographic-report-shows-vaccine-racial.

4. https://hrc-prod-requests.s3-us-west-2.amazonaws.com/LGBTQ-Recommendations-Mon keypox-Recommendations.pdf.

5. Aris Folley, "Biden's Request for Emergency COVID, Monkeypox Funds Missing from Funding Bill," *The Hill*, September 7, 2022, https://thehill.com/homenews/senate/3662862-bidens -request-for-emergency-covid-monkeypox-funds-missing-from-funding-bill/.

6. https://www.who.int/news/item/28-11-2022-who-recommends-new-name-for-monkeypox -disease.

7. Elizabeth Bibi, "Kelly Robinson to Serve as President of the Human Rights Campaign," Human Rights Campaign, September 20, 2022, https://www.hrc.org/press-releases/kelley-robin son-to-serve-as-president-of-the-human-rights-campaign.

8. Interview with a program manager at an economic justice organization, February 2023.

9. As I described in chapter 3, these policy foci derive from the CRP's *category codes*— classifications of organizations' main policy emphases.

10. As I described in chapter 3, I assigned each proposed regulation appearing in the *Collaborative Advocacy Dataset* a major policy topic code according to the Policy Agendas Project's common coding scheme and guidelines.

11. More precisely, I rely on gamma regression models with log link functions. This modeling choice is appropriate because of the distribution of the dependent variable under study in this chapter and related chapters; this variable, textual similarity between comment–final rule pairs, is bound at 0. This condition rules out the use of simpler models—such as ordinary least squares linear regression—which require continuous dependent variables. Other aspects of the models I deploy, including sample size, further validate my modeling choice. For instance, statisticians encourage the use of MLE when the number of observations in the model is greater than 200 and when at least twenty observations per parameter are present (Long 1997). Throughout this book, the models in which I apply this approach generously satisfy these conditions.

12. Summary statistics pertaining to each of these variables are available in appendix C.

13. Using the dispersion parameter set using Stata defaults. More details are available at https://www.stata.com/support/faqs/statistics/gee/.

14. The corresponding regression table is available in appendix D. Due to the high prevalence of Native American tribes in my sample, I also estimated Model 1 excluding observations by Native American tribes. The results of this reestimation, available in appendix P, remain consistent with those presented in the main text. This reestimation should thus lend confidence

in the results presented above by demonstrating that they are not sensitive to the inclusion of Native American tribes in the data.

15. The corresponding regression table is available in appendix D. As with Model 1, because of the high prevalence of Native American tribes in the data, I reestimated this model excluding observations by Native American tribes. The results of this reestimation, available in appendix P, are consistent with those presented in the main text.

16. Interview with a cofounder of a formal coalition of social justice groups, February 2023.

17. Data compiled by the author from ProPublica records, https://projects.propublica.org/nonprofits/).

18. These levels of complexity were measured through the total number of distinct major policy topics encompassed by each proposed rule, according to the Policy Agendas Project's common coding scheme and coding guidelines. This procedure is described in greater detail in chapter 3.

19. See chapter 3 for a discussion of the operationalization of the policy salience variable.

20. Interview with a former communications director at a social justice organization, January 2023.

Chapter Five

1. "Governor Signs Landmark Energy Legislation, Establishing New Mexico as a National Leader in Renewable Transition Efforts," Office of the Governor Michelle Lujan Grisham, March 22, 2019, https://www.governor.state.nm.us/2019/03/22/governor-signs-landmark-energy-legislation-establishing-new-mexico-as-a-national-leader-in-renewable-transition-efforts/.

2. Interview with a former director of communications and strategy at the National Audubon Society, January 2023.

3. https://www.nmlegis.gov/Handouts/ALFC%20071823%20Item%204%20Strategic%20Plan%20for%20Expending%20Energy%20Transition%20Act%20(ETA)%20Funds.pdf.

4. U.S. Energy Information Administration 2021, https://www.eia.gov/state/analysis.php?sid=NM.

5. Interview with a current program manager at an economic justice organization, February 2023.

6. U.S. Small Business Administration 2023, https://www.sba.gov/federal-contracting/contracting-assistance-programs/women-owned-small-business-federal-contract-program.

7. Interview with a former director of communications and strategy at the National Audubon Society, January 2023.

8. Interview with a policy director at a racial justice organization, February 2023.

9. Interview with an agency official with rulemaking duties, February 2023.

10. Jason Brill, "Coalition Calls on FDA to Outline Meaningful Reforms in Announcement on Foods Program," January 30, 2023, *Quality Assurance and Food Safety*, https://www.qualityassurancemag.com/news/coalition-calls-onfda-to-outline-meaningful-reforms-in-announcement-on-foods-program/.

11. "Coalition Has Many Questions about How FDA Commissioner Will Protect Consumers with New Organizational Chart," *Food Safety News*, February 7, 2013, https://www.foodsafetynews.com/2023/02/coalition-has-many-questions-about-how-fda-commissioner-will-protect-consumers-with-new-organizational-chart/.

12. Rick Rojas, "As the Flag Comes Down, 'Looking for a New Mississippi,'" *New York Times*, July 10, 2020, https://www.nytimes.com/2020/07/10/us/mississippi-confederate-flag.html.

13. Interview with an agency official with rulemaking duties, April 2022.

14. Interview with an agency official with rulemaking duties, March 2023.

15. The correlation coefficient (Pearson's r) between the coalition-level variables *representational diversity* and *strange bedfellows* is 0.05.

16. As I described in chapter 3, these policy foci derive from the CRP's *category codes*—classifications of organizations' main policy emphases.

17. Using the dispersion parameter set using Stata defaults. More details are available at https://www.stata.com/support/faqs/statistics/gee/.

18. The corresponding regression table is available in appendix E. As with Models 1 and 2, because of the high prevalence of Native American tribes in my sample, I also estimated Model 3 excluding observations by Native American tribes. The results of this reestimation maintain support of the findings presented in-text and are available in appendix P.

19. The corresponding regression table is available in appendix E. It is important to note that this model does not satisfy the minimum conditions for maximum likelihood estimation (MLE) (sample size of 200 or greater, at least twenty observations per parameter). Its sample size ($N = 127$) is considerably smaller than those of previous models. Thus, I have estimated this model using ordinary least squares (OLS) linear regression—an approach that is considered similar and superior to MLE in cases of small samples (Long 1997). Further, I am unable to produce a reestimation of Model 4 excluding observations by Native American tribes (as provided for Model 3) because of its more limited sample size ($N = 43$) and concerns for statistical power. In lieu of this reestimation, I have produced a means comparison of advocacy influence (the dependent variable of the model) across the data appearing in Model 4 inclusive and exclusive of Native American tribes. This comparison, along with a density plot of the dependent variable respective to each dataset, is available in appendix Q. These descriptive statistics demonstrate that the dependent variable's values are not substantially different across the data inclusive and exclusive of Native American tribes and thus convey no reason to suspect that the model's results would be substantially different if tribes were excluded.

20. Interview with a policy director at a racial justice organization, February 2023.

21. These discussions are also applicable to the analyses of chapter 4, as the data underlying chapters 4 and 5 are identical.

22. See chapter 3 for a detailed explanation of the calculation of this index.

23. These levels of complexity were measured through the total number of distinct major policy topics encompassed by each proposed rule, according to the Policy Agendas Project's common coding scheme and coding guidelines. This procedure is described in greater detail in chapter 3.

24. Interview with a program director at a social justice organization, February 2023.

Chapter Six

1. Source: OpenSecrets, Top Lobbying Organizations, https://www.opensecrets.org/fede ral-lobbying/top-spenders?cycle=2022.

2. Interview with an agency official with rulemaking duties, March 2023.

3. Letter to Chiquita Brooks-LaSure, Administrator, Centers for Medicare and Medicaid Services, February 13, 2013, https://www.aafp.org/dam/AAFP/documents/advocacy/coverage /medicare/LT-CMS-MedicareAdvantageProposedRule2024-021323.pdf.

4. "A 7-Point Plan to Increase Black Homeownership by 3 Million Households by 2030," Black Homeownership Collaborative, https://nhc.org/wp-content/uploads/2021/06/Black-Homeowner ship-7-Point-Plan-FINAL-6-18-21-FINAL-1.pdf.

5. "Program Seeks to Add 3 Million Black Homeowners," Realtor Magazine, February 3, 2022, https://www.nar.realtor/magazine/real-estate-news/program-seeks-to-add-3-million-black-homeowners.

6. Source: OpenSecrets, Top Lobbying Organizations, https://www.opensecrets.org/federal-lobbying/top-spenders?cycle=2022.

7. See chapter 3 for a more detailed explanation of this definition and my sampling procedure.

8. Interview with a former communications director at an industry group, March 2022.

9. Timothy Cama, "Oil Industry, Green Groups Join to Oppose Trump's Ethanol Plan," *The Hill*, October 10, 2018, https://thehill.com/policy/energy-environment/410675-oil-industry-green-groups-join-to-oppose-trumps-ethanol-plan.

10. David Pitt, "Court Strikes Trump EPA Rule for Full-Year 15% Ethanol Sales," AP, July 2, 2021, https://apnews.com/article/courts-business-c64fc205ffe03a4848e2a55c5e4d16b4.

11. Interview with a program manager at an economic justice organization, February 2023.

12. A figure depicting the policy breakdown of these proposed rules by the status of the corresponding final rule—as of September 2022—is available in appendix H.

13. As I described in chapter 3, these policy areas derive from the CRP's *category codes*—classifications of organizations' main policy emphases. These policy areas are the categories appearing in table 6.2.

14. The correlation coefficient (Pearson's r) between the coalition-level variables *representational diversity* and *strange bedfellows* is 0.09.

15. Summary statistics pertaining to each of these variables are available in appendix H.

16. In this chapter, the variable *strange bedfellows* is defined as the occurrence of a coalition that unites mainstream advocates with organizations advocating on behalf of women, people of color, low-income people, LGBTQ+ individuals, and/or immigrant communities, according to the constituency coding scheme detailed in chapter 3.

17. The corresponding regression table is available in appendix I.

18. The corresponding regression table is available in appendix I.

19. The corresponding regression table is available in appendix I.

20. The results of these supplemental analyses (Models 8, 9) are available in appendix I.

21. The results of these reestimations are available in appendix J.

22. The variable *proportion business* is defined according to the coding scheme detailed in chapter 3 (see table 3.5).

Chapter Seven

1. It is worth nothing that while intersectionally marginalized communities *do* have shared interests with broader communities, many social and economic justice organizations do not approach their lobbying on broad issues with an intersectional lens (Brower 2024; Dwidar, Marchetti, and Strolovitch, forthcoming; English 2019, 2020; Marchetti 2014, 2019; Strolovitch 2006, 2007). Thus, their disproportionate focus on broader—more "winnable"—policy work causes the vast majority of these advocates to fall short in promoting the interests of their multiply marginalized constituencies (Brower 2024; Dwidar, Marchetti, and Strolovitch, forthcoming; Marchetti 2014, 2019).

2. This search was executed by building a query within Regulations.gov returning all comments containing the keyword "National Organization for Women" during the period in question (January 1, 2017 to December 31, 2020) and reviewing the content of each comment.

3. This subset was initially introduced in chapter 3 and corresponds to the sample of social and economic justice–oriented organizations under study in chapters 4 and 5.

4. Summary statistics pertaining to each of these variables are available in appendix C. See chapter 3 for a detailed description of the operationalization of the variable *intersectional mission*.

5. The corresponding regression table is available in appendix O. As with the analyses of chapters 4 and 5, because of the high prevalence of Native American tribes in this subset of the *Collaborative Advocacy Dataset*, I reestimated this model excluding observations by Native American tribes. The results of this reestimation, available in appendix R, maintain support of the findings presented in the main text. This reestimation should thus lend confidence in the results presented in the main text through its illustration that the results are not sensitive to the inclusion of Native American tribes in the data.

6. These levels of complexity were measured through the total number of distinct major policy topics encompassed by each proposed rule, according to the Policy Agendas Project's common coding scheme and coding guidelines. This procedure is described in greater detail in chapter 3.

7. I coded this variable by navigating to the website of each group in my sample and searching for whether or not they maintained a paying membership in the year of comment submission (e.g., by way of providing a login page for members, a page that encouraged visitors to "become a member," etc.) using archives of their organizational websites accessible through the Wayback Machine. If the group maintained a paying membership, I assigned the *paying membership* variable a value of 1; otherwise, I assigned it a value of 0.

8. The corresponding regression table is available in appendix O.

9. Janet Murguía, "Latino and Black Americans Are Allies in the Fight for Racial Justice," *The Hill*, June 12, 2020, https://thehill.com/opinion/civil-rights/502465-latinos-allies-are-fighting-for-social-and-economic-justice/.

10. Nikayla Jefferson, "It's Our Party Now," Sunrise Movement, November 7, 2020, https://www.sunrisemovement.org/movement-updates/its-our-party-now/.

11. Taylor Griggs, "Organizing Portland: Local Labor Organizers See Surge in Union Solidarity, Diversity," *Portland Mercury*, September 14, 2023, https://www.portlandmercury.com/labor/2023/09/14/46720874/organizing-portland-local-labor-organizers-see-surge-in-union-solidarity-diversity.

Chapter Eight

1. Interview with a program manager at an economic justice organization, February 2023.

2. Interview with a former communications director at a social justice organization, January 2023.

3. Interview with a program director at a racial justice organization, March 2023.

4. Interview with a policy director at an economic justice organization, November 2022.

5. Tessa Stewart, "Her Team Helped Beat Back Kansas' Abortion Ban," *Rolling Stone*, August 6, 2022, https://www.rollingstone.com/politics/politics-news/kansas-abortion-vote-prochoice-lessons-1393192/.

6. Letter to Melanie Fontes Rainer, Director, Office for Civil Right, Department of Health and Human Services, June 16, 2023, https://www.pregnancyjusticeus.org/wp-content/uploads/2023/06/HIPAA-Coalition-Letter-6.16.23-Final.pdf.

7. Rebecca Pifer, "HHS Proposes Rule Shoring Up HIPAA to Protect Reproductive Health Data, Including around Abortions," HealthcareDive, April 12, 2023, https://www.healthcaredive.com/news/hhs-ocr-hipaa-proposed-rule-abortion/647469/.

8. It is important to note that while a growing proportion of agency rules are finalized outside of the scope of this process, the vast majority of agency policymaking occurs through notice-and-comment rulemaking (approximately 71 percent of all published final rules) (see "Federal Rulemaking: Agencies Could Take Steps to Respond to Public Comments," GAO 13-21, December 2012, available at https://www.gao.gov/assets/660/651052.pdf). Adherence to this process is of paramount importance to federal agencies because of both its legal requirement (as per the APA, with few exceptions, all agencies are required to engage in notice-and-comment rulemaking) *and* its facilitation of the degree of public participation historically encouraged by the courts (Lowande 2018; Potter 2019; and West 2004).

9. Interview with an agency official with rulemaking duties, April 2022.

10. Interview with an agency official with rulemaking duties, November 2022.

11. Interview with an agency official with rulemaking duties, April 2022.

12. Interview with an agency official with rulemaking duties, February 2023.

13. Interview with a program manager at an economic justice organization, February 2023.

14. Interview with a former communications director at a social justice organization, January 2023.

15. Interview with a former policy director at an economic justice organization, November 2022.

16. Interview with an executive director at a racial justice organization, November 2022.

17. Interview with an executive director of a social justice organization, February 2023.

18. Interview with a cofounder of a formal coalition of social justice–oriented groups, February 2023.

19. Interview with a leader of a coalition of racial justice organizations, February 2023.

20. Taylor Giorno, "Federal Lobbying Spending Reaches $4.1 Billion in 2022," Open Secrets, January 26, 2023, https://www.opensecrets.org/news/2023/01/federal-lobbying-spending-reaches-4-1-billion-in-2022-the-highest-since-2010/.

21. Interview with an agency official with rulemaking duties, April 2023.

References

Aberbach, Joel D., and Bert A. Rockman. 2006. "The Past and Future of Political-Administrative Relations: Research from *Bureaucrats and Politicians* to *In the Web of Politics*—and Beyond." *International Journal of Public Administration* 29 (12): 977–95.

Agranoff, Robert, and Michael McGuire. 2001. "Big Questions in Public Network Management Research." *Journal of Public Administration Research and Theory* 11 (3): 295–326.

Alexander, Jeffrey A., Maureen E. Comfort, and Bryan J. Weiner. 1998. "Governance in Public-Private Community Health Partnerships: A Survey of the Community Care Network Demonstration Sites." *Nonprofit Management and Leadership* 8 (4): 311–32.

Amenta, Edwin. 2006. *When Movements Matter: The Townsend Plan and the Rise of Social Security*. Princeton, NJ: Princeton University Press.

Andrews, Kenneth T., Neal Caren, and Todd Lu. 2020. "Racial, Ethnic, and Immigration Protest during Year One of the Trump Presidency." In *Racialized Protest and the State*, edited by Hank Johnston and Pamela Oliver, 208–226. London: Routledge.

Ansell, Chris, and Alison Gash. 2007. "Collaborative Governance in Theory and Practice." *Journal of Public Administration Research and Theory* 18 (4): 543–71.

Bachrach, Peter, and Morton S. Baratz. 1962. "Two Faces of Power." *American Political Science Review* 56 (4): 947–52.

Bäckstrand, Karin. 2006. "Democratizing Global Environmental Governance? Stakeholder Democracy after the World Summit on Sustainable Development." *European Journal of International Relations* 12 (4): 467–98.

Baggetta, Matt, Hahrie Han, and Kenneth T. Andrews. 2013. "Leading Associations: How Individual Characteristics and Team Dynamics Generate Committed Leaders." *American Sociological Review* 78 (4): 544–73.

Baumgartner, Frank R., Jeffrey M. Berry, Marie Hojnacki, Beth L. Leech, and David C. Kimball. 2009a. *Lobbying and Policy Change: Who Wins, Who Loses, and Why*. Chicago: University of Chicago Press.

Baumgartner, Frank R., Christian Breunig, Christoffer Green-Pedersen, Bryan D. Jones, Peter B. Mortensen, Michiel Nuytemans, and Stefaan Walgrave. 2009b. "Punctuated Equilibrium in Comparative Perspective." *American Journal of Political Science* 53 (3): 603–20.

Baumgartner, Frank R., and Bryan D. Jones. 1993. *Agendas and Instability in American Politics*. Chicago: University of Chicago Press.

Baumgartner, Frank R., and Bryan D. Jones. 2005. *The Politics of Attention: How Government Prioritizes Problems*. Chicago: University of Chicago Press.

Baumgartner, Frank R., and Bryan D. Jones. 2009. *Agendas and Instability in American Politics*. Chicago: University of Chicago Press.

Baumgartner, Frank R., and Beth L. Leech. 1998. *Basic Interests: The Importance of Groups in Politics and in Political Science*. Princeton, NJ: Princeton University Press.

Baumgartner, Frank R., and Beth L. Leech. 2001. "Issue Niches and Policy Bandwagons: Patterns of Interest Group Involvement in National Politics." *Journal of Politics* 63 (4):1191–1213.

Beim, Deborah, and Jonathan P. Kastellec. 2014. "The Interplay of Ideological Diversity, Dissents, and Discretionary Review in the Judicial Hierarchy: Evidence from Death Penalty Cases." *Journal of Politics* 76 (4): 1074–88.

Berry, Jeffrey M. 1977. *Lobbying for the People: The Political Behavior of Public Interest Groups*. Princeton, NJ: Princeton University Press.

Berry, Jeffrey M. 1989. *The Interest Group Society*. Northbrook, IL: Scott Foresman.

Berry, Jeffrey M., and David F. Arons. 2005. *A Voice for Nonprofits*. Washington, DC: Brookings Institution Press.

Boehmke, Frederick, and Richard Witmer. 2012. "Indian Nations as Interest Groups: Tribal Motivations for Contributions to U.S. Senators." *Political Research Quarterly* 65 (1): 179–91.

Boehmke, Frederick J., and Richard C. Witmer. 2020. "Representation and Lobbying by Indian Nations in California: Is Tribal Lobbying All about Gaming? *Interest Groups and Advocacy* 9 (1): 90–101.

Box-Steffensmeier, J. M., B. W. Campbell, D. P. Christenson, and Z. Navabi. 2018. "Role Analysis Using the Ego-ERGM: A Look at Environmental Interest Group Coalitions." *Social Networks*,52:213–27.

Boydstun, Amber E., Shaun Bevan, and Herschel F. Thomas. 2014. "The Importance of Attention Diversity and How to Measure It." *Policy Studies Journal* 42 (2): 173–96.

Brady, Henry E., Sidney Verba, and Kay Lehman Schlozman. 1995. "Beyond SES: A Resource Model of Political Participation." *American Political Science Review* 89 (2): 271–94.

Bressman, Lisa S. 2007. "Procedures as Politics in Administrative Law." *Columbia Law Review* 107 (8): 1749–1821.

Brierly, Sarah, Kenneth Lowande, Rachel Augustine Potter, and Guillermo Toral. 2023. "Bureaucratic Politics: Blind Spots and Opportunities in Political Science." *Annual Review of Political Science* 26:271–90.

Brower, Margaret P. 2024. *Intersectional Advocacy: Redrawing Policy Boundaries around Gender, Race, and Class*. New York: Cambridge University Press.

Brown, Nadia. 2014. *Sisters in the Statehouse: Black Women and Legislative Decision Making*. Oxford: Oxford University Press.

Brown, Melissa, Rashawn Ray, Ed Summers, and Neil Fraistat. 2017. "#SayHerName: A Case Study of Intersectional Social Media Activism." *Ethnic and Racial Studies* 40 (11): 1831–46.

Browne, William P. 1990. "Organized Interests and Their Issue Niches: A Search for Pluralism in a Policy Domain." *Journal of Politics* 52 (2): 477–509.

Bryson, John M., Barbara C. Crosby, and Melissa Middleton Stone. 2006. "The Design and Implementation of Cross-Sector Collaborations: Propositions from the Literature." *Public Administration Review* 66 (1): 44–55.

Carlson, Kirsten Matoy. 2021. "Rethinking Legislative Advocacy." *Maryland Law Review* 90 (4): 960–1020.

Carlson, Kirsten Matoy. 2022. "Beyond Descriptive Representation: American Indian Opposition to Federal Legislation." *Journal of Race, Ethnicity, and Politics* 7 (1): 65–89.

Carpenter, Daniel P. 2002. "Groups, the Media, Agency Waiting Costs, and FDA Drug Approval." *American Journal of Political Science* 46 (3): 490–505.

Carpenter, Daniel. 2017. "On the Emergence of the Administrative Petition: Innovations in Nineteenth-Century Indigenous North America." In *Administrative Law from the Inside Out: Essays on Themes in the Work of Jerry L. Mashaw*, edited by Nicholas R. Parrillo, 349–72. Cambridge: Cambridge University Press.

Carpenter, Daniel P., Angelo Dagonel, Devin Judge-Lord, Christopher T. Kenny, Brian Libgober, Steven Rashin, Jacob Waggoner, and Susan Webb Yackee. 2022. "Inequality in Administrative Democracy: Methods and Evidence from Financial Rulemaking." Paper presented at the American Political Science Association's annual meeting, 2021.

Cheyns, Emmanuelle, and Lone Riisgaard. 2014. "Introduction to the Symposium: The Exercise of Power through Multi-stakeholder Initiatives for Sustainable Agriculture and Its Inclusion and Exclusion Outcomes." *Agriculture and Human Values* 31:409–23.

Chubb, John E. 1983. *Interest Groups and the Bureaucracy: The Politics of Energy*. Palo Alto, CA: Stanford University Press.

Clough, Paul, and Mark Stevenson. 2011. "Developing a Corpus of Plagiarised Short Answers." *Language Resources and Evaluation* 45 (1): 5–24.

Coaston, Jane. 2019. "The Intersectionality Wars." *Vox*, May 28, 2019. https://www.vox.com/the-highlight/2019/5/20/18542843/intersectionality-conservatism-law-race-gender-discrimination.

Collins, Patricia Hill. 1990. *Black Feminist Thought: Knowledge, Consciousness, and the Politics of Empowerment*. New York: Routledge.

Combahee River Collective. 1977. *Combahee River Collective Statement*. https://www.blackpast.org/african-american-history/combahee-river-collective-statement-1977/.

Corntassel, Jeff, and Richard Witmer. 2008. *Forced Federalism: Contemporary Challenges to Indigenous Nationhood*. Norman: University of Oklahoma Press.

Costain, Anne N. 1992. *Inviting Women's Rebellion: A Political Process Interpretation of the Women's Movement*. Baltimore: Johns Hopkins University Press.

Costain, Anne N. 2005. "Social Movements as Mechanisms for Political Inclusion." In *The Politics of Democratic Inclusion*, edited by Christina Wolbrecht and Rodney E. Hero, 108–21. Philadelphia: Temple University Press.

Cowger, Thomas. 2011. *The National Congress of American Indians: The Founding Years*. Lincoln: University of Nebraska Press.

Crenshaw, Kimberlé. 1989. "Demarginalizing the Intersection of Race and Sex: A Black Feminist Critique of Antidiscrimination Doctrine, Feminist Theory and Antiracist Politics." *University of Chicago Legal Forum* 1989 (1): 139–67.

Crenshaw, Kimberlé. 1991. "Mapping the Margins: Intersectionality, Identity Politics, and Violence against Women of Color." *Stanford Law Review* 43 (6): 1241–99.

Crepelle, Adam. 2021. "White Tape and Indian Wards: Removing the Federal Bureaucracy to Empower Tribal Economies and Self-Government." *University of Michigan Journal of Law Reform* 54 (3): 563–609.

Croley, Steven P. 1998. "Theories of Regulation: Incorporating the Administrative Process." *Columbia Law Review* 98 (1): 1–168.

Cropper, Maureen L., William N. Evans, Stephen J. Berardi, Maria M. Duclasoares, and Paul R. Portney. 1992. "The Determinants of Pesticide Regulation: A Statistical Analysis of EPA Decision Making." *Journal of Political Economy* 100 (1): 175–97.

Davies, Elizabeth J. 2023. "Alienated: Anti-Blackness and the Process of Radical Organizing." Unpublished manuscript.

Davis, Angela. 1981. *Women, Race and Class.* New York: Random House.

Dentoni, Domenico, Varena Bitzer, and Greetje Schouten. 2018. "Harnessing Wicked Problems in Multi-stakeholder Partnerships." *Journal of Business Ethics* 150 (2): 333–56.

Drutman, Lee. 2015. *The Business of America Is Lobbying: How Corporations Became Politicized and Politics Became More Corporate.* New York: Oxford University Press.

Drutman, Lee, and Steven M. Teles. 2015. "Why Congress Relies on Lobbyists Instead of Thinking for Itself." Atlantic, March 10, 2015.

Dwidar, Maraam A. 2022a. "Diverse Lobbying Coalitions and Influence in Notice-and-Comment Rulemaking." *Policy Studies Journal* 50 (1): 199–240.

Dwidar, Maraam A. 2022b. "Coalitional Lobbying and Intersectional Representation in American Rulemaking." *American Political Science Review* 116 (1): 301–21.

Dwidar, Maraam A., and Kathleen Marchetti. 2023. "Tribal Coalitions and Lobbying Outcomes." *Presidential Studies Quarterly* 53 (3): 354–82.

Dwidar, Maraam A., Kathleen Marchetti, and Dara Z. Strolovitch. Forthcoming. "Organizational Leaders and Intersectional Advocacy." *Politics, Groups, and Identities.* https://www.maraamdwidar.com/uploads/8/1/2/9/81297114/dwidarmarchettistrolovitch_orgleaders.pdf.

English, Ashley. 2019. "She Who Shall Not Be Named: The Women That Women's Organizations Do (and Do Not) Represent in the Rulemaking Process." *Politics and Gender* 15 (3): 572–98.

English, Ashley. 2020. "Where Are All the Single Ladies? Marital Status and Women's Organizations' Rule-Making Campaigns." *Politics and Gender* 16 (2): 581–607.

Epstein, David, and Sharyn O'Halloran. 1996. "Divided Government and the Design of Administrative Procedures: A Formal Model and Empirical Test." *Journal of Politics* 58 (2): 373–97.

Epstein, David, and Sharyn O'Halloran. 1999. *Delegating Powers: A Transaction-Cost Approach to Policymaking under Separate Powers.* New York: Cambridge University Press.

Fagan, E. J., and Zachary M. McGee. 2022. "Problem Solving and the Demand for Expert Information in Congress." *Legislative Studies Quarterly* 47 (1): 53–77.

Evans, Laura. 2011. *Power from Powerlessness.* New York: Oxford University Press.

Farhang, Sean, and Gregory J. Wawro. 2010. "Indirect Influences of Gender on the U.S. Court of Appeals: Evidence from Sexual Harassment Law." All Faculty Scholarship 2767, Penn Carey Law, Legal Scholarship Repository. https://scholarship.law.upenn.edu/cgi/viewcontent.cgi?article=3770&context=faculty_scholarship.

Foster-Fishman, Pennie G., Shelby L. Berkowitz, David W. Lounsbury, Stephanie Jacobson, and Nicole A. Allen. 2001. "Building Collaborative Capacity in Community Coalitions: A Review and Integrative Framework." *American Journal of Community Psychology* 29 (2): 241–61.

Fox, Jonathan, and John Gershman. 2000. "The World Bank and Social Capital: Lessons from Ten Rural Development Projects in the Philippines and Mexico." *Policy Sciences* 33:399–419.

Frymer, Paul. 1999. *Uneasy Alliances: Race and Party Competition in America.* Princeton, NJ: Princeton University Press.

Gailmard, Sean. 2002. "Expertise, Subversion, and Bureaucratic Discretion." *Journal of Law, Economics, and Organization* 18 (2): 536–55.

Gause, LaGina. *The Advantage of Disadvantage: Costly Protest and Political Representation for Marginalized Groups.* of *Cambridge Studies in Contentious Politics.* Cambridge: Cambridge University Press, 2022.

Gelbman, Shamira. 2021. *The Civil Rights Lobby: The Leadership Conference on Civil Rights and the Second Reconstruction.* Philadelphia: Temple University Press.

Gerber, Elisabeth R. 1999. *The Populist Paradox: Interest Group Influence and the Promise of Direct Legislation.* Princeton, NJ: Princeton University Press.

Gershon, Sarah A., Celeste Montoya, Christina Bejarano, and Nada Brown. 2019. "Intersectional Linked Fate and Political Representation." *Politics, Groups, and Identities* 7 (3): 642–53.

Gilens, Martin. 2004. *Affluence and Influence: Economic Inequality and Political Power in America.* Princeton, NJ: Princeton University Press.

Gilens, Martin, and Benjamin I. Page. 2014. "Testing Theories of American Politics: Elites, Interest Groups, and Average Citizens." *Perspectives on Politics* 12 (3): 564–81.

Gillion, Daniel Q. 2013. *The Political Power of Protest: Minority Activism and Shifts in Public Policy.* New York: Cambridge University Press.

Golden, Marissa Martino. 1998. "Interest Groups in the Rule-Making Process: Who Participates? Whose Voices Get Heard?" *Journal of Public Administration Research and Theory* 8 (2): 245–70.

Goodnow, Frank J. 1900. *Politics and Administration: A Study in Government.* London: Macmillian.

Gray, Barbara. 1989. *Collaborating: Finding Common Ground for Multiparty Problems.* San Francisco: Jossey-Bass.

Gray, Barbara, and Jenna P. Stites. 2013. "Sustainability through Partnerships: Capitalizing on Collaboration." Network for Business Sustainability. https://nbs.net/wp-content/up loads/2022/01/NBS-Systematic-Review-Partnerships.pdf.

Gray, Virginia, and David Lowery. 1996. *The Population Ecology of Interest Representation: Lobbying Communities in the American States.* Ann Arbor: University of Michigan Press.

Gray, Virginia, and David Lowery. 1998. "To Lobby Alone or in a Flock: Foraging Behavior among Organized Interests." *American Politics Quarterly* 26 (1): 5–34.

Grimmer, Justin, and Brandon M. Stewart. 2013. "Text As Data: The Promise and Pitfalls of Automatic Content Analysis Methods for Political Texts." *Political Analysis* 21 (3): 267–97.

Grose, Christian R. 2011. *Congress in Black and White: Race and Representation in Washington and at Home.* New York: Cambridge University Press.

Guinier, Lani. 1994. *The Tyranny of the Majority: Fundamental Fairness in Representative Democracy.* New York: Free Press.

Haeder, Simon F., and Susan Webb Yackee. 2015. "Influence and the Administrative Process: Lobbying the U.S. President's Office of Management and Budget." *American Political Science Review* 109 (3): 507–22.

Haider-Markel, Donald P. 2006. "Acting as Fire Alarms with Law Enforcement? Interest Groups and Bureaucratic Activity on Hate Crime." *American Politics Research* 34 (1): 95–130.

Hall, Richard L., and Alan V. Deardorff. 2006. Lobbying as Legislative Subsidy. *American Political Science Review*, 100 (1): 69–84.

Hall, Richard L., and Kristina C. Miler. 2008. "What Happens after the Alarm? Interest Group Subsidies to Legislative Overseers." *Journal of Politics* 70 (4): 990–1005.

Han, Hahrie, Elizabeth McKenna, and Michelle Oyakawa. 2021. *Prisms of the People: Power and Organizing in Twenty-First-Century America*. Chicago: University of Chicago Press.

Hansen, John Mark. 1991. *Gaining Access: Congress and the Farm Lobby, 1919–1981*. Chicago: University of Chicago Press.

Heaney, Michael T. 2004. "Issue Networks, Information, and Interest Group Alliances: The Case of Wisconsin Welfare Politics, 1993–99." *State Politics & Policy Quarterly* 4 (3): 237–70.

Heinz, John P., Edward O. Laumann, Robert L. Nelson, and Robert H. Salisbury. 1993. *The Hollow Core: Private Interests in National Policy Making*. Cambridge, MA: Harvard University Press.

Hero, Rodney E., and Robert R. Preuhs. 2013. *Black-Latino Relations in U.S. National Politics: Beyond Conflict and Cooperation*. Cambridge: Cambridge University Press.

Hertel-Fernandez, Alexander, and Theda Skocpol. 2015. "Asymmetric Interest Group Mobilization and Party Coalitions in U.S. Tax Politics." *Studies in American Political Development* 29 (2): 235–49.

Hojnacki, Marie. 1997. "Interest Groups' Decisions to Join Alliances or Work Alone." *American Journal of Political Science* 41 (1): 61–87.

Hojnacki, Marie. 1998. "Organized Interests' Advocacy Behavior in Alliances." *Political Research Quarterly* 51 (2): 437–59.

Hojnacki, Marie, Kathleen M. Marchetti, Frank R. Baumgartner, Jeffrey M. Berry, David C. Kimball, and Beth L. Leech. 2015. "Assessing Business Advantage in Washington Lobbying." *Interest Groups & Advocacy* 4 (3): 205–24.

Holden, Matthew. 2014. "'Imperialism' in Bureaucracy." *American Political Science Review* 60 (40): 943–51.

hooks, bell. 1981. *Ain't I a Woman: Black Women and Feminism*. New York: Routledge.

Hoxie, Frederick. 2012. *This Indian Country: American Indian Activists and the Place They Made*. New York: Penguin Books.

Hrebenar, Ronald J. 1997. *Interest Group Politics in America*. Armonk, NY: M. E. Sharpe.

Huber, John D., and Charles R. Shipan. 2002. *Deliberate Discretion? The Institutional Foundations of Bureaucratic Autonomy. of Cambridge Studies in Comparative Politics*. Cambridge: Cambridge University Press.

Hula, Kevin. 1999. *Lobbying Together: Interest Group Coalitions in Legislative Politics*. Washington, DC: Georgetown University Press.

Huxham, Chris, and Siv Vangen. 2004. *Managing to Collaborate: The Theory and Practice of Collaborative Advantage*. London: Routledge.

Imig, Douglas R. 1996. *Poverty and Power: The Political Representation of Poor Americans*. Lincoln: University of Nebraska Press, Lincoln.

Jones, Bryan D., Sean M. Theriault, and Michelle Whyman. 2019. *The Great Broadening: How the Vast Expansion of the Policymaking Agenda Transformed American Politics*. Chicago: University of Chicago Press.

Junk, Wiebke Marie. 2019. "When Diversity Works: The Effects of Coalition Composition on the Success of Lobbying Coalitions." *American Journal of Political Science* 63 (3): 660–74.

Kastellec, Jonathan P. 2013. "Racial Diversity and Judicial Influence on Appellate Courts." *American Journal of Political Science* 57 (1): 167–83.

Kerwin, Cornelius, Scott R. Furlong, and William West. 2011. "Interest Groups, Rulemaking, and American Bureaucracy." In *The Oxford Handbook of American Bureaucracy*, edited by Robert Durant, 590–611. New York: Oxford University Press.

Kessler, David. 2001. *A Question of Intent: A Great American Battle with a Deadly Industry*. New York: PublicAffairs.

Kingdon, John W. 1973. *Congressmen's Voting Decisions*. Ann Arbor, MI: University of Michigan Press.

Kitchener, Caroline. 2020. "'How Many Women of Color Have to Cry?': Top Feminist Organizations Are Plagued by Racism, 20 Former Staffers Say." *Washington Post*, July 13, 2020.

Kroeger, Mary. 2016. "Plagiarizing Policy: Model Legislation in State Legislatures."Paper presented at the 2018 meeting of the American Political Science Association.

Laperrière, Marie, and Eleonore Lépinard. 2016. "Intersectionality as a Tool for Social Movements: Strategies of Inclusion and Representation in the Québécois Women's Movement." *Politics* 36 (4): 374–82.

LaPira, Timothy M., Lee Drutman, and Kevin R. Kosar. 2020. *Congress Overwhelmed: The Decline in Congressional Capacity and Prospects for Reform*. Chicago: University of Chicago Press.

LaPira, Timothy M., and Herschel F. Thomas. 2020. "The Lobbying Disclosure Act at 25: Challenges and Opportunities for Analysis." *Interest Groups and Advocacy* 9 (1): 257–71.

LaPira, Timothy M., Herschel F. Thomas, and Frank R. Baumgartner. 2014. "The Two Worlds of Lobbying: Washington Lobbyists in the Core and on the Periphery." *Interest Groups and Advocacy* 3 (3): 219–45.

LaVelle, John P. 2011. "Strengthening Tribal Sovereignty through Indian Participation in American Politics: A Reply to Professor Porter." *Kansas Journal of Law and Public Policy* 10 (3): 533–80.

Leech, Beth L., Frank R. Baumgartner, Timothy M. La Pira, and Nicholas A. Semanko. 2005. "Drawing Lobbyists to Washington: Government Activity and the Demand for Advocacy." *Political Research Quarterly* 58 (1): 19–30.

Levi, Margaret, and Gillian H. Murphy. 2006. "Coalitions of Contention: The Case of the WTO Protests in Seattle." *Political Studies* 54 (4): 651–70.

Levine, Peter. 2022. *What Should We Do? A Theory of Civic Life*. New York: Oxford University Press.

Lewallen, Jonathan. 2020. *Committees and the Decline of Lawmaking in Congress*. Ann Arbor: University of Michigan Press.

Lindblom, Charles. 1977. *Politics and Markets: The World's Political Economic Systems*. New York: Basic Books.

Lorenz, Geoffrey. 2019. "Prioritized Interests: Diverse Interest Group Coalitions and Congressional Committee Agenda-Setting." *Journal of Politics* 82 (1): 225–40.

Long, J. Scott. 1997. *Regression Models for Categorical and Limited Dependent Variables*. Thousand Oaks, CA: Sage.

Lowery, David, Frank R. Baumgartner, Joost Berkhout, Jeffrey M. Berry, Darren Halpin, Marie Hojnacki, Heike Klüver, Beate Kohler-Koch, Jeremy Richardson, and Kay Lehman Schlozman. 2015. "Images of an Unbiased Interest System." *Journal of European Public Policy* 22 (8): 1212–31.

Lowande, Kenneth. 2018 "Who Polices the Administrative State?" *American Political Science Review* 11 2 (4): 874–90.

Lowi, Theodore J. 1964. "American Business, Public Policy, Case Studies, and Political Theory." *World Politics* 16 (4): 677–715.

Lyon, Caroline, James Malcolm, and Bob Dickerson. 2001. "Detecting Short Passages of Similar Text in Large Document Collections." Paper read at the Conference on Empirical Methods in Natural Language Processing, June 3–4, 2001, Pittsburgh, Pennsylvania.

Magat, Wesley A., Alan J. Krupnick, and Winston Harrington. 1986. *Rules in the Making*. Washington, DC: RFF Press.

Mahoney, Christine. 2007. "Networking vs. Allying: The Decision of Interest Groups to Join Coalitions in the US and EU." *Journal of European Public Policy* 14 (3): 366–83.

Mahoney, Christine, and Frank R. Baumgartner. 2004. "The Determinants and Effects of Interest-Group Coalitions." Paper presented at the Annual Meeting of the American Political Science Association, Chicago, September 2–5, 2004 https://fbaum.unc.edu/papers/Mahoney_Baumgartner_APSA_2004_Coalitions.pdf.

Marchetti, Kathleen. 2014. Crossing the Intersection: The Representation of Disadvantaged Identities in Advocacy. *Politics, Groups, and Identities* 2 (1): 104–19.

Marchetti, Kathleen. 2019. "Intersectional Advocacy and Policymaking across US States." In *The Palgrave Handbook of Intersectionality in Public Policy: The Politics of Intersectionality*, edited by Olena Hankivsky and Julia S. Jordan-Zachery, 451–69. Cham, Switzerland: Palgrave Macmillan.

Martinez, Dierdre. 2009. *Who Speaks for Hispanics? Hispanic Interest Groups in Washington*. Albany, NY: State University of New York Press.

Mason, Dale W. 1998. "Tribes and States: A New Era in Intergovernmental Affairs." *Publius* 28 (1): 111–30.

Mason, Dale W. 2000. *Indian Gaming*. Norman: University of Oklahoma Press.

Mayhew, David R. 1974. *Congress: The Electoral Connection*. New Haven, CT: Yale University Press.

McAdam, Doug. 1982. *Political Process and the Development of Black Insurgency, 1930–1970*. Chicago: University of Chicago Press.

McAlevey, Jane. 2016. *No Shortcuts: Organizing for Power in the New Gilded Age*. New York: Oxford University Press

McCammon, Holly and Karen Campbell. 2002. "Allies on the Road to Victory: Coalition Formation between the Suffragists and the Woman's Christian Temperance Union." *Mobilization: An International Quarterly* 7 (3): 231–51.

McConnaughy, Corrine M. 2013. *The Woman Suffrage Movement in America: A Reassessment*. New York: Cambridge University Press.

McConnell Grant. 1966. *Private Power and American Democracy*. New York: Knopf.

McCubbins, Matthew D., Roger G. Noll, and Barry R. Weingast. 1987. "Administrative Procedures as Instruments of Political Control." *Journal of Law, Economics, and Organization* 3:243–77.

McCubbins, Matthew D., Roger G. Noll, and Barry R. Weingast. 1989. "Structure and Process as Solutions to the Politician's Principal Agency Problem." *Virginia Law Review* 74:431–82.

McCubbins, Mathew D., and Thomas Schwartz. 1984. "Congressional Oversight Overlooked: Police Patrols versus Fire Alarms." *American Journal of Political Science* 28 (1): 165–79.

McGarity, Thomas O. 1992. "Some Thoughts on 'Deossifying' the Rulemaking Process." *Duke Law Journal* 41 (6): 1385–462.

McGarity, Thomas O. 1997. "The Courts and the Ossification of Rulemaking: A Response to Professor Seidenfeld." *Texas Law Review* 75 (3): 525–58.

McKay, Amy, and Susan Webb Yackee. 2007. "Interest Group Competition on Federal Agency Rules." *American Politics Research* 35 (3): 336–57.

Meier, Kenneth J., and Laurence J. O'Toole. 2006. *Bureaucracy in a Democratic State: A Governance Perspective*. Baltimore, MD: Johns Hopkins University Press.

Mena, Sébastien, and Guido Palazzo. 2012. "Input and Output Legitimacy of Multi-Stakeholder Initiatives." *Business Ethics Quarterly* 22 (3): 527–56.

Minta, Michael D. 2011. *Oversight: Representing the Interests of Blacks and Latinos in Congress.* Princeton, NJ: Princeton University Press.

Nelson, David, and Susan Webb Yackee. 2012. "Lobbying Coalitions and Government Policy Change: An Analysis of Federal Agency Rulemaking." *Journal of Politics* 74 (2): 339–53.

Nilsson, Warren. 2019. "Social Innovation as Institutional Work." In *Handbook of Inclusive Innovation,* edited by Gerard George, Ted Baker, Paul Tracey, and Havovi Joshi, 83–105. Cheltenham: Edward Elgar.

Niskanen, William A. 1971. *Bureaucracy and Representative Government.* New York: Routledge.

Nixon, David C., Robert M. Howard, and Je R. DeWitt. 2002. "With Friends Like These: Rule-Making Comment Submissions to the Securities and Exchange Commission." *Journal of Public Administration Research and Theory* 12 (1): 59–76.

Nownes, Anthony J. 2007. *Total Lobbying: What Lobbyists Want (and How They Try to Get It).* New York: Cambridge University Press.

Oeser, Michael D. 2010. "Tribal Citizen Participation in State and National Politics: Welcome Wagon or Trojan Horse?" *William Mitchell Law Review* 36 (2): 793–858.

Olson, Mancur. 1965. *The Logic of Collective Action.* Cambridge, MA: Harvard University Press.

Ostrom, Elinor. 1990. *Governing the Commons: The Evolution of Institutions for Collective Action.* New York: Cambridge University Press.

Phinney, Robin. 2017. *Strange Bedfellows: Interest Group Coalitions, Diverse Partners, and Influence in American Social Policy.* New York: Cambridge University Press.

Pinderhughes, Diane. 1995. "Black Interest Groups and the 1982 Extension of the Voting Rights Act." In *Blacks and the American Political System,* edited by Huey L. Perry and Wayne Parent, 203–24. Gainesville: University Press of Florida.

Piven, Frances F., and Richard A. Cloward. 1977. *Poor People's Movements: Why They Succeed, How They Fail.* New York: Pantheon Books.

Porter, Martin F. 1980. "An Algorithm for Suffix Stripping." *Program: Electronic Library and Information Systems* 14 (3): 130–37.

Potter, Rachel A. 2019. *Bending the Rules: Procedural Politicking in the Bureaucracy.* Chicago: University of Chicago Press.

Purdie-Vaughns, Valerie, and Richard P. Eibach. 2008. "Intersectional Invisibility: The Distinctive Advantages and Disadvantages of Multiple Subordinate-Group Identities." *Sex Roles* 59 (5/6): 377–91.

Rabin, Robert L. 1986. "Federal Regulation in Historical Perspective." *Stanford Law Review* 38 (5): 1189–326.

Reingold, Beth, Kerry Haynie, and Kirsten Widner. 2020. *Race, Gender, and Political Representation: Toward a More Intersectional Approach.* Oxford: Oxford University Press.

Reingold, Beth, Kirsten Widner, and Rachel Harmon. 2019. "Legislating at the Intersections: Race, Gender, and Representation." *Political Research Quarterly* 73 (4): 819–33.

Rourke, Francis E. 1984. *Bureaucrats, Politics, and Public Policy.* Boston: Little, Brown.

Salisbury, Robert H. 1990. "The Paradox of Interest in Washington: More Groups, Less Clout." In *The New American Political System.* Washington, DC: AEI Press.

Salisbury, Robert H. 1992. *Interests and Institutions: Substance and Structure in American Politics.* Pittsburgh: University of Pittsburgh Press.

Sanchez, Gabriel R. 2021. *What Might We Expect from Native American Voters in the Upcoming 2022 Election?* Technical report, The Brookings Institution, 12.

Schattschneider, E. E. 1960. *The Semi-Sovereign People.* New York: Rinehart & Winston.

Schlozman, Kay L. 1984. "What Accent the Heavenly Chorus? Political Equality and the American Pressure System." *Journal of Politics* 46:1006–32.

Schlozman, Kay L., and John T. Tierney. 1983. "More of the Same: Washington Pressure Group Activity in a Decade of Change." *Journal of Politics* 45:351–77.

Schlozman, Kay L., and John T. Tierney. 1986. *Organized Interests and American Democracy.* New York: HarperCollins.

Schlozman, Kay L., Sidney Verba, and Henry Brady. 2012. *The Unheavenly Chorus: Unequal Political Voice and the Broken Promise of American Democracy.* Princeton, NJ: Princeton University Press.

Schneider, A. L., and H. M. Ingram. 1997. *Policy Design for Democracy.* Lawrence: University Press of Kansas.

Schneider, Anne, and Helen Ingram. 1993. "Social Construction of Target Populations: Implications for Politics and Policy." *American Political Science Review* 87 (2): 334–47.

Schroering, Caitlin, and Suzanne Staggenborg. 2022. "Volunteer and Staff Participants in Social Movements: A Comparison of Two Local Coalitions." *Social Movement Studies* 21 (6): 782–97.

Seidenfeld, Mark. 1997. Demystifying Deossification: Rethinking Recent Proposals to Modify Judicial Review of Notice and Comment Rulemaking. *Texas Law Review* 41 (6): 1385–462.

Shapiro, Martin. 1988, *Who Guards the Guardians? Judicial Control of Administration.* Athens: University of Georgia Pressa.

Shugerman, Emily. 2020. " 'Don't Forget the White Women!': Members Say Racism Ran Rampant at NOW." *Daily Beast*, June 6, 2020, updated August 12, 2020. https://www.thedaily beast.com/national-organization-for-women-members-say-racism-ran-rampant.

Simon, Herbert. 1972. "Theories of Bounded Rationality." In *Decision and Organization*, edited by C. B. McGuire and Roy Radner, 161–76. Amsterdam: North-Holland.

Skocpol, Theda. 1992. *Protecting Soldiers and Mothers: The Political Origins of Social Policy in the United States.* Cambridge, MA: Harvard University Press.

Skrentny, John David. 2002. *The Minority Rights Revolution.* Cambridge, MA: Harvard University Press.

Smith, Mark A. 2000. *American Business and Political Power: Public Opinion, Elections, and Democracy.* Chicago: University of Chicago Press.

Staggenborg, Suzanne. 1986. "Coalition Work in the Pro-Choice Movement: Organizational and Environmental Opportunities and Obstacles." *Social Problems* 33 (5): 374–90.

Staggenborg, Suzanne. 1998. "Social Movement Communities and Cycles of Protest: The Emergence and Maintenance of a Local Women's Movement." *Social Problems* 45 (2): 180–204.

Staggenborg, Suzanne. 2015. "Event Coalitions in the Pittsburgh G20 Protests." *Sociological Quarterly* 56 (2): 386–411.

Steinman, Erich. 2004. "American Federalism and Intergovernmental Innovation in State-Tribal Relations." *Publius* 34 (1): 95–114.

Strolovitch, Dara Z. 2006. "Do Interest Groups Represent the Disadvantaged? Advocacy at the Intersections of Race, Class, and Gender." *Journal of Politics* 68 (4): 894–910.

Strolovitch, Dara Z. 2007. *Affirmative Advocacy: Race, Class, and Gender in Interest Group Politics.* Chicago: University of Chicago Press.

Strolovitch, Dara Z. 2018. "Intersectional Advocacy and Activism in Time." Paper read at the 2018 annual meeting of the American Political Science Association. Boston.

Strolovitch, Dara Z., and David M. Forrest. 2010. "Social and Economic Justice Movements and Organizations." In *The Oxford Handbook of American Political Parties and Interest Groups,* edited by L. Sandy Maisel, Jeffrey M. Berry, and George C. Edwards, 468–84. New York: Oxford University Press.

Swain, Carol M. 1993. *Black Faces, Black Interests: The Representation of African Americans in Congress*. Cambridge, MA: Harvard University Press.

Szulecki, Kacper, Philipp Pattberg, and Frank Biermann. 2011. "Explaining Variation in the Effectiveness of Transitional Energy Partnerships." *Governance* 24 (4): 713–36.

Tattersall, Amanda. 2020. *Power in Coalition: Strategies for Strong Unions and Social Change*. London: Routledge.

Truman, David B. 1951. *The Governmental Process*. New York: Alfred A. Knopf.

Truth, Sojourner. 1851. "Ain't I a Woman?" Speech delivered at the Women's Convention in Akron, Ohio, May 28–29, 1851.

Viola, Herman J. 1995. *Diplomats in Buckskins: A History of Indian Delegations in Washington City*. Bluffton, SC: Rivilo Books.

Walker, Jack L. 1983. "The Origins and Maintenance of Interest Groups in America." *American Political Science Review* 77 (2): 390–406.

Walker, Jack L. 1991. *Mobilizing Interest Groups in America*. Ann Arbor: University of Michigan Press.

Warren, Kenneth F. 2018. *Administrative Law in the Political System*. London: Routledge.

Weldon, Laurel. 2011. *When Protest Makes Policy: How Social Movements Represent Disadvantaged Groups*. Ann Arbor: University of Michigan Press.

Werner, Timothy, and John J. Coleman. 2014. "Citizens United, Independent Expenditures, and Agency Costs: Reexamining the Political Economy of State Antitakeover Statutes." *Journal of Law, Economics, and Organization* 31 (1): 127–59.

West, William F. 1984. "Structuring Administrative Discretion: The Pursuit of Rationality and Responsiveness." *American Journal of Political Science* 28 (2): 340–60.

West, William F. 2004. "Formal Procedures, Informal Processes, Accountability, and Responsiveness in Bureaucratic Policy Making: An Institutional Policy Analysis." *Public Administration Review* 64 (1): 66–80.

West, William F. 2009. "Inside the Black Box: The Development of Proposed Rules and the Limits of Procedural Controls." *Administration and Society* 41 (5): 576–99.

Whitford, Andrew B. 2003. "The Structures of Interest Coalitions: Evidence from Environmental Litigation." *Business and Politics* 5 (1): 45–64.

Wilkinson, Charles F. 2006. *Blood Struggle: The Rise of Modern Indian Nations*. New York: W. W. Norton.

Wilson, John. 1973. *Introduction to Social Movements*. New York: Basic Books.

Witmer, Richard, and Frederick Boehmke. 2007. "American Indian Political Incorporation in the Post-Indian Gaming Regulatory Act Era." *Social Science Journal* 44 (1): 127–45.

Wilson, James Q. 1989. *Bureaucracy: What Government Agencies Do and Why They Do It*. New York: Basic Books.

Witmer, Richard, Joshua Johnson, and Frederick Boehmke. 2014. "American Indian Policy in the States." *Social Science Quarterly* 95 (4): 1043–63.

Woodly, Deva R. 2015. *The Politics of Common Sense: How Social Movements Use Public Discourse to Change Politics and Win Acceptance*. New York: Oxford University Press.

Woodly, Deva R. 2021. *Reckoning: Black Lives Matter and the Democratic Necessity of Social Movements*. New York: Oxford University Press.

Wolff, Thomas. 2001. "A Practitioner's Guide to Successful Coalitions." *American Journal of Community Psychology* 29 (2): 173–91.

Workman, Samuel. 2015. *The Dynamics of Bureaucracy in the U.S. Government*. New York: Cambridge University Press.

Workman, Samuel, and JoBeth S. Shafran. 2015. "Communications Frameworks and the Supply of Information in Policy Subsystems." In *Policy Paradigms in Theory and Practice*, edited by John Hogan and Michael Howlett, 239–67. London: Palgrave Macmillan.

Yackee, Susan Webb. 2006. "Sweet-Talking the Fourth Branch: The Influence of Interest Group Comments on Federal Agency Rulemaking." *Journal of Public Administration Research and Theory* 16 (1): 103–24.

Yackee, Susan Webb. 2012. "The Politics of Ex Parte Lobbying: Pre-Proposal Agenda Building and Blocking during Agency Rulemaking." *Journal of Public Administration Research and Theory* 22 (2): 373–93.

Yackee, Susan Webb. 2019. "The Politics of Rulemaking in the U.S." *Annual Review of Political Science* 22:37–57.

Yackee, Susan Webb. 2020. "Hidden Politics? Assessing Lobbying Success During US Agency Guidance Development." *Journal of Public Administration Research and Theory* 30 (4): 548–62.

Zack, Elizabeth, and Lynsy Smithson-Stanley. 2024. "Designing Effective, Resilient Coalitions." *The Good Society: A Journal of Civic Studies* 31 (1/2): 62–85.

Zack, Elizabeth, Lynsy Smithson-Stanley, Jane Booth-Tobin, and Hahrie Han. 2023. *Designing Resilient Coalitions*. Baltimore: The P³ Lab at Johns Hopkins University. https://assets.na tionbuilder.com/hahrie/pages/1229/attachments/original/1679672631/Designing_Resilient _Coalitions_%28P3_Lab%29.pdf?1679672631.

Index

www.ingramcontent.com/pod-product-compliance
Lightning Source LLC
Chambersburg PA
CBHW032134020426
42334CB00016B/1161